Steppin' Out

An African American Entertainment Guide to Our 20 Favorite Cities

by Carla Labat

AVALON
TRAVEL
publishing

Avalon Travel Publishing
5855 Beaudry Street, Emeryville, CA 94608

Copyright © 2000 by Carla Labat
Cover copyright © 2000 by Avalon Travel Publishing
All rights reserved.

Printed in the United States of America
First edition. First printing September 2000

Library of Congress Cataloging-in-Publication data

Labat, Carla, 1959-
    Steppin' out : an African American guide to our 20 favorite
cities / by Carla Labat.—1st ed.
        p. cm.
    Includes index.
    ISBN 1-5661-252-0 (pbk.)
        1. United States—Guidebooks. 2. Afro-Americans—
    Travel—United States—Guidebooks. 3. Cities and
    towns—United States—Guidebooks. I. Title.

    E158.L235 2000
    917.304'929'08996073—dc21
                                                    00-058281

Editors: Angelique Clarke, Peg Goldstein, Elizabeth Wolf
Cover & Interior Design: Kathleen Sparkes, White Hart Design
Cover Art: *Atlanta Reflection* by Corey Barksdale
Artwork Courtesy of Art Licensing Properties, LLC (800/227-1666)
Typesetter: Kathleen Sparkes, White Hart Design
Index: Vera Gross
Printer: Publishers Press

All photos by Carla Labat unless otherwise noted.

Distributed to the book trade by
Publishers Group West
Berkeley, California

Acknowledgments

I would like to thank everyone involved in helping me pull this book together, especially the restaurant and nightclub owners, the festival promoters, church administrators, museum curators, and historians who took time out of their busy schedules to assist me any way they could. Many thanks to all my friends across the country who helped me identify some of the best eateries and clubs nationwide, with special recognition to Howlie R. Davis, Judy Cothran, Patrice Green, Melvin and Johnetta Hardy, Darrell Pitts, and Cy Prince. A big thank you to the staffs of the various city convention and visitors bureaus for providing me with additional information on their cities' sights and attractions.

I am also grateful for assistance from my agent, Wanda Akin, and especially indebted to my literary consultant and advisor, D. Kamili Anderson. Of course, this book could not have been completed without the loving support of my family: my father, Victor J. Labat, my mom, Dorothy M. Labat, my sister, Lori Labat-Scott, and my brother, Yancey C. Labat.

Contents

Introduction

Tired of arriving in an unfamiliar city on business or vacation with no clue where to go to relax and take in a little local flavor, to hear the best in live jazz, or to enjoy the latest dining trends? Looking to do a little celebrity watching in Manhattan, some museum hopping in Chicago, and a lot of barbecue eating in Kansas City? Always wanted to attend a major music festival, but were afraid the kids would be bored? As they say today, "No problem, mon!" The answers to these concerns and many more are found right here in the book you're holding in your hands.

Steppin' Out is the first comprehensive source book written with the African American traveler in mind. It concentrates on specific events and establishments that cater to or may be of particular interest to African American road warriors. We have done the legwork for you: The information in this book was gathered firsthand. Covering 20 major metropolitan areas across the United States, *Steppin' Out* includes more than 800 entries on where to go, what to do, and when to go there. Each chapter provides an in-depth look at the soul of a city—what makes it tick, how it will lure you in, and what about it will make your trip memorable. Each city, venue, and event included was selected for its potential to make your travel experience as enjoyable and meaningful as possible.

Only recently has the African American traveler received recognition as a viable consumer. In the past, the travel industry thought that African Americans took only the occasional trip by car or bus to visit relatives. Enjoyable journeys, for sure, but hardly noteworthy to those in the multibillion-dollar travel business. Not until the summer of 1994, when two African American music festivals made their debuts, did the industry sit up and take notice. Sinbad's Soul Music Festival and the *Essence* Music Festival proved that Black folk have and know how to spend money away from home! During the four days New Orleans hosted the first *Essence* festival, for example, African Americans spent $75 million in a city tourists usually avoid in hot and humid July. (It was rumored that some of those dollars were dropped at a well-heeled ladies' specialty store on Canal Street—which, in fact, sold out of practically every pair of shoes in stock during those four days! Needless to say, the store was ready for the festival the following year with additional merchandise.) After news of the *Essence* festival's spectacular success hit the wires, a new travel consumer group was born and, at last, given the respect it deserves.

Today's trends in African American travel, dining, and entertainment have brought national attention to the way we like to live and play. Travel clubs across the country now offer Afrocentrically themed cruises to the Caribbean and Black-interest ski packages. National minority professional and trade associations frequently mix in a little pleasure with business by holding their conventions in desirable locations complete with golf, tennis, and day spa facilities. Whatever the venue, there are more opportunities today for African American travelers to network and play with other savvy sojourners, and we are taking every opportunity to do so.

This book was written for the adventurous vacationer as well as the serious business traveler. I have personally visited every city included in this book, dined and danced at nearly every restaurant and nightclub noted, and attended almost every festival described to give you firsthand accounts of each. The majority of restaurants and nightclubs included are African American–owned, identified by an "AA" symbol. Other venues were included because they welcome and cater to African American travelers.

The star symbol ✳ identifies an event or establishment that's strongly recommended. Dollar amounts indicate the approximate cost, per person, for an entrée, appetizer, beverage, and tip. But note that prices, menu selections, performers, gallery exhibits, and other details of business operation are subject to change. Before visiting any of the listed restaurants, nightclubs, museums, festivals, or churches, it is wise to call to confirm specifics such as hours of operation, location, cover charges, menu offerings, and special events.

Atlanta

tlanta. Anointed the proverbial Promised Land for African Americans, Atlanta remains the destination of choice for many. The recent exodus from the North to Atlanta started in the early 1980s. No longer considered the genteel capital of the South, Atlanta is today a thriving metropolis, home to Fortune 500 companies like UPS and Home Depot, media giants like Ted Turner's CNN, and musical millionaires like Babyface and his LaFace Records. With the near guarantee of outstanding professional opportunities, prominent status within the business community, and acres of posh, affordable homes in quiet, affluent, predominantly Black suburban neighborhoods, the mad dash to "Hotlanta" continues.

Atlanta... where every other street is named Peachtree, where a cold drink called Coca-Cola made its debut in a little soda fountain millions of bottles ago, and where a man named Martin Luther King Jr. inspired the world with his hopes and dreams. In the heart of the city is "Sweet Auburn," a flourishing avenue that earned its nickname during the '30s and '40s, when life for Black businesses and residents, despite segregation, was oh-so-sweet. Instead of neglecting this slice of American history (the way many other cities have), contemporary Atlantans view Sweet Auburn as a living monument to the enduring strength of African American communities and as a living testament to the city's number-one son, Dr. King.

Indeed, the most significant memorial on Sweet Auburn is the Martin Luther King Jr. Center for Nonviolent Social Change. A tour

Dr. King was born in Atlanta in 1929 in this house on Auburn Avenue.

of this inspiring facility will have you holding your heart, and you'll be fighting back tears at the sight of Dr. King's white marble tomb, illuminated by an eternal flame. The Ebenezer Heritage Baptist Church, across the street, is where Dr. King served as co-pastor with his father from 1960 to 1968. There, he and 11 other ministers founded the Southern Christian Leadership Conference (SCLC). At the far end of Sweet Auburn is the spacious Victorian home, now a historical landmark, where Dr. King spent the first 12 years of his life.

Before setting off to explore Sweet Auburn, "set yo'self down" and enjoy a down-home breakfast of smothered fish, grits, and fresh biscuits at the Beautiful Restaurant. Later on, if the midday sun hasn't gotten to you, take a walk around the corner to Moshood, where the sexy, Afrocentric-style clothing is guaranteed to accentuate your positive. En route to the Atlanta University Center, stop for lunch at the Busy Bee Café and soak up a little local flavor along with a mess of collard greens, tender fried chicken, and sweet potato pie.

Then take a spin around the campuses of historically Black

Morehouse, Spelman, and Morris Brown Colleges. Be sure to check out the Hammonds House Galleries' impressive collection of fine African American and Haitian art and antiques. A couple of blocks away at the Shrine of the Black Madonna Bookstore, next to the Pan-African Orthodox Christian Church, you can find an eclectic array of contemporary and classic African American books and art. To lighten up your afternoon, cut across town to Little Five Points, one of Atlanta's funkiest multicultural neighborhoods. Peruse the vintage clothing stores and the real and not-so-real antique boutiques, and enjoy a cup of Blue Mountain Jamaican java at one of the terrific outdoor cafés.

A quiet dinner in Atlanta may be hard to find, so forget about it! Instead, head on over to Buckhead, where barhopping has been elevated to a fine art form. And if you're out of practice, Partyin' 101 is taught along "the Strip" nightly. Justin's is where Atlanta's PYTs ("pretty young thangs") are stylin' and profilin' these days, dining on upscale soul food and spying to see if proprietor Sean "Puffy" Combs and his posse fall through for some Cajun-fried catfish, macaroni and cheese, and bread pudding. Sambuca Jazz Café is a hot spot for cool jazz. For the late, late crowd, Tongue & Groove is the dance club of the second, where the beautiful people can be seen shakin' it on down to the ground all night long.

Restaurants

Although Atlanta has evolved into a city of international proportions, the cuisine most desired by locals and tourists remains strictly southern—and always good for the soul. Whether the names of individual dishes have been changed to protect the guilty—who attempt to make good ol' soul food sound like more than it is—or the fare is based on simple family recipes handed down through generations, the menus remain basically the same: Sweet-smellin' chitterlings, tender barbecued ribs, baked turkey wings with cornbread dressing, old-fashioned meatloaf, and fresh, flaky hand-rolled biscuits are just a few favorites you can find in most eateries around town. And let's not leave town without having a li'l peach cobbler, peach pie, peach ice cream, or peach preserves, now. After all, honey, this is Atlanta!

Fine Dining

*Bacchanalia
1198 Howell Mill Rd., 404/365-0410

Locals argue which is more satisfying: Bacchanalia's gorgeous new setting or its rack of Colorado lamb with fresh lima bean ragout. Considered Atlanta's best restaurant, Bacchanalia forces the diner to experience its creative American cuisine by offering prix fixe menus. The six-course tasting menu with matched wines is accented by wonderful cheeses, fruits, salads, and a lush tangerine sorbet. Bacchanalia has little arm twisting to do—diners make reservations two weeks in advance. • **$60**

*Food Studio
887 W. Marietta St. NW, 404/815-6677

Widely considered the most visually exciting restaurant in the city, the Food Studio is as appetizing to the eye as its innovative entrées are pleasing to the palate. The menu of bold American cuisine features a wonderful sweet-potato-crusted salmon with baby bok choy and tantalizing apple-stuffed smoked pork loin. • **$35+**

Fusebox
3085 Piedmont Rd., 404/233-3383

With an ultra-chic interior too gorgeous for words, Fusebox is one of the latest and greatest entries onto the Atlanta dining scene. Its menu is an exotic and elaborate fusion of Asian and American cuisine. Standouts include the Bento Box, a traditional Japanese lunch box filled with not-so-common delicacies; a tuna chop surrounded by editable flowers; and a fragrant Chilean sea bass preserved in a bamboo steamer. No doubt, superstar music producer and investor L. A. Reid's mark is firmly stamped on Fusebox. The DJ-spun happy hours, specialty drinks, and cigar-friendly lounge attract Atlanta's slickest clientele. • **$35+/AA-invested**

Hairston's Dinner Club
1273 S. Hairston Rd., Stone Mountain, 770/322-9988

Hairston's is a sophisticated restaurant/bar/nightclub that attracts a professional, over-30 crowd made up of local politicians, corporate executives, celebrities, athletes, and other area residents.

Hairston's specializes in delicious New Orleans-style cuisine, including oyster, crab, andouille sausage, and shrimp gumbo and fried crawfish tails. Main courses include a Cajun shrimp platter and chicken étouffée, both of which come with dirty rice or Cajun fries. • **$25+/AA**

✻South City Kitchen
1144 Crescent Ave. NE, 404/873-7358
People will wait forever to dine alfresco at South City Kitchen, but if you can secure an unreserved table on any given night, sit while you can! One of Atlanta's most sophisticated *restaurants du jour*, South City Kitchen serves exciting southern cuisine like pan-roasted duckling with Georgia peach chutney and barbecued swordfish atop creamy, stone-ground grits. • **$35+**

Casual Dining

✻Café Intermezzo
1845 Peachtree Rd. NE, 404/355-0411
Sure, they serve sandwiches, pasta, salads, and other light fare, but it's all about the desserts at Café Intermezzo. A wraparound glass case shows off the more than a hundred varieties of worthwhile calories in grand style. A wide selection of gourmet coffees complements the cakes, pies, and cookies at this popular after-dinner spot. • **$10+**

✻Chanterelle's
646 Evans St., 404/758-0909
Chanterelle's interior is not as fancy as its name suggests. The restaurant is modest but clean, and the menu reflects a unique marriage of "country French with a southern flair." Everything is sautéed, broiled, or steamed, and no pork is added to the vegetables. The menu changes daily; specialties include baked rosemary chicken, curried turkey, and a wide variety of sautéed vegetables, with homemade cheesecake and carrot cake for dessert. • **$10/AA**

Justin's
2200 Peachtree Rd., 404/603-5353
Do people go to Justin's to dine or to show off their new Dolce & Gabbona outfits? There is definitely some stylin' and profilin' going

You've Got to Have Soul (Food, That Is!)

Beautiful Restaurant, 2260 Cascade Rd. SW, 404/223-0080; 397 Auburn Ave., 404/223-0080—Scores of local and national business executives, celebrities like Denzel Washington, and politicians including Vice President Al Gore have made breakfast at this Atlanta establishment a "must" before important events. The casual interior is clean and offers a friendly, Christian-oriented dining atmosphere. · $10/AA

Busy Bee Café, 810 Martin Luther King Jr. Dr., 404/525-921—We're talking small, we're talking down-home, we're talking cheap and cheerful. The Busy Bee specializes in southern favorites like fried chicken, Mama's beef stew, and a heart-smart veggie plate with some 15 veggies from which to choose. · $10/AA

Gladys & Ron's Chicken & Waffles, 529 Peachtree St., 404/874-9393—How does one classify a meal of fried chicken and waffles? Breakfast? No, Gladys & Ron's Chicken & Waffles doesn't open until 11 a.m. Dinner? Then what are salmon croquettes, chicken omelettes, and three wings, grits, one egg, and toast doing on the menu? Legendary proprietors Gladys Knight and gospel singer Ron Winans figure it's all good, no matter what time you eat. And we agree. Open until 4 a.m. on weekends. · $10+/AA

on at Justin's, the second location in Sean "Puffy" Combs's growing restaurant empire. Flirting across the busy bar, keeping an eye out for Puff Daddy himself, and people watching are the reasons most folks pack Justin's nightly. Oh, and the sophisticated soul food on the menu is quite good. • **$35+/AA**

*✴Mumbo Jumbo
596 E. Paces Ferry Rd. NE, 404/523-0330
Mumbo Jumbo is Atlanta's ultimate ultra-cool, oh-so-sexy, see-and-be-seen spot, where stylishly presented dishes of nouvelle American cuisine overshadow the stunning abstract sculptures and extravagant wall murals. Seared tuna with eggplant basil compote, young

Satterwhite's Restaurants, 851 Oak St. SW, 404/756-0963; 3131 Campbellton Rd., 404/344-6401; 590 Cascade Ave., 404/758-9825—Some 10,000 orders of Satterwhite's legendary baked chicken and dressing are sold each week in these casual, cafeteria-style settings. Other favorites include stir-fried shrimp, stuffed trout, meatloaf, pot roast, and macaroni and cheese. · $10–$25/AA

Soul Vegetarian Restaurant, 879 Ralph D. Abernathy Ave. SW, 404/752-5194; 652 N. Highland Ave., 404/875-0145—Soul Vegetarian specializes in vegan-style dishes including a tasty split pea soup, Megedeem (sandwiches) ranging from lentil burgers to crunchy battered tofu filet, battered mushrooms, tofu, or cauliflower and Soul Vegetarian's famous onion rings. · $10/AA

Sylvia's of Atlanta, 241 Central Ave., 404/529-9692—Harlem's favorite daughter, Sylvia Woods, headed south to set up shop in ultra-modern digs in downtown Atlanta. Now that simply every celebrity who's passing through town stops in for dinner, it's getting harder and harder to get a table! · $20+/AA

Thelma's Kitchen, 768 Marietta St., 404/688-5855—Open only until 4:30 p.m. weekdays, Thelma's serves a soulful home-style breakfast and lunch menu that features beef liver, baked ham, pork chops, and barbecued ribs. Cafeteria-style service; casual family-style dining area. · $10/AA

chicken with grits and fried collard greens, and roast rabbit with lobster and sautéed spinach are just a few of the items on Mumbo Jumbo's eclectic menu. • **$35**

Murphy's Restaurant
997 Virginia Ave. NE, 404/872-0904
If you come to Murphy's around 11:30 any Sunday morning, be prepared to wait at least 20 minutes for a table. Breakfast/brunch is what Murphy's is known for, so cop a squat outside with the day's newspaper and nosh on bread or pastry from the wonderful bakery until they call your name. It's worth the wait for Atlanta's best biscuits-and-bacon breakfast. • **$15 Breakfast/$25+ Dinner**

Paschal's
830 Martin Luther King Jr. Dr. SW, 404/577-3150

Paschal's is arguably the most famous African American-owned restaurant in Atlanta. Legend has it that brothers Robert and James Paschal left their home in Jackson, Georgia, in 1946 with all of three dollars between them and headed to Atlanta to make their fortune. When they opened Paschal's, little did they know their humble restaurant would one day serve fried chicken to every president of the United States from Kennedy to Clinton. Martin Luther King Jr., who frequently used Paschal's as a meeting place, is said to have organized the March on Selma from one of its booths. Today, the restaurant is owned by Clark-Atlanta University, which is committed to continuing the tradition of good food and good service established more than 50 years ago. Paschal's menu features traditional southern-style family meals, including all the favorites. Breakfast at Paschal's is popular with local folks. • **$10/AA**

Patti Hut Café
554A Piedmont Ave., 404/892-5133

Patti Hut Café is locally recognized for fixing the best oxtails in the city as well as the best jerk chicken. But it's the Jamaican meat patties, once sold out of the back of the owner's truck, that put the Patti Hut on the map. The café sponsors poetry readings every Thursday evening and live reggae on weekends. • **$10/AA**

Shark Bar
571 Peachtree St., 404/815-8333

This is where the beautiful people wait, and wait, and wait to enjoy an upscale soul food menu of shrimp étouffée, jerked Cornish hen, and Big Easy chicken and sausage gumbo. The decor is sensuous and the food is good, but the service is inconsistent. Is it all that? You decide. • **$30+/AA-invested**

*Showcase Eatery
5549 Old National Hwy., College Park, 404/669-0504

The Showcase Eatery is a delightful, eclectic, upscale restaurant that not only pays tribute to African American heritage but also makes people from all walks of life feel welcome. The extensive international menu boasts original, freshly prepared, health-conscious dishes (no fried foods). The "Chef's Fantasy" dishes include champagne chicken, New Orleans-style colossal shrimp, sassy salmon, crab leg feast, whole Maine lobster, and Greek-style mahi mahi. • **$30+/AA**

Nightclubs

Atlanta's Buckhead and Five Points sections are popular with the international crowd, so where do the folks hang out? Today's party people have no allegiance to any particular nightclub—you'll find them in that week's latest place to be. So bring your own party and start your own commotion!

Café Echelon
5831 Memorial Dr., Stone Mountain,
404/292-5539
Café Echelon's deejays pump out the very best in contemporary R&B, house, hip hop, and old-school music to a young crowd that really *knows* how to party. In addition, the club features nationally known acts like Howard Hewitt, Silk, SOS Band, the Whispers, and CeCe Peniston, to name just a few. • **Cover charge/AA**

Crowe's Nest
5495 Old National Hwy., College Park, 404/767-0123
The Crowe's Nest has showcased big-name acts such as Regina Belle, Pieces of a Dream, George Howard, and Roy Ayers. It features a sports bar for catching the game and a large dance floor for the party crowd. For late-night bites, the Crowe's Nest has got all your cravings covered, with selections of classic American cuisine. • **Cover charge/AA**

✳Kaya
1068 Peachtree St., 404/874-4460
Up front, Kaya's cute bistro offers a taste of the European old country with tapas, pastas, and salads. But in the back, it's all about the party—with everything from live contemporary jazz to house, funk, and old school. • **Weekend cover charge**

Shaken, Not Stirred

✳Cosmopolitan, 45 13th St., 404/873-6189—As silky smooth as its lethal cocktail namesake, Cosmopolitan is yet another sexy bar/lounge where Atlanta's young professionals go to chill after a taxing day at the j-o-b. Live music nightly.

✳Tongue & Groove, 3055 Peachtree Rd., 404/261-2325—Where Atlanta sophisticates rub martini glasses with local sports celebrities, Tongue & Groove is the cocktail lounge/dance club of the moment. Dress to excess. Sushi bar menu.

✳Martini Club, 2391 Peachtree Rd., 404/842-1010; 1140 Crescent Ave., 404/873-0794—With more than 50 different martinis to choose from—with names like "The Dog Bites Back"—dozens of premium cigars, al fresco dining, and a little piano music to help dissolve the day's worries, the Martini Club provides extra-strength pain relief. Light appetizer menu.

✳Royal Peacock Club
186 Auburn Ave., 404/880-0745
Jimi Hendrix, Chuck Berry, Little Richard, James Brown, Aretha Franklin—these are some of the folks who shaped and forever changed American music. And they all graced the stage of the Royal Peacock. Today, new talent tries to fill their shoes every week, with local and national acts filling the bill with everything from alternative rock to jazz, hip hop, funk, reggae, and world music. With so many great sounds going on all the time, the proud Peacock will not soon lose its feathers. • **Music charge**

✳Sambuca Jazz Café
3102 Piedmont Rd., 404/237-5299
Sambuca marries the "Harlem Nights" attitudes of the 1930s and '40s to funky, modern lifestyles to deliver a jazz club the way it ought to be: cool, sleek, and *trés* sophisticated. Sambuca serves a wonderful continental dinner and offers live jazz nightly. • **Music charge/Dinner $35+**

✳Ying Yang Café
64 Third St., 404/607-0682
A funky little spot where the music is hot and the food is better than most music joints', the Ying Yang club lives up to its name by featuring everything from acid jazz to funk, rap, and straight-ahead jive. Call for a performance schedule. • **Music charge/Dinner $30+**

Festivals

Hotlanta really heats up in the summertime. Loads of outdoor festivals fill parks from one end of the city to the other with music, arts and crafts, laughter, food, and fun.

Atlanta Caribbean Folk Festival
Various venues, 404/344-2567
The entire city starts feelin' that island beat when the Atlanta Caribbean Folk Festival's infectious rhythm and energy shake the city. Thousands of folks crowd the downtown area to hear their favorite reggae bands or catch a glimpse of the latest hot calypso dance troops. Art exhibits, soccer and cricket tournaments, and a colorful Caribbean marketplace add to the weekend's festivities. • **Memorial Day weekend/Free**

Atlanta Jazz Festival
Piedmont Park, 404/817-6951
Atlanta sure knows how to treat its people right! Once limited to free concerts over the Memorial Day weekend, the Atlanta Jazz Festival now kicks off festivities a week early with concerts, art and photography exhibits, poetry, and late-night jam sessions. Area jazz clubs and concert halls host more than 30 local and big-name talents such as Nancy Wilson and Little Jimmy Scott. Brown Bag Concerts, held at Woodruff Park during lunchtime and featuring some of Atlanta's finest musicians, make it difficult to return to the office. Free all-night jam sessions, starting at midnight in area hotels and nightclubs, make it even harder to get up and go to work the next day!

The main event starts on Saturday, and the festival rolls on until late Monday night. Chick Corea, Stanley Jordan, Roy

Hargrove, Pharaoh Sanders, Max Roach, and the Dirty Dozen Brass Band are just a few of the major talents who have graced the Piedmont Park stage. So bring a blanket, a picnic basket, your family, and your best friends and enjoy one of the best free concerts in the country. • **Memorial Day weekend/Admission charge for some events**

Black Arts Festival
Various venues, 404/730-7315
The Black Arts Festival, 10 days of celebration, education, and fun, is one of the most comprehensive events of its kind in the country. It celebrates the African Diaspora in all its complex creativity, bringing together the finest in contemporary and fine art; traditional African art; jazz, blues, urban contemporary, and Caribbean music; film; theater; literature; and dance.

Recent festival events have included evenings with poet Maya Angelou and vocal stylists Abbey Lincoln and Regina Carter, performances of August Wilson's new play *Jitney*, and World Drums for Peace, an ensemble of more than 200 drummers from around the world. Midnight jam sessions complemented live musical entertainment during the day. Free events included the Artists' Market and the Vendors' Market, which showcased scores of African artifacts and original handmade crafts. • **Mid-July/Biannual/Admission charge for most events**

Sweet Auburn Heritage Festival
Auburn Ave., 404/525-0205
When they throw a party on Sweet Auburn, everybody and their grandmother shows up! In 1998, more than 350,000 people from around the world joined together to celebrate not just a neighborhood but a legacy—a legacy that will live on because of Sweet Auburn's preservation. In addition to open doors at area businesses and historic homes, four entertainment stages stir up excitement with acts such as the Great Atlanta Blues Review and Country Western Jamboree, as well as a gospel jubilee. The accompanying Taste of Sweet Auburn event plies plenty of soul food for the party. And what's a street fair without vendors? You'll find everything from handmade jewelry to incense and African masks by way of the Abidjan. • **Third weekend in October**

GDITT/Atlanta CVB

Located in the historic Sweet Auburn district of Atlanta, the APEX Museum displays African art, African American history and exhibitions by local and national artists.

Museums

African-American Panoramic Experience (APEX) Museum
135 Auburn Ave. NE, 404/523-2739

This innovative museum, located within the Sweet Auburn historical corridor, tells many stories of the Black Experience through audiovisual displays, photography, and fascinating artifacts. The APEX focuses on Atlanta history and the Sweet Auburn community. It also features replicas of the trolley that once ran up and down Auburn Avenue and of the Gate City Drugstore, Atlanta's first Black-owned pharmacy. • **Admission charge**

Gallery Hoppin'

Camille Love Gallery, 309 E. Paces Ferry Rd., Suite 120, 404/841-0446—A premier gallery dedicated to the greater exposure of African American artists, featuring original paintings, quilts, crafts, and mixed-media sculptures. AA

Hammonds House Galleries & Resource Center of African-American Art, 503 Peeples St. SW, 404/752-8730—Located in a beautifully restored Victorian house formerly owned by the late Dr. Otis T. Hammonds, a prominent Atlanta physician, this is the only museum in Georgia devoted to the preservation of African American fine art. AA

William Tolliver Art Gallery, 2300 Peachtree Rd., Suite C-203, 404/350-0811—This gallery features original pieces along with prints of Tolliver's popular earthy-colored paintings depicting scenes from African American life. AA

Ebenezer Baptist Church–Heritage Sanctuary
407 Auburn Ave. NE, 404/688-7263
At Ebenezer Heritage Baptist Church, founded in 1886, three generations of pastors not only preached the gospel but changed the course of history as fierce civil rights advocates. The Reverend A. D. Williams, Martin Luther King Jr.'s grandfather, encouraged economic self-sufficiency within the African American community while serving as pastor there. "Daddy" King Sr., founded the Southern Christian Leadership Conference (SCLC) within the church, and Martin Luther King Jr., gave his first and last sermon from Ebenezer's pulpit. Daily tours available. • **Free (donations welcome)**

Herndon Home
587 University Pl. NW, 404/581-9813
The Corinthian-columned home of Atlanta Life Insurance Company founder and president—and Atlanta's first Black millionaire—is more a symbol of achievement and accomplishment than it is a house. Alonzo Franklin Herndon is credited with strengthening the Sweet

Auburn neighborhood by rallying residents and encouraging a strong sense of fiscal responsibility within the local Black community. To tour Herndon's home is to feel a sense of pride and triumph over adversity. • **Admission charge**

Martin Luther King Jr. Center for Nonviolent Social Change
449 Auburn Ave., 404/524-1956
One's reactions while touring the Martin Luther King Jr. National Historical Site will undoubtedly run the course of an emotional roller coaster. The walk through Exhibition Hall, which houses many of Dr. King's awards and accolades—including a replica of his Nobel Peace Prize, copies of his speeches, and other artifacts from the struggle for civil rights—evokes a mixture of excitement, pride, sorrow, and outrage. Most probably you'll be moved to tears viewing the video documentary on King's assassination or while standing in the shadow of his white marble crypt. It is inscribed with his most famous words: "Free at last. Free at last. Thank God Almighty, I'm free at last." An extension of the center includes Ebenezer Heritage Baptist Church and the home where Dr. King was born. • **Free (donations welcome)**

Churches

Big Bethel AME Church
220 Auburn Ave. NE, 404/659-0248
Founded in 1847, Big Bethel was the sanctuary of former slaves who left the segregated white church to be a part of Atlanta's first Black church. Morris Brown College, named after Bishop Morris Brown, the second bishop of the AME church, was founded in the basement of this church back in 1881.

Butler Street CME Church
23 Butler St., 404/659-8745
Tiger Flowers, the first Black middleweight boxing champion, was once a deacon at Atlanta's oldest CME church, founded in 1882.

Ebenezer Baptist Church–New Horizon Sanctuary
400 Auburn Ave. NE, 404/688-7263
This magnificent new sanctuary holds 1,700 worshipers. Two

On the Avenue, Auburn Avenue

Excitement abounds as Sweet Auburn celebrates its past and welcomes the challenges of the new millennium. Check out these sights and attractions:

APEX Museum, 135 Auburn Ave., 404/521-2739

Atlanta Daily World, 145 Auburn Ave., 404/659-1110

Atlanta Life Insurance Company, 100 Auburn Ave., 404/659-2100

Big Bethel AME Church, 220 Auburn Ave., 404/659-0248

Ebenezer Baptist Church-Heritage Sanctuary, 407 Auburn Ave., 404/688-7263

Ebenezer Baptist Church-New Horizon Sanctuary, 400 Auburn Ave., 404/688-7263 (No tours, Sunday service only)

King's Birth Home, 501 Auburn Ave., 404/331-3920

Martin Luther King Jr. Center for Nonviolent Social Change, 449 Auburn Ave., 404/524-1956

Wheat Street Baptist Church, 359 Auburn Ave., 404/659-4328

Sunday morning services are offered, at 7:45 and 11. No tours are available at this facility.

Friendship Baptist Church
437 Mitchell St., 404/688-0206
Founded in 1866, Friendship is Atlanta's oldest African American Baptist church. Ever committed to the education and enlightenment of Black youth, Friendship Church was the site of the first classes of the Atlanta Baptist Seminary in 1879. Spelman College was founded in Friendship's basement in 1881.

Our Lady of Lourdes Catholic Church
25 Boulevard Dr. N.E., 404/522-6776
Founded in 1912, Our Lady of Lourdes is the oldest African American Catholic church in Atlanta.

Recreation

Six Flags Over Georgia
7561 Six Flags Rd., Mableton, 770/948-9290
This amusement complex features eight roller coasters, countless rides, games, children's rides, and scores of other diversions to entertain the family all day long!

Stone Mountain Park
Hwy. 78, Stone Mountain, 770/498-5600
More than 3,200 acres of outdoor recreation activities including fishing, golf, tennis, and a skylift surround the world's largest exposed mass of granite—hence, the name.

White Water Atlanta
250 Cobb Pkwy. N., Marietta, 770/424-9283
The only way to beat the southern heat! White Water Atlanta offers a 90-foot, free-fall Cliffhanger water slide, a 735-foot Run-A-Way River raft ride, a wading pool, a children's water playground, and a new toddler pool.

The San Francisco Bay Area

S an Francisco. Arguably, the most panoramic city in the United States, San Francisco is sweet eye-candy for the soul. This lovely city by the Bay demands and deserves at least a full weekend of your undivided attention to appreciate its abundant attributes. Start your morning downtown with a walk around the financial district, where the imposing, modern skyline fights for attention with the charming structures of yesteryear and where shopaholics' fantasies are realized on every corner. Union Square is where you will find retail's finest seductions. On Maiden Lane, a chic, little alley off the square, stop in Mocca's for a wonderful *al fresco* lunch of jumbo shrimp salad, and the live jazz sounds courtesy of San Francisco's best street musicians. But all is not flawless in paradise. San Francisco's homeless problem is a sad and unfortunate situation. And like many other cities in America, a solution for this quandary is not easy, nor appears to be imminent.

Walk over to Powell and experience the charm of San Francisco's most celebrated attraction; the cable cars. Tell the conductor to let you off at Chinatown, but a word of caution; the two block walk from Powell to Grant Avenue is one of the steepest in the city, so leave your "look cute, but not for walking shoes" at home! Grant Avenue, the oldest street in San Francisco, which runs through the center of Chinatown, is home to hundreds of intriguing storefronts filled with unusual charms, figurines, and spiritual idols, as well as food markets selling pungent spices and every type of animal edible by man. Step into any restaurant for traditional dim sum, best described as a buffet that comes to you. Don't try to taste every delicacy offered by the constant parade of metal rolling carts, and don't worry if you don't recognize some of the items—it's all *good*! At the end of this cable line is another of the city's most famous attractions: Fisherman's Wharf. Now here's the read: it is the tackiest, most unimpressive spot in the city. The only motivation to go at all is to indulge in the fresh, fat Dungeness Crabs that awaits you at every outdoor seafood stall.

By car, there's even more to experience in San Fran At Lyon and Broadway in the breathtaking Pacific Heights district, well-trained joggers tackle a challenging flight of steep, stone steps, with little regard to the palatial homes, and the magnificent view of the Bay and the marina below. The exterior design and property surrounding the Palace of Fine Arts Exploratorium and the Palace of the Legion of Honor museums are equally as impressive as the museum's treasured collections. Vista Point, the first exit once across the Golden Gate Bridge, offers a spectacular view of the city's skyline, the ominous island of Alcatraz, and the sparkling, white-sailed yachts littering that dazzling Bay. And no trip to the area is complete without a drive to the Sonoma and Napa Valley, where after a day of vineyard hopping and wine tasting, finding your way back to San Fran may be a bit of a challenge, but well worth it!

Oakland. Oakland is considered by many to be San Francisco's homely stepsister. The national consensus is that "nobody goes there except to visit relatives." Sad but true. "Oaktown" doesn't have the 24-7 thrill of San Francisco, the quaintness of Sausalito, just across Golden Gate Bridge, or Berkeley's quirkiness. Yet despite these shortcomings, Oakland is a great place to live. The weather is always agreeable, and the residents represent an extremely diverse mix of folks who, for the most part, seem to get along.

Settled by the Spanish in 1820, dubbed "Oaktown"—the "Land of the Oak Trees" by Native Americans—Oakland is best known today as the city where Huey P. Newton and Bobby G. Seale terrified as well as electrified a nation by establishing the Black Panthers. More recently, the city gained notoriety when the local school board recognized the African American dialect called "Ebonics." And it's the place where the Oakland Raiders show the rest of the NFL "This is how *we* do it!" most every Sunday in the fall.

A Hill with a View

You'd be hard pressed to find a bad view while toolin' around the city. Try not to have an accident as you drive around slack-jawed in awe of its beauty. (P.S. Don't forget to put on the emergency brake when you park your car. The thing about those hills? They're steep, very steep.) For particularly impressive vistas, check out the following:

Alamo Square, Hayes and Steiner Sts., Mission District—Located in the heart of the African American community, these quaint Victorian row houses provide a stunning contrast to downtown skyscrapers, which seem like visitors from another world at the city's most photographed location.

Lombard Street—"The crookedest street in America."

Nob Hill, California and Powell Sts.—Best view of the San Francisco Bay.

Telegraph Hill—Take the elevator up 210 feet to the top of Coit Tower.

Twin Peaks—Amazing 360-degree view of the city.

From San Francisco, it's an easy ride to downtown Oakland on BART (Bay Area Rapid Transit), the area's convenient quick-rail. Get off at City Center, where modern mirror-and-chrome skyscrapers stand side by side with some of the most exquisite examples of art deco in the region. Walk north on Broadway for more examples of extraordinary architecture, such as the old I. Magnin store, the Fox Theater (the exterior of which resembles a Buddhist Temple), and the stunning 110-foot-high multicolored mosaic façade of the Paramount Theater. As you walk back down Broadway, cross over to Webster Street and explore the sights and smells of Oakland's Chinatown. Jack London Square, at the base of the Oakland seaport, is an all-inclusive waterfront entertainment center, with restaurants, mainstream retail shops, and appealing boutiques. While there, check out the Ebony Museum of Arts, with its engaging collection of African art and artifacts, and the symbolic World Wall for Peace. A terrific way to end the day is at the ultra-modern sushi bar at Yoshi's, Oakland's premier jazz club, where the spicy tuna rolls are rivaled only by the good musical vibes. Who said there was nothing to do in Oakland?

Restaurants

It is said that if the entire population of San Francisco went out to dinner on the same night, everyone could be seated! With more restaurants per capita than any other city in the United States, the "City by the Bay" is a mecca of great dining. Pan-Asian cuisine, featuring roasted Dungeness crabs and carts loaded with varieties of dim sum, was the darling of the nineties, a decade that forever changed the way America regarded Asian dining. In the East Bay, Berkeley chefs concocted "California cuisine," which combines traditional French food with fresh local seasonings and herbs. But the Bay Area's two greatest contributions to the nineties restaurant scene were the resurrection of California wines and the revival of the martini. Let's face it, any city claiming to have jump-started the notorious gin kicker is aw-right with us!

Fine Dining: San Francisco

✳Aqua
252 California St., San Francisco, 415/956-9662
If food is the sex of the new millennium, then Aqua is arguably San Francisco's most exciting young lover. Seducing nightly with a tantalizing five-course tasting menu, some of Aqua's gloriously, wicked delights may include plump, sensuous Dungeness crab cakes; luscious raw oysters drenched in a frozen Margarita marinade; an irresistible black mussel soufflé drizzled with a light Chardonnay cream sauce; and an orgy of seared foie gras, spinach, and rare Ahi tuna. An assortment of the most sinful desserts imaginable brings the meal to its oh, so satisfying climax. Was it good for you, too? • **$60+**

✳Boulevard
1 Mission St., San Francisco, 415/543-6084
Although the entrées change daily, Boulevard's classic California menu leans more towards beef than fish dishes. No matter, Boulevard can still please the seafood lover with a wonderful appetizer of crispy

softshell crab complemented by a shrimp remoulade or a pan-roasted halibut with jumbo prawns. Keep your fingers crossed that the celebrated roasted rack of lamb with an English pea risotto is on the menu the night you dine here. • **$40+**

✳Farallon
450 Post St., San Francisco, 415/956-6969
The decor is an idealistic, modern version of *20,000 Leagues Under the Sea*, complete with fluid jellyfish chandeliers, and octopus-shaped bar stools. But the food and presentation at Farallon is even more spectacular than the decor, serving up aquatic delights like the rich, seafood chowder; a tempura skate wing atop a bed of Soba noodles and Asian vegetables in a curry mussel sauce; and a pan roasted Alaskan halibut on a bed of asparagus risotto. Desserts are simply outrageous. Consider going for lunch, when the prices are more manageable and the food and the service is just as wonderful. • **$45+**

Fine Dining: Oakland and Berkeley

Bay Wolf Restaurant
3853 Piedmont Ave., Oakland, 510/655-6004
The pretty Victorian setting may make you forget you're in Oakland, but the delicious California cuisine, heavily and heavenly inspired by the Mediterranean, brings you right back to the bay. The menu changes frequently, but if you're lucky, the seafood stew filled with cracked Dungeness crab, and the rockfish entrée will be on the menu, both guaranteed to delight. • **$35+**

Café at Chez Panisse
1517 Shattuck Ave., Berkeley, 510/548-5525
Café at Chez Panisse is where the moniker "California cuisine" was coined and chef Alice Waters crowned the queen of this fresh approach to cooking. To experience the simple but complex seasoning techniques featured on Panisse's four-course prix fixe menu, make reservations at least two weeks in advance. • **$65+**

✳Oliveto
5655 College Ave., Oakland, 510/547-5356
An award-winning restaurant famous for its northern Italian cuisine,

Oliveto is the one reason many San Francisco restaurant snobs venture to Oakland. Oliveto serves the best spit-roasted meats, thin pizzas, and handmade pastas in the Bay area. Try the fall-off-the-bone osso buco, the tender split-roasted pigeon, and the house specialty: taglietelle alla bolognese. • **$35+**

✳TJ's Gingerbread House
741 Fifth St., Oakland, 510/444-7373
Living up to its name, this larger-than-life gingerbread house looks like it jumped off the pages of a Grimm's fairy tale. Adorned with dancing gingerbread men and red-and-white candy-cane poles, the Gingerbread House is one of Oakland's most popular dining spots. Doing their best to make food fantasies come true, the restaurant specializes in Cajun-Creole cuisine. Delicious highlights include Louisiana fancy filé gumbo, smoked prime rib, whiskey stuffed lobster, pheasant bon temps (bathed in coconut milk), and red snapper stuffed with crab. • **$30+/AA**

Casual Dining: San Francisco

The Fly Trap
606 Folsom St., San Francisco, 415/243-0590
Don't let the unpalatable name shoo you away. While this charming bistro can sometimes be a little cramped, the kitchen a little slow, and the dining room a little loud, the Continental cuisine at The Fly Trap is straightforward and good. The menu is heavy on grill items and meats, so stick with what they do best. • **$30+**

Leon's Bar-B-Que
2800 Slope Blvd., San Francisco, 415/681-3071
"If you have been around as long as we have, your food has got to be good!" Leon's serves pork and beef ribs, hot links, chicken, boneless pork, barbecue beef, chili, and Cajun-style jambalaya. Their homemade barbecue sauce, seasonings, and hot links are on sale at the on-site shop. • **$10+/AA**

✳Mozell's Kitchen
6286 Third St., San Francisco, 415/467-1682
This tiny soul food restaurant is one of San Francisco's favorite

Around the World in the Bay

✳**Keur Baobab**, 3386 19th St., San Francisco, 415/643-3558—OK, so it doesn't look like much, but this small, friendly Senegalese eatery serves authentic fare so delicious, you'd swear you were in Dakar. Try the *tieboudien*— fish, vegetables, and rice prepared all in one pot. · $15+/AA

Massawa, 1538 Haight St., San Francisco, 415/621-4129—This funky, modern Eritrean restaurant features traditional East African fare, all served with *injera*, a spongy flatbread, in place of traditional utensils, just as they do back east. (And we don't mean Manhattan!) Beef, lamb, chicken, and lots of vegetarian dishes tantalize the taste buds. · $15+/AA

places to enjoy a meal even your grandmother would approve of (and you know Grandma thinks *no* one can burn like she can!). Mozell's proudly serves fried chicken, smothered steak in oniony gravy, tender baby backs, fried catfish, mac and cheese, and black-eyed peas. Mmm! • **$10/AA**

✳**Powell's Place**
511 Hayes St., San Francisco, 415/863-1404
This funky little spot is right at home on infamous Hayes Street, offering soul cooking peppered with lots of sass. Powell's serves up their famous fried chicken, smothered pork chops, liver and onions, barbecue pork and meatloaf, along with plenty of sides. Save room for a slice of their beautiful homemade banana, lemon, coconut, peach, or sweet potato pie. • **$10+/AA**

✳**Scala's Bistro**
432 Powell St., San Francisco, 415/395-8555
One of the city's most popular hot spots, this modern, Italian bistro knows how to work a sweet onion. Lovin' it, whether they're lightly fried with the crispy calamari, fennel and green beans appetizer; or on top of the fresh tomato, garlic and ricotta salata pizza; or mixed with the roasted duck, covering a housemade pappardella pasta. But it is Scala's wonderfully diverse menu and spacious, 'bring the gang'

dining room that packs the place in nightly, so don't forget to make those reservations. • **$30+**

✷Zuni Café
1658 Market St., San Francisco, 415/552-2522
It's all about the simple pleasures in life at Zuni Café. Tell the waiter to keep the menu, because this is all you need to know: Order one dozen assorted raw oysters with a champagne sauce, the freshly prepared classic Caesar salad, and the roasted brick oven chicken, beautifully poised over a warm, garlicky bread salad laced with currants and pine nuts, please. Only thing missing is a side of veggies. And, in an eatery that boasts organically grown produce, they should be able to hustle up a side of spinach, don't you think? • **$30+**

Casual Dining: Oakland/Berkeley

✷Asmara Restaurant
5020 Telegraph Ave., Oakland, 510/547-5100
For more than 10 years, Asmara has catered to Oakland's diverse culinary appetites. Specializing in Eritrean and Ethiopian cuisine, Asmara offers such dishes as *gored gored* (cubes of tenderloin tips served rare in a spicy butter dip), *ye-beg Alicha* (cubes of lamb stewed with curry), *tebsi* (pan-roasted strips of beef simmered in onion), and *ye-gomen Alicha* (mustard greens simmered in Asmara's special spices). • **$15+/AA**

Caribbean Spice Restaurant
1920 San Pablo Ave., Berkeley, 510/843-3035
The decor at Caribbean Spice pays homage to the islands with flags of Caribbean nations serving as tablecloths and posters of reggae icons on the walls. Local artists' work, much of it available for sale, also adorns the walls. The menu features Caribbean delicacies such as oxtails, Jamaican jerk chicken, curried beef, Lambada-fried fish with sexy rice, crazy goat, and Ghana-style escoveitch fish. A DJ and dancing liven things up on the weekends. • **$15+/AA**

✷Lois the Pie Queen
851 60th St., Oakland, 510/658-5616
This old-fashioned lunch counter, an Oakland institution for 45

years, is known citywide for its great breakfasts and delish pies. How about starting the day with the Reggie Jackson special (two pork chops, eggs, and grits), a tender rib-eye steak with scrambled eggs, or fried chicken with hash browns? Early dinner selections (Lois closes at 2 p.m. weekdays, 3 p.m. Saturdays, and 4 p.m. Sundays) include baked ham, smothered pork chops, and meatloaf. It's impossible to leave without a slice of lemon ice-box, French apple, or sweet potato pie. • **$10+/AA**

*Red Sea Restaurant & Bar
5200 Claremont Ave., Oakland, 510/655-3757
Voted four times the World's Best African Restaurant by *San Francisco Focus* magazine in conjunction with American Express, the Red Sea offers an extensive menu of poultry, lamb, seafood, vegan, and pasta dishes. House specialties include *kilwa dorho* (chicken sautéed in spices), *kitfo* (spicy chopped beef with spiced butter), *sebhi* shrimp (sautéed in spicy red pepper sauce), and *atakilt alitcha* (a mixture of vegetables sautéed with garlic and ginger root). • **$20+/AA**

Soul Brothers Kitchen
5239 Telegraph Ave., Oakland, 510/655-9367
Soul Brothers Kitchen features Creole specialties such as jambalaya, catfish Creole, and crawfish étouffée. Fried chicken, smothered steak, fried oysters, and stuffed red snapper are among other delicious entrées on the lunch and dinner menus. If you can't wait 'til then, breakfast starts at 8 a.m. with salmon croquettes, New York strip, or shrimp with eggs. Now that's the way to start a day! • **$10+/AA**

Take-Out Food: San Francisco

*Big Nate's Barbeque
1665 Folsom St., San Francisco, 415/861-4242
Big Nate (Thurmond, as in one of the top-50 basketball players of all time) serves good pork ribs, Memphis pork butt, beef brisket, links, and chicken from his canary yellow warehouse all day long. Sides include Nate's mean greens, country beans, potato salad, and corn muffins. But the crowd pleaser is the stuffed baked potato, piled high with tender Memphis-style pork, green onions, and barbecue sauce. • **$15/AA**

Brother's in Law Bar-B-Que
705 Divisadero St., San Francisco, 415/931-RIBS
2666 Geneva Ave., San Francisco, 415/467-9335
These two restaurants may not be much to look at on the outside, and the insides are no better, but the barbecue they fix is good and tasty! The menu at Brother's in Law is short but sweet: pork ribs, links, beef brisket, and bird (that's short for chicken). Classic sides like greens, barbecue baked beans, and cornbread round out the meal. • **$10+/AA**

Take-Out Food: Oakland and Berkeley

✳Everett & Jones
296 A St., Hayward, 510/581-3222
1955 San Pablo, Berkeley, 510/548-8261
2676 Fruitvale Ave., Oakland, 510/533-0900
3415 Telegraph Ave., Oakland, 510/601-9377
8740 E. 14th St., Oakland, 510/638-6400
126 Broadway, Jack London Square, Oakland, 510/336-7021
(Family-style dining)
Where "the meat is smoked so pretty, it has a pink glow," Everett & Jones offers a neat, narrow menu of pork ribs, beef brisket, chicken, and beef links, with three sauces to choose from: mild, medium, or Watch Out! The portions are hefty, the meat is fresh, and the taste is like none to be had anywhere else in Northern California. • **$10+/AA**

✳Your Black Muslim Bakery
5832 San Pablo Ave., Oakland, 510/658-7080
365 17th St., Oakland, 510/839-1313
7200 Bancroft Ave., Oakland, 510/568-6024
1474 University Ave., Berkeley, 510/644-3043
160 Eddy St., San Francisco, 415/929-7082
"*As-salaam alaikum*" ("Peace be unto you") is the greeting you'll hear from the friendly staff when you enter any Your Black Muslim Bakery location. Each outlet offers all-natural, egg-free baked goods, a variety of natural whole wheat breads, delicious cobblers, carrot cakes, and their famous bean pies. Fish and tofu burgers are best-sellers among the lunch crowd, as are the spiced pound cake and the cookies (oatmeal, carob chip, and chocolate chip). • **$10/AA**

Nightclubs

Mention the music scene in the Bay area and many will still recall the sixties, when San Francisco was synonymous with hippies, drugs, and rock 'n' roll. However, it was the Fillmore district, formerly an African American neighborhood, that birthed the most influential musical mecca of that decade: the Fillmore Theater. Jimi Hendrix, Aretha Franklin, Marvin Gaye, and Oakland's Tower of Power turned this little local club into a prestigious showcase for some of the best talent of that generation. Today, with the reopening of the Fillmore and other clubs along the strip, the district is trying to relive those infamous days. But, as we all know, lightning rarely strikes twice in the same place.

San Francisco

Asia SF
201 Ninth St., San Francisco, 415/255-2742
In these politically correct days, those once referred to as "drag queens" are now called "gender illusionists," and boy, does Asia SF know how to work those girls! More classy than campy, waitresses do double duty as they jump in and out of character from server to songstress, stepping into the spotlight to strut their stuff. After dinner, these international club kids dance the night away to the rhythms of dance, house, soul, and old-school music. • **Admission charge**

Biscuits & Blues
401 Mason St., San Francisco, 415/292-2583
Sometimes there's nothing better than a big plate of fried catfish, greens, mac and cheese, and for dessert, an order of live down-and-dirty blues. Biscuit & Blues, the Bay area's premier blues/supper club, offers live music nightly and a decent-sized dance floor for when the groove gets to ya. If that space is packed, just kick back your chair and get your dance on right there. • **Music charge**

The Blue Bar
501 Broadway, San Francisco, 415/981-2233
The Blue Bar, located on the first level of the Black Cat Restaurant and featuring, yes, blue walls, is a lively little jazz lounge showcasing

local talent nightly. What's great about the Blue Bar is that the kitchen serves eclectic bar fare until 1:30 a.m.! A much-appreciated courtesy in a city with lots of partying to do. • **Music charge**

The Bubble Lounge
714 Montgomery St., San Francisco, 415/434-4204
This is where you need to start your the evening. With a menu of 300-plus champagnes and sparkling wines to choose from, 30 by the glass, and oysters, beluga caviar, sushi, and other edible aphrodisiacs to savor, the ultra-chic Bubble Lounge knows how to end the day and start the evening right.

John Lee Hooker's Boom Boom Room
1601 Fillmore, San Francisco, 415/673-8000
Legendary bluesman John Lee Hooker brought the blues right back to where it belongs on Fillmore with his "blues lights in the basement" Boom Boom Room. National and local acts turn out the club with live blues, funk, and soul acts every night. • **Music charge/AA-invested**

✳Rasselas Jazz Club
2801 California St., San Francisco, 415/567-5010
A great place to be on a sleepy Monday night, Rasselas is one of the city's best kept secrets for live music and good Ethiopian cuisine. And no cover charge! How can that be? Live music nightly. • **AA**

Storyville Classic Jazz Club
1751 Fulton St., San Francisco, 415/441-1751
Hosting terrific national and local acts playing everything from Latin to straight-ahead jazz, Storyville is San Francisco's premier jazz club. The menu serves—what else?—Creole cuisine, and the gumbo is pretty darn close to the real thing. • **Music charge**

Oakland and Berkeley

Bluesville
131 Broadway at Second St., Jack London Square, Oakland, 510/893-6215
Regional and national acts heat up this club nightly—and they play nothing but the blues. • **Music charge most nights**

The spectacular Martin Luther King Jr. Memorial fountain at the Yerba Buena Gardens in San Francisco.

Casino San Pablo
13255 San Pablo Ave., San Pablo, 510/215-7888
Lots of big names have appeared here, making Casino San Pablo the Bay area's hot spot for urban contemporary artists such as Eric Benoit, his lady love Halley Barry in the audience cheering him on, and the Temptations. The Casino serves a classic American menu for lunch and dinner. • **Music charge**

Eli's Mile High Bar & Club
3629 Martin Luther King, Oakland, 510/655-6661
This is a real-deal blues joint, no frills, no overpriced cocktails, just good down-and-dirty blues. Monday nights host the house jam ses-

sion, the rest of the week features local favorites who've been playing at Eli's for eons. Barbecue, beer, and blues—what else do you need? • **Music charge most nights/AA**

Jimmie's Entertainment Complex
1731 San Pablo Ave., Oakland, 510/268-8445
Sweet Jimmie, as he is known around town, knows how to take care of his patrons, especially the female ones. Exotic male dancers raise the blood pressure, while old-school, R&B, and funk favorites rock the house. Nationally known acts like the Chi-Lites and the Dramatics, as well as local talents, have performed here. Jimmie's also serves first-rate soul food, but what else would you expect from Oakland's most "ghetto fabulous" hot spot! • **Cover charge/Dinner $10/AA**

Yoshi's
510 Embarcadero, Jack London Square, Oakland, 510/238-9200
This club is too cool, too slick, too smart to be in touristy Jack London Square. When Yoshi's moved to its new digs, they installed a state-of-the-art lighting and sound system, a 1998 Steinway nine-foot Concert D grand piano, and a modern smoke-free dining room/bar area with a sensuous decor. Yoshi's features live jazz nightly and a deliciously modern sushi/Pan-Asian menu. • **Music charge**

Festivals

The Bay Area has always been known for colorful street parades and music festivals. The scandalously entertaining Gay Pride Parade; the Nihonmachi Street Fair, featuring the thunderous sounds of taiko drums; and the uplifting Juneteenth celebration are just three of numerous events that animate the Bay Area's already lively streets.

Carnaval
Mission District, San Francisco, 415/826-1401
Carnaval is a big, noisy, outrageous kaleidoscope of costumes, steel-drum players, cultures, and big fun. Foot-stompin', hip-gyratin' dancers strut their stuff through the city's most diverse neighborhood. Parade goers and spectators come out to represent and cheer on their

Juneteeth Celebrations

Berkeley Juneteenth Festival, 510/534-2054—The festival attracts more than 40,000 to the streets of Berkeley for live national and local musical acts, stage performances, and educational forums. One of Berkeley's largest festivals, the event is produced by the Adeline-Alcatraz Merchants Association for the purpose of "promoting the economic and social well-being of residents and small businesses in the South Berkeley community." · Third weekend in June/Most events are free

Juneteenth Celebration, Kimball Park, San Francisco, 415/346-2634, www.sfjuneteenth.com—Introduced to the Bay area in 1945 by Texas club-owner Wesley Johnson, Juneteeth has evolved into a four-day celebration that features a Ms. Juneteenth "Inner Beauty" Pageant, the Invitational Black Rodeo, the Juneteenth Film Festival, a parade, and musical performances featuring top R&B and gospel entertainers. · Third weekend in June/Many events are free

favorite country and culture. Bolivia, Brazil, Jamaica, the Philippines, Trinidad and Tobago, and Puerto Rico are just a few of the 70-plus contingents sashaying their rumbas to the infectious Caribbean beat. At the end of the parade route, revelers find great food, arts, crafts, and more music. Par-tae! • **Memorial Day weekend/Free**

Blues Alley Barbecue and Beer Festival
Jack London Square, Oakland, 510/532-0373
This big throw down is sponsored by one of our favorite culinary establishments, barbecue king Everett & Jones. Talented local musicians take to the stage for an all-out party to celebrate Oakland's rich musical heritage. Blues, jazz, hip-hop, and R&B get everyone in the partyin' groove. • **Third weekend in June**

Blues & Art on the Bay
Historic Old Oakland District, Broadway to Clay from Eight to Tenth Sts., Oakland, 415/249-4640
Oakland takes it to the streets when the Blues & Art fest unveils the

Bay area's most accomplished musicians for an all-out blow-up weekend of music, crafts, food, and big fun. In addition to paying homage to America's greatest art form, the fest features unique African artifacts, original paintings and photography, and handmade crafts. And what's an outdoor festival without lots of good food? Blackened shrimp and crawfish étouffée, African *suya* (chicken) and jolof rice, barbecued oysters, and roasted corn on the cob are among the goodies you'll find. • **Labor Day weekend/Free**

San Francisco Blues Festival
Great Meadow at Fort Mason, San Francisco, 415/979-5588
Since 1972, the San Francisco Blues Festival has thrilled audiences with its all-star lineups. Past legendary rockers have included John Lee Hooker, Jimmie Vaughan, Dr. John, Deborah Coleman, Geoff Muldaur, Robert Cray Band, Taj Mahal, Irma Thomas, Marcia Ball, Mavis Staples, Magic Slim & the Teardrops, and Walter "Wolfman" Washington. • **Third weekend in September**

San Francisco Jazz Festival
Various venues, 415/398-5655
Acid, bebop, straight ahead, Afro-Cuban, and avant garde are just a few of the melodious variations derived from the original American musical form known as jazz. For 12 glorious days, San Francisco brings together more than 50 local and national acts to celebrate jazz. In fields, auditoriums, and intimate, smoky clubs, jazz devotees and novices alike gather to relish the complexity of jazz music. Past performers have included Al Jarreau, Diana Krall, John Pizzarelli, Gato Barbieri, and Tito Puente. • **Last two weeks in October/Admission charge**

Museums

African American Museum and Library (AAMLO)
Charles Greene Building, 659 14th St., Oakland, 510/238-3281
Located on the edge of historic Preservation Park, the museum and library have settled into their new renovated digs in the stunning Charles Greene Building. Founded in 1965 as the East Bay Negro Historical Society, AAMLO focuses on the history of African

Americans in Northern California, with emphasis on the Bay area. The library houses some 300 original manuscripts, 10,000 photographs, and 8,000 books, and it hosts a thought-provoking lecture series and Black History Film Series during February. While at the museum, pick up a map of the African American walking tour of downtown Oakland; later, investigate some of the sites where African Americans contributed to the development of this city. • **Free**

Center for African and African American Art and Culture
762 Fulton St., San Francisco, 415/928-8546
A main goal of this visionary center is to expose children to the art and culture of African ancestry within African and American experience. This effort is realized through revolving exhibits as well as permanent collections representing the diversity of the African Diaspora. Additionally, programs that reinforce these positive images and recognize local and national heroes, present and past, are also offered. • **Admission charge**

Ebony Museum
Jack London Square, Oakland, 510/763-0745
This small, delightful museum features an exhibit on Black stereotypes filled with more portayals of Little Black Sambo and mammies than you care to acknowledge. Other collections include contemporary African American art and unusual African artifacts. • **Free/AA**

Martin Luther King Jr. Memorial Fountain
Yerba Buena Gardens, Fourth and Mission Sts., San Francisco
One of the most spectacular tributes erected to the memory of Dr. King, the Martin Luther King Jr. Memorial Fountain is a study of the man in water, granite, and glass. The thunderous water that falls from the fountain's 50-foot height shields a "floating bridge" walkway where 12 glass panels are inscribed with some of King's most compelling quotations. Beneath each inscription is a translation into one of the 12 languages spoken by San Francisco's international sister cities. The fountain is surrounded by the beautiful Yerba Buena gardens, on the sprawling grounds of the Yerba Buena Center for the Arts.

Gallery Hoppin'

Bomani Gallery, 251 Post St., Suite 600, San Francisco, 415/296-8677—Proprietors Asake Bomani and her husband, film actor Danny Glover, own this gallery showcasing the works of highly acclaimed African American artist. · AA

Expressions Art Gallery, 815 Washington St., Oakland, 510/451-6646—A unique collection of local multicultural artists including an unusual assortment of pieces illustrated by local prisoners. · AA

Thelma Harris Art Galleries, 5940 College Ave., Oakland, 510/654-0443—An exciting collection of contemporary multicultural pieces from the country's most influential and emerging artists. · AA

San Francisco African American Historical and Cultural Society Museum
Building C-165, Fort Mason Center, 415/441-0640
www.fortmason.org.
The museum and gallery house a fairly extensive range of artifacts from the African disapora, including various textiles, masks, sculptures, and elaborate headdresses. Traveling exhibits, publications, manuscripts, and audio and videotapes are just a few of the items in the collection. • **Admission charge**

San Francisco Museum of Modern Art
151 Third St., San Francisco, 415/357-4000
The best in 20th century contemporary art and photography. • **Admission charge**

California Palace of the Legion of Honor
Lincoln Park, 34th and Clement Sts., San Francisco
415/863-3330
Before you head in, check out the spectacular view of the Pacific Ocean and the coast at the scenic overlook. Rodin's Thinker greets you at the museum's entrance. • **Admission charge**

Palace of Fine Arts Exploratorium
3601 Lyon St., San Francisco, 415/561-0360
One of the city's most awesome structures, the Exploratorium houses a "please touch" scientific museum. • **Admission charge**

Churches

Allen Temple Baptist Church
8500 A Street, Oakland, 510/569-9418, www.allen-temple.org
One of the largest congregations in the Oakland area, this 4,000-plus-member community boasts a Family Life Center that provides recreational facilities, an AIDS ministry, and youth outreach programs.

Bethel African Methodist Episcopal Church
916 Laguna St., 415/921-4935
Founded in 1854, Bethel was the first AME in the Bay area. Today, Bethel's outreach work includes child-care programs and support of a credit union and investment club.

Evergreen Baptist Church
408 W. MacArthur Blvd., Oakland, 510/654-2976
The first African American congregation of any denomination in Alameda, California, Evergreen Baptist was organized in 1947 at the home of the Reverend J. L. Richard along with a group of 20 parishioners. Over the years, Evergreen moved a half a dozen times, finally settling in its current location in 1957. Evergreen's outreach programs include weekly Sunday evening radio broadcasts and a spacious housing facility for seniors and those with disabilities.

First African Methodist Episcopal Church
Telegraph and 37th, Oakland, 510/655-1527
Founded in 1858, the First African Methodist Episcopal Church is credited with establishing the first school for African Americans in the East Bay.

Glide Memorial United Methodist Church
330 Ellis St., 415/771-6300
Glide Memorial is located in the Tenderloin, a neighborhood littered

with society's unwanted denizens and purposely omitted from every San Francisco city tour. Led over the past 35 years by the outspoken and controversial Reverend Cecil Williams, Glide is the only hope and inspiration to many here, feeding more than 3,500 needy people three times a day, 365 days a year. Glide parishioners are required to volunteer their time and efforts to many outreach programs.

Third Baptist Church
1399 McAllister St., 415/346-4426
Third Baptist, the first African American Baptist congregation west of the Rockies, was established in 1854. Founded as the First Colored Baptist Church, Third Baptist occupied a site at Clay and Hyde, now a National Historic Landmark, from 1908 to 1956. The Reverend Amos C. Brown is active in San Francisco community politics and a confidant to Mayor Willie Brown.

Recreation

Alcatraz
Immortalized on film by Clint Eastwood, Alcatraz is almost as much trouble to get to as it was for the original prisoners to escape from. First, you have to make reservations three days in advance. Second, you must arrive no later than 20 minutes before the boat's departure to "the Rock." Make sure you bring a sweater since the trip across the bay can be cold, and wear comfortable shoes because there are hills to climb and a long walkway to the prison. • **Admission charge**

Golden Gate Park
This sprawling three-mile park is where the city comes to play. Tennis courts, horse stables, soccer fields, tranquil lakes, a children's playground including a handsome carousel, and a golf course are among this gorgeous park's main amenities. Make sure you stop to smell the roses at the Conservatory of Flowers, say a prayer at the National AIDS Memorial Grove for those remembered there, and take in the rest of the lovely sights as you travel the length of Martin Luther King Jr. Drive from one end of the park to the other.

Enjoying the beauty of Wilhemina's Garden, located in Golden Gate Park.

Lake Merritt/Lakeside Park
Grand and Bellevue Aves., Oakland, 510/238-6876

Smack in the middle of downtown Oakland is Lake Merritt, where one can escape from the humdrum of everyday life. Glide across its tranquil waters in a paddleboat, bird watch at the sanctuary, or take the kids to the Children's Fairyland. At dusk, the enchantment of the lake turns up a notch when the "Necklace of Lights" surrounding it illuminates the night.

The Presidio
Lombard St., San Francisco, 415/561-4323
This scenic historical park was once one of the oldest military bases in the nation. Seventeenth-century cannons, World War II bunkers, and deserted surface-to-air missile sites provide an eerie backdrop and a stark contrast to the nearby Presidio golf course, bike trails, and Baker beachfront.

Birmingham

Birmingham. "Such a sleepy town," folks say. "Not much going on there. Well, it is in the South, and you know how slow the South moves." Perhaps, but "back in the day" Black Birminghamians were lucky to get any sleep at all for fear of being jolted awake in the middle of the night by bombs exploding and neighbors crying "Fire!" as their homes burned to the ground.

Birmingham today is still cooling down from its early incendiary years, when residents didn't get along quite as well as they do now. Today, the tragedies and triumphs of the city's past have been distilled and preserved for all the world to see in what is now called Birmingham's "Civil Rights District." This historic downtown area is bounded by Fourth and Sixth Avenues and 15th and 18th Streets. Once the hub of local African American business activity and prosperity, it was also the center of acute social injustice and police brutality.

Kelly Ingram Park, the site of many demonstrations, sits in the middle of the Civil Rights District. Disturbing yet impressive sculptures positioned along a circular path called Freedom's Trail tell the moving story of Black Birmingham residents' struggle for freedom from racial oppression. These memorials include statues of Black children and youth being attacked by vicious police dogs, sprayed by high-powered fire hoses, and jailed when the intentions of their peaceful demonstrations were lost on local authorities.

The Birmingham Civil Rights Institute's museum continues the story in more detail, concentrating on several important events that took place throughout Alabama. It chronicles the sufferings and suc-

This shocking bronze portrayal of police brutality during the civil rights riots is immortalized in Kelly Ingram Park.

cesses of the Civil Rights movement: the historic March on Selma, the Montgomery Bus Boycott, the establishment of the Alabama Christian Movement for Human Rights, and the bombing of Birmingham's Sixteenth Street Baptist Church. This byzantine African American church, which sits across the street from the Institute, received national notoriety in 1963 when a bomb blew up in its basement, killing four young Black girls waiting to attend Sunday school.

Upon leaving Sixteenth Street Baptist Church and the Civil Rights Institute, walk back through Kelly Ingram Park to the Fourth Avenue Black Business District, a restored three-block area that during segregation was the center of all Black activities. Hosie's Bar-b-que & Fish is *the* place for lunch. Hosie himself might even come out to make sure your plate of cornmeal-fried whiting slathered with hot sauce, collard greens, and tangy potato salad is prepared to your liking.

After such a meal, you'll no doubt want to take a nice, long walk. Wander around the district and check out the old-fashioned barber shops, boutiques, and soul food restaurants. Just about every little take-out place in the neighborhood boasts a juke box that plays R&B oldies-but-goodies to serenade you while you wait for your order. No surprise—music plays an important role in Alabama's history. The intimate Alabama Jazz Hall of Fame, located in the old Carver Theater at Fourth Avenue and 17th Street, pays tribute to the impressive musical talent the state has shared with the world over the decades.

After touring the Civil Rights District, head to the south side of the city, past the University of Alabama campus to Lakefront, a newly developed area where antique bazaars filled with other people's junk sit next to ultra-sophisticated furniture showrooms. Don't worry if you fall in love with that caramel brown chenille sofa, they'll ship it anywhere in the United States for a small charge.

Time for a quick nap before dinner; the hot Birmingham sun takes a toll on everyone's energy. Tonight, enjoy an evening of fine dining at Azalea, one of Birmingham's choicest restaurants, located on the south side of the city. The restaurant features a fried-catfish appetizer that's big enough to share with others—though it's so good you might not want to. After dinner, head to Ona's Music Room to hear the best in local jazz. Oh, sleepy Birmingham, you've got a lot to be proud of today!

Restaurants

Funny thing about dining in the South: One's self-restraint seems to fly out the window once a menu is in hand. Just below the Mason-Dixon line, the typical breakfast order of cereal, toast, and juice explodes into an all-out orgy of smothered pork chops, grits and gravy, biscuits, scrambled eggs. It just can't be helped! Many of Birmingham's simple neighborhood restaurants subscribe to this style of eating. Is it a conspiracy against the bagel and gourmet coffee industry? Nah, it's just their way of welcoming you home.

Fine Dining

*Azalea
1218 20th St. S., 205/933-8600
Azalea does its patrons a disservice as soon as they walk in the door: The dining room is so dimly lit, you have to strain your eyes to appreciate the beautiful decor. With brighter lighting, diners also could better see and enjoy Azalea's fabulous sizzling whole-catfish appetizer, the luscious tomato bisque with dollop of crabmeat, and the lightly fried grouper tittering on a bed of extra rich and buttery Boursin-whipped potatoes. If you're the type who squirms when ordering wine to complement your meal, you're in luck: Azalea's menu suggests the perfect vintage to accompany each entrée. • **$35+**

*Highlands Bar & Grill
2011 11th Ave., 205/939-1400
Considered by locals to be Birmingham's best restaurant, Highlands main dining area is certainly one of the loveliest, with a strong accent on French decor and appointments. The cuisine is nouvelle American with entrées such as Appalachicola oysters on the half shell with two sauces for dipping, lump crabmeat with golden potatoes, grilled shrimp and tuna, and a lovely veal chop with caramelized sweet Vidalia onions, white asparagus, and Madeira redeye gravy. • **$35+**

Casual Dining

*Dreamland Bar-B-Que Ribs
1400 15th St. S., 205/933-2133
Since 1958, John "Big Daddy" Bishop served nothing but his famous ribs with warm piquant sauce on the side, barbecue pork sandwiches, and soft white bread. In fact, his slogan was "No slaw, no beans, no potato salad—don't ask!" Well, someone whispered the right words in his ear because just before Bishop passed away in 1997, he added vegetable sides and barbecued chicken to his menu. Thank goodness, the additional pressure on the kitchen did not jeopardize the integrity of the meats. In other words, the eatin's all good at Dreamland! Grab a seat by the window, ask for plenty of napkins, keep the sweet tea coming! • **$15/AA-invested**

Black Business District Eateries

Fancy they are not, but plenty of down-home goodness comes out of the kitchens of these African American-owned, cheap-and-cheerful take-out restaurants:

Green Acres Café, 1705 Fourth Ave. N., 205/251-3875—Chicken livers, wings smothered in hot sauce, fried whitefish, and pork chop sandwiches.

La' Vase Fine Foods, 328 16th St. N., 205/328-9327—Soul food dinners.

Nelson Brothers Café, 312 17th St. N., 205/254-9098—Breakfast, chicken, fish, and sides.

Gorin's of Southside
1101 20th St. S., 205/933-5220
This is one old-fashioned ice cream parlor that takes ice cream seriously. Even the frozen yogurt and the fat-free ice creams are rich enough to give Bill Gates a toothache. If you're looking to cut back on calories, don't even tempt yourself by walking through the doors. For the rest of us, Gorin's works out just fine, with lots of great gourmet deli sandwiches, vegetarian burgers, salads, and baked goods—just in case ice cream isn't enough! • **$10**

*Hosie's Bar-b-que & Fish
321 17th St. N., 205/326-3495
The most popular Black-owned restaurant in Birmingham has to be Hosie's. We're talkin' about cornmeal-fried whiting dinners with sides—tender, tasty collard greens and way-too-cheesy macaroni and cheese—the way your mama made them. The barbecued pork sandwich is large and sloppy, just the way you like it, and served with cole slaw and sweet baked beans. The fried chicken wings can be combined with fish or ribs or served alone. Sure, there are other items on the menu, but what more do you need to know? Located in the center of Birmingham's Black business district, Hosie's is cheap and cheerful, and so is its decor. Just keeping it real! • **$10+/AA**

Jim N Nick's Barbecue
744 29th St. S., 205/323-7082

Fancier than most barbecue joints you'll ever visit, Jim N Nick's caters to those who enjoy the simple things in life but still want "a little flash for their cash." The restaurant's bar area rivals any trendy martini bar, as does its main seating area. A meal of flaky barbecued pork, tender barbecued chicken, or smoked turkey, accompanied by cheese biscuits and lemon ice box pie, is the way to go! • **$15+**

The Mill Brewery, Eatery & Bakery
1035 20th St., 205/939-3001

The Mill, as this multi-venue restaurant in Five Points is known, is reminiscent of a favorite campus hangout where everyone meets after class and the food is always good and cheap. The dinner menu features peppered pork tenderloin with tangy mustard sauce and Cajun jambalaya penne pasta with chicken, shrimp, and sausage. Late night, the Mill becomes the place to be when the house band does their best Neville Brother's imitation and the pesto chicken pizza goes head-to-head (no pun intended) with the on-site-brewed beer. • **$15+**

Niki's West Steak & Seafood Restaurant
233 Finely Ave. W., 205/252-5751

Niki's West exemplifies the diversity that is Birmingham today. Truck drivers and downtown executives, mothers and kids, rich folks and folks down on their luck—they all dine at Niki's. Here the food is strictly southern and the portions are huge. Breakfast is all about fried pork chops, grits, scrambled eggs, and wonderfully sweet sticky buns. Lunch is cafeteria-style with smothered chicken, fried fish, and barbecue, with plenty of sides to choose from. The dining room is modest, and the waitresses take cigarette breaks at the few empty tables available, but that's OK. There's no pretense at Niki's, and that's aw'right! • **$10+**

Nightclubs

Birmingham's south side, especially the Five Points area, caters to the college crowd with live local rock bands performing at restaurants, bars, and night spots. High-tech dance clubs in this neighborhood stay open until the wee hours. A smattering of African American party-goers visits these establishments, but most frequent the downtown clubs on North Second Avenue or Ona's Music Room, also on the south side.

*Blue Monkey Lounge
1318 Cobb Ln., 205/933-9222

This is a slick cocktail bar where straight-up martinis are the drink of choice, hand-rolled cigars are enjoyed by men and women alike, and live jazz adds to the already ultra-cool ambience.

French Quarters
1630 Second Ave. N., 205/322-1700

There's plenty of room to party at this large, two-story dance club. Live R&B and deejay-spun old-school and urban contemporary music rock the house all night long. • **Cover charge/AA**

*Ona's Music Room
423 20th St. S. 205/322-4662

Ona's Music Room is reminiscent of the old-fashioned juke joints of the South: a simple interior with a splash of red on the walls for color, a bar against the back wall, a stage in the center of the room. What makes Ona's special is the caliber of musicians who perform here Wednesdays through Saturdays, including proprietor Ona Watson himself. His smooth, silky voice, coupled with terrific local bands like Eric Essex & Modern Man, makes Ona's Music Room Birmingham's number-one spot for live jazz and R&B. • **Music charge/AA**

Wellington's Bistro 1500
Second Ave. N., 205/324-2345

White lights twinkle in the windows of the dining room at Wellington's, an upscale eatery popular for its live jazz and soul food menu. • **Music charge/AA**

Festivals

Music, music, and more music is what Birmingham festivals are all about. With an emphasis on urban contemporary sounds, jazz, and blues, Birmingham summers pound with plenty of "dancing in the streets."

City Stages
Linn Park, 888/290-5795
The entire city of Birmingham rolls out for City Stages, the party extravaganza of the year. With more than 270 acts performing on 16 stages throughout the city, City Stages has something for everyone. Blues, gospel, world beat, reggae, alternative, rock, and R&B stars light up the night and dazzle the day with concerts starting at 12 noon and continuing until 11 p.m. Big-name performers have included Isaac Hayes, Chaka Khan, T. S. Monk, Robert Cray, Donna Summer, Irma Thomas, Phil Collins, the Neville Brothers, Take 6, the Doobie Brothers, Ohio Players, and the Gap Band. And that's just the short list! Local restaurants make sure everyone has enough to eat, and vendors sell jewelry and crafts. • **Third weekend in June/Admission charge**

Function at Tuxedo Junction Jazz Festival
Erskine Hawkins Park, 205/788-3672
Honoring the alumni of Alabama's most famous group of musicians, the Function at Tuxedo Junction Jazz Festival features local yet legendary bands, stage performers, and dance troupes. Held in Erskine Hawkins Park, named in honor of the big band conductor himself, festival honorees include Fess Whatley, Amos Gordon, and Sammy Lowe. "Doc" Frank Adams, executive director of the Alabama Jazz Hall of Fame, still gets out there and blows a mean clarinet! • **Last Saturday in July/Free/AA**

Birmingham Heritage Festival
Civil Rights District, 205/324-3333
When George Duke, Kenny Latimore, and Rachelle Ferrell came on stage together to kick off the first night of the 1999 Birmingham Heritage Festival, the crowd knew the evening was going to be "all the way live." The artists took turns helping each other out: Latimore and Ferrell sang sweet backup to Duke's "No Rhythm or No Reason," and Duke played musical director to Latimore's "For You." Then he sang backup for Ferrell, who turned it out with her sultry "What Did I Do to Deserve This?" Nearly everyone jumped to their feet when

Young performers celebrate their heritage at the Birmingham Heritage Festival.

Duke rolled out his anthem "Dookie Stick"! Almost three hours of old-school jams and sexy ballads, and this was only one of six stages. Other performers in 1999's impressive lineup included Bobby Blue Bland, Foxy Brown, Michael McDonald, Joe Sample, Michael Franks, Nas, and Busta Rhymes.

This fest has something for everyone. In addition to the main stage, there is a gospel stage, a jazz and reggae stage, a blues and R&B stage, a hip hop stage, and a poets' stage. Festival veterans sling collapsible chairs in canvas tubes on their backs—very smart: The music stages are set up in the street, and the hard, hot concrete quickly punishes one's behind. Although the festival begins around 3 p.m., most folks don't arrive until 8 p.m. (That Birmingham heat will get you every time!)

Of course, the festival also features the obligatory vendors selling African artifacts and jewelry and plenty of so-so food (mostly giant polish sausages and fried catfish). But it's the folks peddling frozen non-alcoholic daiquiris in bizarre, foot-tall plastic containers that make out like bandits. Again, blame it on the heat! • **First weekend in August/Admission charge/AA**

A Family Affair
Kelly Ingram Park, 205/322-5646
The Birmingham Civil Rights District rocks with the biggest names in the entertainment industry when they turn out for A Family Affair, held Labor Day weekend. Past performers include such notables as Lauryn Hill, LL Cool J, Barry White, the Temptations, Brandy, and Monica. The purpose of this event is not just to celebrate great music but to celebrate the history and future of the African American family. In addition to several stages for gospel and jazz performers, the festival also offers a children' s pavilion and a comedic stage for those who need a good laugh. • **Labor Day weekend/Admission charge/AA**

Museums and Attractions
Civil Rights District

Birmingham Civil Rights Institute
520 16th St. N., 205/328-9696
"Wow!" Chances are, that's what you'll say after touring the Birmingham Civil Rights Institute. Most folks are awed or overwhelmed by the permanent exhibits. But the Institute is about much more than exhibits, it's about teaching. It reminds us where we came

Think You've Seen It All?

Barber Vintage Motorsports Museum, 2721 Fifth Ave. S., 205/252-8377—Born to be wild? This is the museum for you. More than 325 motorcycles from the very first one to the baddest ones on the market today are on display. · Admission charge

Birmingham Museum of Art, 2000 Eighth Ave., 205/254-2565—An interesting collection of art from different cultures including African, Asian, and American works. The atrium displays a collection of gorgeous colorful glass sculptures that resemble amoebas dressed for Mardi Gras. · Free

Southern Museum of Flight, 4343 73rd St. N., 205/833-8226—Before you get back on the plane to go home, check out the Southern Museum of Flight. The World War II Tuskegee Airmen are prominently featured here, along with other early aviation milestones. · Admission charge

from and who paved the way for our smooth successes, it points us in the right direction and helps us realize our battles are nothing compared to those our heroes fought.

This museum honors those heroes. Some of them we already know: Rosa Parks, Martin Luther King Jr., Adam Clayton Powell. Others are less familiar to us, like the Rev. Fred Shuttlesworth, pastor of Bethel Baptist Church and founder of the Alabama Christian Movement for Human Rights, the group that stepped into the gap when the NAACP was kicked out of town. The museum also recognizes the thousands of protesters, activists, parents, working-class citizens, children, and youth who marched peacefully for equal rights and in return were confronted with attack dogs, fire hoses, and jail time. Many of their names we will never know, but after a visit to this museum, their actions and bravery are forever engraved in our minds.

The journey into the past starts with a short film recalling slavery and other manifestations of racism in the United States. The interactive galleries engage visitors in viewing videos, photographs, and newspaper clippings that chronicle the era of segregation, failed and successful integration efforts, Freedom Fighters, the March on Selma, church bombings, and voter registration drives, ending with the 1963 March on Washington. Wow! • **Admission charge**

Fourth Avenue Business District
Fourth Ave. N. between 15th and 18th Sts.
During segregated times, African Americans developed the downtown area between 15th and 18th Streets and set up businesses including barber shops, churches, restaurants, and a funeral home. This strip, part of the city's Civil Rights District, is being preserved to remember those prosperous yet turbulent times. Also known as the Black Business District, it is home to several casual restaurants and barber shops, where patrons and friends sit outside and talk the talk, as they have for years.

Kelly Ingram Park
Sixth Ave. at 16th St.
Identified by former Birmingham mayor Richard Arrington as "a place of revolution and reconciliation," Kelly Ingram Park saw numerous peaceful marches turn violent during the turbulent 1960s. Stone, bronze, and steel sculptures placed at the entrance of the park and along a path named Freedom's Trail pay tribute to Civil Rights heroes in Birmingham, both revered and unsung. The most controversial sculptures depict frightened but courageous children being attacked by police dogs and fire hoses that resemble machine guns. One wonders why these images are considered controversial by some when, in fact, they simply retell historical truths.

Sixteenth Street Baptist Church
1530 Sixth Ave. N., 205/251-9402
Founded in 1873 as the First Colored Baptist Church of Birmingham, Sixteenth Street Baptist Church was also the city's first Black church, period. The current sanctuary was built by African American architect Wallace Rayfield in 1911. Over the years, the church has served as a social and meeting place for members of its congregation and others. In the early 1960s, it became the headquarters for Civil Rights movement activities, rallies, and meetings. Some of the more violent and memorable events of that era occurred in or in front of Sixteenth

Street Baptist Church. On September 15, 1963, a bomb exploded at the church, killing four young girls waiting to attend Sunday school. This act of cowardice and malice shocked not only Birmingham but the world. More than $300,000 was raised to rebuild the church. The people of Wales donated a stunning stained-glass window depicting a Black Christ as a symbol of peace and a memorial to that awful day. Today, Sixteenth Street Baptist Church holds worship services every Sunday and offers guided tours upon advance notification. • **Free (donations welcome)**

Other Museums

Alabama Jazz Hall of Fame
1631 Fourth Ave. N., 205/254-2731
Inside the historic Carver Theater is the Alabama Jazz Hall of Fame, the first museum of its kind. Neon pink and blue lights welcome jazz enthusiasts. This museum honors a pleasant aspect of Alabama history: the music that held folks together during desperate times and that continues today to unite people of all races. The eras of down 'n' dirty blues, the big band, sultry vocal stylings, and straight-ahead jazz are all represented. The first inductees included Fess Whatley, Erskine Hawkins, Haywood Henry, Sammy Lowe, Amos Gordon, and "Doc" Frank Adams, the only musician living of the original six and the current executive director of the hall. Adams still performs, and his CDs are proudly played throughout the intimate museum, which showcases photographs, wax figures, paintings, costumes, sheet music, and posters. An interactive "juke box" commemorates some 170 of Alabama's finest jazz musicians. • **Free (donations welcome)**

Churches

Bethel Baptist Church
3200 28th Ave. N., 205/322-5360
Pastor Fred Shuttlesworth founded the Alabama Christian Movement for Human Rights at Bethel Baptist Church when the NAACP was banned from Birmingham. During Shuttlesworth's tireless campaign for equal rights for African Americans, Bethel Baptist Church, originally located at 3191 29th Avenue North in

The Power of the Black Church

In 1958, under the direction of Rev. Fred Shuttlesworth, the Alabama Christian Movement for Human Rights (ACMHR) rallied the parishioners of 55 Black churches to attend mass meetings every Monday night to gain support for integration in Birmingham. By 1961, the police began infiltrating meetings and taping the proceedings to use as evidence against Shuttlesworth. Needless to say, this only fueled the fire that ACMHR had already lit. Below is a short list of ACMHR-member churches still located in Birmingham and active today:

Metropolitan AME Zion Church, 1530 Fourth Ave. N., 205/252-8503

St. Luke AME Church, 2803 21st St. N., 205/252-3717

St. Paul (United) Methodist Church, 1500 Sixth Ave. N., 205/252-3236

Sixteenth Street Baptist Church, 1530 Sixth Ave. N., 205/251-9402

The following churches have relocated to these new addresses since the movement years:

First Baptist Church, 1508 19th St., Ensley, 205/788-2494

New Pilgrim Baptist Church, 708 Goldwire Place S.W., 205/326-0923

St. James Baptist Church, 1300 24th St. N., 205/251-5342

St. John AME Church, 708 15th St. N., 205/251-3764

Seventeenth Street A.O.H. Church, 1120 24th St. N., 205/252-4270

Sixth Avenue Baptist Church, 1101 Martin Luther King Jr. SW, 205/251-5173

Collegeville, served as a meeting place and refuge for Civil Rights movement organizers and workers. The church was bombed on Christmas Day 1956, in response to Shuttlesworth's protest of the segregation of public transportation.

Sixteenth Street Baptist Church
1530 Sixth Ave. N., 205/251-9402
Filmmaker Spike Lee's documentary film *4 Little Girls* tells the story that changed race relations in Birmingham forever and brought

Tee Time

Beacon Hill, 333 16th Ave. SW, 205/328-8545

Eagle Point, 4500 Eagle Point Dr., 205/995-2000

Oxmoor Valley Golf Club, 100 Sunbelt Pkwy., 205/942-1177
   (Robert Trent Jones Golf Trail course)

worldwide attention to the plight of African Americans. The movie recounts an event that took place in this church on that fateful Sunday in September 1963 when a homemade bomb thrown into a basement window at the church killed four young girls. Services are held every Sunday. (See also page 55.)

Recreation

Visionland Theme Park
5051 Prince St., Bessemer, 205/783-6040
The brainchild of African American Larry Langford, Visionland is the first major theme park to open in the Birmingham area since 1993. Geared toward family fun, Visionland boasts an old-fashioned-looking wooden roller coaster (remember the one on Coney Island?), a water park, a picnic and park area, a 120-foot Ferris wheel, and, of course, plenty of rides and cotton candy for the kids.
• **Admission charge**

Boston

oston. "Baah-ston," as the locals pronounce it, is one of the most charming cities in the United States. For one thing, the city boasts extraordinary parks, such as the famed Boston Commons, the oldest public park in the nation. Visitors to the Commons can stop to smell the fragrant roses scattered throughout the gardens, finger pop to the groove of a lunch-time jazz performance, or glide across a lagoon in a boat shaped like a giant white swan. A walk along elegant Commonwealth Avenue can make you feel greener than the perfectly planted trees lining that boulevard—green with envy, that is, at the people who actually live in those fabulous brick mansions. Try not to cause a car accident driving down Storrow Drive as you steal a quick glimpse of the Charles River sparkling beneath the noon-day sun. Cambridge, just over the Massachusetts Bridge, preserves the bohemian-radical image it earned in the '60s, but it's the stunning spectacle of Harvard and MIT each fall, when brilliant leaves blanket the sprawling campuses, that attracts thousands of admirers each year.

But all that glitters is not gold in Beantown. Boston's reputation for entrenched racism is a civic embarrassment, and its neglect of its own African American neighborhoods—including the infamous Roxbury area, early stomping grounds of the young Malcolm X—is the stuff of urban legends. Quite frankly, many Black people do not feel comfortable in Boston and remain cautious of the racist remnants of the city's past. While other cities have grown beyond their violent histories, many fear that Boston still holds tight to a deplorable legacy of prejudice and discrimination.

So why visit Boston, a city whose European American residents have historically shown that they have little regard or need for Blacks? Because of its African American heritage. Black Bostonians have many stories to share about their role in shaping New England. Boston's Museum of Afro-American History (MAAH) is committed to telling those stories, through exhibits and the Black Heritage Trail, an engaging self-guided discovery of 10 landmarks and sites relating to the Beacon Hill community prior to the Civil War. The museum is located on Beacon Hill in the African Meeting House, the oldest surviving Black church edifice in the nation. Long before the bluebloods moved in, Beacon Hill was the center of Boston's African American community; today it is one of the toniest areas of the city, a neighborhood of red brick sidewalks and Doric-columned townhouses with petite Juliet balconies. Beacon Hill was also home to the first public school built expressly for the education of Black students, and where notables such as Frederick Douglass and Sojourner Truth waged many early battles for Black civil rights.

Down the street from the historical attractions on Beacon Hill, in front of the Old State House, lie a ring of cobblestones marking the site of the Boston Massacre. When British troops opened fire on the group of defiant colonists, igniting the Revolutionary War, Crispus Attucks, a runaway slave, was the first man killed.

Present-day Boston has just as much to offer. Visitors can easily lose track of time in the sophisticated art galleries, outdoor cafés, and exclusive boutiques and haberdasheries located downtown on Boylston and Newbury Streets.

Well, here we go again: Where to eat? If you came to New England for seafood, Turner Fisheries guarantees to serve some of the best clam chowder in town, not to mention a lush Bouillabaisse brimming with *fur de mer*. Bob the Chef's is the only Black-owned restaurant downtown, and while Bob doesn't know from clam chowder, he does know a thing or two about "glori-fried" fried chicken, collard greens, and sweet candied yams. To check out some of the local "flava," late-night jazz enthusiasts head over to Wally's, a little joint in the heart of the city where local musicians wail until all hours of the night.

Restaurants

When you're a city known worldwide for clam chowder and baked beans, it can be hard to convince gourmands to take your other culinary offerings seriously. So, in the 1980s, restaurants began luring some of the country's brightest chefs to Beantown. These kitchen magicians conjured up seafood dishes so fresh and savory, they could make a lobster clap on the way to the pot. Adding more flavor to Boston's culinary scene, a generous sprinkling of neighborhood ethnic eateries opened during the '80s, and *voilà!* Boston became the Northeast's latest gastronomic sensation.

Fine Dining

✳Biba's
272 Boylston St., 617/426-7878
Considered by many to be the best restaurant in Boston, Biba sets the bar so high, other restaurants wish they could just qualify for the preliminaries. Biba's menu is classified as "eclectic New American," borrowing the best spices and influences from other ethnic kitchens, and designing creative dishes that are strictly Biba's own. With a pinch of Mediterranean seasoning here, something baking in a tandoori oven over there, what turns out to be Biba's signature dish? How does lobster pizza sound for a modern New England dish? • **$40+**

✳Hammersley's Bistro
553 Tremont St., 617/423-2700
This charming country French-American bistro, one of Boston's crown jewels, serves some of the most palate-pleasing dishes in town. Try the petite tart of lobster, a full, crispy-skin roast chicken, or the beef filet with fried oysters and garlic mashed potatoes. Yum! • **$35+**

✳Radius
8 High St., 617/426-1234
Sure, Radius is snooty and pertinacious, and you can't get an 8 o'clock reservation on a Friday night for love or money, but hey, who cares? If you have to call a week in advance for a table, so be it—this modern

More Than Just Clam Chowder

Jae's Café and Grill, 520 Columbus Ave., 617/965-7177—In addition to an exciting menu of Japanese and Korean delights, Jae's features traditional Korean flat tabletop grilling. · $30+

✳**Tiger Lily**, 8 Westland Ave., 617/267-8881—Wonderful upscale Malaysian cuisine in a bamboo village environment. Love the jumbo shrimp fried in ground coconut batter! · $20+

American menu is just too good to miss. So, if you've just got to see what all the fuss is about, not to mention need a place to sport those sexy new black threads, Radius is it. At least for this week. • **$35+**

Casual Dining

✳Black Crow Caffé
2 Perkins St., Jamaica Plain, 617/983-9231
In racially strained Boston, Black Crow Caffé is a neighborhood bistro that attracts a multicultural clientele and appears refreshingly free of any hint of ethnic tension. This colorful meeting place packs 'em in on Sunday and Monday nights with live jazz. The menu changes monthly specializing in light bistro fare. Entrées include breaded crusted Atlantic salmon, wood-grilled chicken with garlic mashed potatoes, and oven-roasted Chilean sea bass with red pepper saffron risotto. • **$20+/AA**

✳Bob the Chef's Jazz Cafe
604 Columbus Ave., 617/536-6204
Since the reopening of Bob the Chef's in 1996, after an upscale renovation, the wait for a table on the weekends is as long as one hour. So arrive early, and start with the Cajun crab cakes and mustard fried catfish. Bob's original "glori-fried" chicken, baby beef liver and onions, barbecued spare ribs, and smothered pork chops keep folks coming back for more. Live jazz Thursday through

Saturday packs the house, and Sunday's all-you-can-eat jazz brunch is not to be missed. • **$20/AA**

✳Chef Lee's
140 Blue Hill Ave., Dorchester, 617/436-6634
Old-fashioned meatloaf, barbecued ribs, collard greens, fired chicken, candied yams, black-eyed peas, potato salad, coconut cake, and sweet potato pie are just a few of the reasons why folks from all over Boston head to Chef Lee's. This modest little spot is known not only for its decadent banana pudding, but also for its makeshift African American Wall of Fame, which displays framed photos of local and national heroes, celebrities, and friends and family. • **$10/AA**

✳Grill 23 & Bar
161 Berkeley St., 617/542-2255
Just because it's been named "Best Steak House" and "Best Seafood Restaurant," is that any reason to eat at Grill 23? Heck, yes! What could be better than a beet-red center filet mignon sitting next to a two-pound Maine lobster? Sharing it with someone you love? Please, let them get their own! • **$50+**

✳Jake's Boss BBQ
3492 Washington St., Jamaica Plain, 617/983-3701
Don't let the desolate surroundings scare you. Once inside this cheery, scarlet-painted take-out joint, you'll understand why Jake's was crowned the "Best BBQ in Boston" by *Boston* magazine. The menu at Jake's Boss includes wonderful pork "Oink" ribs, "Moo Brisket," a smoked Jamaican rubbed jerk chicken, rib tips, wings, and chopped BBQ. Real sides include collard greens, mac 'n' cheese, and award-wining cowboy beans. • **$10+/AA**

Keith's Place
469 Blue Hill Ave., Dorchester, 617/427-7899
"Come with an appetite and leave with a smile" is how Keith's Place welcomes its patrons. Owners Cheryl Straughter and Keith Motley's serve up a varied menu from hot and cold wrappers to down-home goodness. Favorites include steak, mushroom, pepper, and onion wrappers; Cajun chicken Caesar salad; country fried chicken with gravy; seafood platter; and more than 20 vegetables and sides. • **$10/AA**

✳Rhythm & Spice Caribbean Grill & Bar
315 Massachusetts Ave., Cambridge, 617/497-0977

MIT students and faculty alike go to relax their brain cells at Rhythm & Spice, located right next to campus. Bringing a sunny slice of Caribbean life to a dreary Boston winter day, Rhythm & Spice's menu combines culinary influences from the Caribbean, Europe, Africa, and Asia. Get started with spicy (and when they say spicy, they're not kidding!) jerk wings, then cool down with a frozen Jamaican voodoo drink. Curried goat, curried sea conch, stewed oxtails, and vegetarian roti are a few campus favorites. Thursday through Saturday nights the tables push back to make room for dancing to live reggae and calypso music. • **$20+/AA**

Stephanie's on Newbury
190 Newbury St., 617/236-0990

When Stephanie's on Newbury sets up their large cream umbrellas and wrought-iron tables, you can be sure spring has sprung in Beantown. A wait for that coveted table can easily run up to 45 minutes on a beautiful sunny afternoon, but who cares? It's worth it to sit and enjoy the sights on famed Newbury Street, to say nothing of savoring the classic American fare—especially the to-die-for warm gingerbread sundae. • **$30+**

✳Tremont 647
647 Tremont, 617/266-4600

How can you not love a place whose claim to fame is great margaritas and fresh baked bread? And the best entrée to complement Tremont's luscious lime concoctions? The Chilean sea bass wrapped tightly in banana leaves wins hands down. Tremont 647 classifies its menu as "new American cuisine." Sounds a little more exotic than Mom's apple pie? Oh, yes, my darlings, that's because it's a new day... and it's about time! • **$35+**

Turner Fisheries
10 Huntington Ave.
617/338-8070

Frequent winner of the Fourth of July's annual Chowderfest "Best Clam Chowder" award, Turner Fisheries specializes in fish served every which way, from a simple grill to a spectacular every-creature-that-roams-the-sea Bouillabaisse. The New England Seafood Medley of lobster, shrimp, and scallops in a lobster cream sauce and the baked ginger-and-garlic-crusted halibut are also necessary indulgences. • **$35+**

Nightclubs

Boston is pretty much a rock 'n' roll kinda town. But for those who seek a mellower sound, downtown offers a number of hotel piano bars as well as a couple of jazz spots to help ease you into the night.

✳House of Blues
96 Winthrop St., Cambridge, 617/491-2100
War, Ziggy Marley, Average White Band, the Radiators, Al Green, Roy Ayers, good southern food, gospel brunch, silky smooth martinis...need we say more? Attracts the Harvard, MIT crowd on weekends—after exams, of course. • **Music charge/Dinner $25+**

✳Regattabar Charles Hotel
1 Bennett St., Cambridge, 617/864-1200
The trend is spreading across the country. Not only is Regatta considered Boston's premier jazz club, it's smoke-free! Shirley Horn, Tito Puente, and Sonny Rollins, to name a few, have rolled through here. • **Music charge some nights**

✳Scullers Jazz Club
DoubleTree Guest Suites Hotel, 400 Soldiers Field Rd., 617/562-4111
Jazz, blues, Latin jazz, R&B, a little bit of soul, and a great view of the Charles River rolling by are reasons why folks head over to Scullers. Big-name giants as well as local talent pack the house nightly. • **Music charge some nights**

✳Wally's
427 Massachusetts Ave., 617/424-7204
With blues, Latin jazz, straight-ahead, and fusion from some of the city's best musicians, Wally's has entertained jazz-hungry Bostonians for years. One of the few spots that is truly integrated, with enthusiasts

that include Blacks, college students, gays, and old jazz heads, this small, unpretentious spot has room enough (although very little) for everyone. • **No music charge/AA**

Festivals

History, fashion, and fun come alive along the banks of the Charles River, as do its parks and byways each spring and summer when a host of parades, fairs, and festivals celebrate Boston's revolutionary history, musical talents, and art scene.

Boston Globe Jazz Festival
Various venues, 617/267-4301
Roll over, Beethoven, and push over, Boston Pops! The Boston Globe Jazz Festival takes over the music scene each June with a weeklong tribute to that most American of musical forms. The festival begins with a celebrated free concert at the Hatch Shell concert hall, which boasts crystal-clear acoustics rivaled only by a spectacular view of the Charles River. Copley Square and Newbury Street host free concerts during the week, while area jazz clubs and performance centers spotlight big-name artist for a nominal fee. Past performers include Terrence Blanchard, Diane Shur, McCoy Tymer & Latin Allstars, and Kenny Garrett, just to name drop a few. • **Third week in June/Music charge**

Chowderfest
City Hall Plaza, 617/227-1528
You don't have to bring your own spoon, but you'd better bring an empty stomach to sample some of the city's top clam chowder contenders. Twelve restaurants pull out all the stops to compete for the title of "Boston's Best Chowder." Past winners include Turner Fisheries Bar and Restaurant of the Westin Hotel, the Chart House, and the Back Bay Restaurant Group. • **Fourth of July weekend/Admission charge**

Caribbean Carnival
Dorchester Franklin Park, Roxbury, 781/380-7559
Boston explodes with the history, sights, and sounds of Trinidad

when the annual Caribbean Carnival takes to the streets. Music, dancing, and elaborate costumes set the stage for the celebration. Friday night sees the crowning of the carnival king and queen, followed by the "Panorama," a competition between steel pan orchestras. The next morning, starting at an eye-opening 5 o'clock, the J'ouvert, or Breaking of the Day, pre-fest gets kicked off by outrageously dressed revelers "wining" in the streets. By 11 a.m. the parade is in full force, with thousands of costumed players strutting their finery for all to enjoy. • **Last weekend in August/Free**

Boston Blues Festival
Hatch Shell, 888/SEE-BOSTON
The Boston Blues Festival weekend at the Hatch Shell is free, so there's no excuse not to go and get your blues on. The festival is all about music appreciation, its number-one goal to turn a new generation on to one of America's most beloved, and, some believe, endangered musical forms. To help keep the blues alive, restaurants and area clubs host a number of local and national acts, prior to the big weekend blowout, just to get the party started right. There's a nominal fee to attend the smaller venues, but so what? Your donation helps fund events like this, and you can have a ball at the same time. Amen. • **Last weekend in September/Free**

Cambridge Jazz Fest
Regatta Bar, 1 Bennett St., Cambridge,
617/864-1200, www.concertix.com
From November through March, the Regatta Bar at the Charles Hotel lights up every evening with the brightest jazz stars around. Ahmad Jamal, Dave Brubeck Quartet, Tommy Flanagan Trio, Ron Gill Sextet, and Tito Puente are just a few of the headliners who've graced the stage at Boston's premier jazz club. • **Admission charge**

Museums

Black Heritage Trail
46 Joy St., 617/742-5415
Bet you didn't know stuffy Beacon Hill was once the center of Boston's African American community? Pick up a guide map from

the Museum of Afro-American History (see page 67) and arrange to take a fascinating walking tour of one of Boston's most scenic and historic neighborhoods. Notable sites:

Robert Gould Shaw and 54th Regiment Memorial–Remember the movie *Glory?* The North's first Black regiment, on which the film was based, is immortalized here in stone.

George Middleton House–Built in 1791, this is the oldest standing house built by a Black person on Beacon Hill.

Phillips School–This is the first integrated school in Boston.

John J. Smith House–Smith's barber shop was the meeting place for abolitionists and fugitive slaves.

Charles Street Meeting House–Formerly the site of the first integrated church in America, Charles Street's pulpit served as a forum for abolitionist Frederick Douglass and Sojourner Truth.

Lewis and Harriet Hayden House–The home of Lewis Hayden, an escaped slave himself, was a major stop on the Underground Railroad.

Coburn's Gaming House–A discreet gambling getaway for select members.

Smith Court Residences–Offers examples of typical, inexpensive, 19th-century brick housing for Black Bostonians.

Abiel Smith School–This National Historic Landmark was the first school built exclusively for the education of Black elementary students.

African Meeting House–The oldest Black church in the United States, the First African Baptist Church was built in 1806, almost entirely by Black laborers. The church was also the site of many antislavery and political meetings.

Cambridge African American History Trail
Cambridge, 617/349-4683

Twenty markers throughout the city of Cambridge guide you to sites where some of the most influential African American authors, abolitionists, and educators changed the course of history. Harvard alumnus W. E. B. Du Bois, William H. Lewis, and Clement G. Morgan, as well as fellow Niagara Movement organizer Emery T. Morris, are just a few of the leaders well represented. Others are:

Richard T. Greener–Harvard's first African American graduate (1870)

Abiel Smith School was the first school built exclusively for the education of black elementary students.

Maria Baldwin–First African American headmaster at Agassiz Grammar School
William Wells Brown–Former escaped slave who became the first African American novelist
Alberta V. Scott–First African American graduate of Radcliffe College

Museum of Afro-American History
African Meeting House
46 Joy St., 617/739-1200
Boston's Museum of Afro-American History (MAAH) illuminates the lives of free African Americans and White abolitionists who fought

Historical Happenings

A. Philip Randolph Memorial Statue and Tribute to Pullman Porters, Back Bay Station, Dartmouth St.—This stunning sculpture by African American sculptor Tina Allen pays tribute to A. Philip Randolph, Civil Rights activist and founder of the Brotherhood for Sleeping Car Porters, the first Black trade union.

Emancipation Group, Park Square and Stuart St.—Modeled after Archer Alexander, the last slave captured under the Fugitive Slave Act, the Emancipation Group memorial was presented to the city of Boston in 1877. The cost of this symbolic monument was raised entirely by freed slaves.

Harriet Tubman House, 566 Columbus Ave., 617/536-8610—In addition to housing an office that provides assistance and services to local women, the Tubman House holds an interesting collection of historical documents, periodicals, and a small art gallery featuring some of the area's best talents.

Old South Meeting House, 310 Washington St., 617/482-6439—Booker T. Washington and W. E. B. Du Bois lectured here. Poet Phillis Wheatley, the first widely recognized African American writer, was a member of the meetinghouse. A copy of her book is on display.

side by side for the rights of those still enslaved. The activists' role in the development of Boston and of New England is depicted through rare documents as well as artifacts, audio visuals, interactive exhibits, and the Black Heritage Trail (see page 65), an enlightening tour of historic Beacon Hill. The third weekend in July, the African Meeting House holds an Abolitionists March and Rally. • **Free**

Museum of the National Center of Afro-American Artists
300 Walnut Ave., Roxbury, 617/442-8614
The intriguing collection of cultural arts from the African Diaspora here includes exhibits, publications, and educational and research materials. Primary works include artifacts, paintings and sculptures

by local and nationally known artists, and revolving exhibits honoring the contributions of today's African Americans educators, activists, artists, and leaders. • **Admission charge**

Churches

Charles Street AME Church
551 Warren St., Dorchester, 617/442-7770
Organized in 1833, the Charles Street AME Church, located on Belknap Street on Beacon Hill, was the site of many abolitionist meetings, including those directed under the leadership of Frederick Douglass and William Lloyd Garrison. When the church moved to Dorchester in 1939, it was the last Black institution to leave Beacon Hill. Today, the Charles Street congregation is known for its many community service programs, including food distribution centers, and tutorial services.

Muhammad's Mosque #11
10 Washington St., Dorchester, 617/442-6082
The Boston headquarters for the Nation of Islam, Muhammad's Mosque #11 was founded by the late Malcolm X in 1954.

Peoples Baptist Church of Boston
830 Tremont St., 617/427-0424
Established in 1805, the Peoples Baptist Church is a direct descendant of the First African Baptist Church. In 1898, First African moved from the Meeting House to Camden and Tremont. The newly relocated congregation became known as St. Paul's Baptist Church. In 1915, three congregations, the Calvary Baptist Church, the Morning Star Baptist Church, and St. Paul's Baptist Church, merged together to form the Peoples Baptist Church of Boston.

Twelfth Baptist Church
160 Warren St., Roxbury, 617/442-7855
The Twelfth Baptist Church was the first church to evolve from the First African Baptist Meeting House. In 1840, 46 members withdrew from the Meeting House to form the Second African Baptist Church. These nonconformists left to become involved with the

Underground Railroad, among other causes, and in 1848, the congregation of the Twelfth Baptist Church was formed.

Recreation

Martha's Vineyard
504/540-2022 (ferry reservations)

Martha's Vineyard was one of the earliest resorts in the nation to welcome African Americans; however, their first arrival was not a day at the beach. Many of the first African American residents on the island were brought over as slaves. The area in which they lived is now recognized as Oak Bluffs, centrally located at the island's northern tip. Today many of the homes in Oak Bluffs are owned by African Africans, passed down from generations. From May to September, the island's mix gets more colorful—in fact, no resort in the nation boasts a more racially diverse population than Martha's Vineyard.

The town of Oak Bluffs exudes charm from every corner, from its signature cotton candy-colored gingerbread houses, sitting pretty all in a row, to the Ocean Park Gazebo, an old-fashioned bower in the seaside park where islanders gather to watch spectacular holiday fireworks displays. On Circuit Avenue, Oak Bluffs's main drag, the cookie-cutter storefronts share ornate trellises with touristy boutiques and rock 'n' roll beer joints. The Flying Horses Carousel, the nation's oldest platform carousel, operating since 1884, still thrills the kids. This is a place to kick back and relax. Savor fried clam rolls and chocolate pecan fudge, take in a movie, or join up with an all-night card party. Relax.

Cousin Rose's, an African American-owned bookstore at the end of the strip, is a must stop for its unique literature by African American authors, beautifully framed prints, and exclusive "Inkwell" T-shirts. The Inkwell, located at the end of Pennacook Avenue in Oak Bluffs, was once the only beach open to African Americans. Certainly not the nicest beach on the island, the Inkwell nevertheless was and probably always will be *the* beach for summer blanket hopping and socializing. South Beach, also a popular meeting spot, is a much nicer stretch of sand, but be forewarned. On blustery days, stay on the north side of the island; South Beach is notorious for flying sand when the wind starts kickin', and it can get downright co-old!

Sugary-sweet gingerbread houses are the pride and joy of Oak Bluffs, Martha's Vineyard.

So, what kind of scene are you looking for? The PYTs and twenty-somethin's descend on the island over the Fourth of July weekend, ready to get their beach on and their groove on at the Atlantic Connection, *the* dance club in the Bluffs. Labor Day weekend traditionally attracts tennis buffs and a slightly more mature crowd, when the annual tennis tournament, among other activities, takes center court. For those who simply want to bask in the island's natural beauty, the best time to visit is late July or early August, when the weather's perfect and the water's warm. But, if you're driving, don't even think about planning a trip without reserving a spot for your car on the ferry. Traveling from the mainland is not too risky, but getting off island without a reservation, especially on a Sunday, can be a nightmare.

Charleston

C harleston. This grand old port city offers more picture-per-
fect postcard views of the old aristocratic South than the law
should allow. Yet the architectural splendor of the august,
pastel mansions lining Charleston's famous Battery (or
"Bat'try," as the locals call it) cannot mask the city's ugly racial history. Although Charleston itself has tried to undo much of the dam-
age of the past, the state of South Carolina has not tried hard
enough to erase the sinister vestiges of slavery and segregation. To
wit, South Carolina officials have refused to lower the Confederate
battle flag that flies over the state capitol. As a result, after numerous
requests for the flag's removal, on January 1, 2000, the National
Association for the Advancement of Colored People (NAACP) issued economic sanctions against the state of South Carolina.

The Confederate flag, often embraced by racist hate groups and
considered by the NAACP and others as a symbol of Whites' rejection of Black civil rights, has been a source of increasing controversy
in South Carolina and other states. The NAACP has asserted that
the people of South Carolina need to have proof that their state
government indeed speaks for all of its people and will not tolerate
the backward mentality suggested by this defiant Civil War symbol.
Until state officials recognize that the Old South will *not* rise again
and decide to put the Confederate battle flag to rest once and for
all, the NAACP's boycott will remain in effect.

Because of the sheer number of slaves imported into the port
of Charles Town, as it was called back then, a majority of African

Down on the Farm

Although those days in 'da land ob' cotton" would rather be forgotten by most African Americans today, these plantation museums offer fascinating insight into the lives of their former enslaved occupants.

Aiken-Rhett House, 48 Elizabeth St., 803/723-1159—One of Charleston's grandest old dames, this antebellum home offers a most impressive account of slave life within the confines of its estate. A must-see. · Admission charge

Boone Hall Plantation, Hwy. 17 N., 803/884-4371—Boone Hall Plantation acknowledges the adversity of slave life in its preservation of 18th-century wooden cabins and historical records pertaining to slavery in the low-country region. · Admission charge

Middleton Plantation, Ashley River Road, 800/782-3608—The history of a low-country African American community is unearthed at Eliza's House on this restored plantation. Named for Eliza Leach, the cabin's last occupant, this humble two-family home was built for the freed slaves who stayed on as tenants after the Civil War and gives visitors a unique look at plantation life. · Admission charge

Americans can trace their roots back to the South Carolina low country. The African American legacy in Charleston is an extraordinary one, so start your day at the Charleston Museum, where the permanent exhibit on African Americans during slavery times sets the tone for a day filled with history and pride.

From the museum, walk a couple of blocks to King Street, a main Charleston byway where small-town America sits side by side with stately Carolina homes and modern retail stores. Stop in Alice's Fine Foods for a slice of local flavor and some delicious down-home, low-country soul food. A block south of Alice's is Gallery Chuma, Charleston's premier African American art studio. Here you'll find the works of some of South Carolina's most celebrated artists. You'll also be captivated by Alphonzo Brown, one of Charleston's most prolific historians. Brown tells the stories of his ancestors, the local

Gullah people, who managed to preserve much of their African culture and language, during slavery and since, as a result of their isolation from the mainland on the Sea Islands off the coast of South Carolina and Georgia.

Charleston's Old City Market, located in the center of the historical district, is a lively, touristy outdoor spot where visitors can find everything from down-South cloth rag dolls to intricate handmade sweetgrass baskets woven in Gullah style. A couple of blocks away is the Old Slave Mart, where enslaved Africans were sold at auction to the highest bidders.

Remember the first Black Broadway play, *Porgy & Bess*, and its controversial interpretation of Black life in the South during the 1920s? Well, Catfish Row, now the site of some of Charleston's most exclusive property, was once one of the poorest sections of Church Street and the inspiration for author DuBose Heyward's stirring novel, which was the inspiration for the play. Today, if you want a firsthand account of what life in Old Charleston was really like, visit the shop of blacksmith Phillip Simmons, known throughout the city as *the* master of his trade. Simmons is responsible for much of the ornate wrought-iron work that graces Charleston's elite homes. He'll stop and tell you a story or two if he's not too busy.

After a day of sightseeing and soaking in the local flavor, stop into Latasha's A Taste of New Orleans for crawfish étouffée and a cup of real South Carolina gumbo. After dinner, enjoy a walk along Charleston's sandy shores and know that this day was made possible courtesy of the proud and resilient African ancestors who lived and worked here long ago.

Restaurants

Low-country cooking has finally found its way out of the South and onto the menus of some of the best restaurants in the country. Two examples are Frogmore Stew, named after a seaside Charleston locale, which combines a complex of spices with hearty portions of regional seafood, and savory stewed shrimp perched atop creamy, cheesy grits. These are just two of the many delicacies from the region's African American culinary repertoire. Finally, delicious credit is being given where it is due!

Casual Dining

✳Abe's Shrimp House
605 William Hilton Pkwy., Hilton Head, 843/785-3675,
www.abeshrimp.com
Just a couple of blocks from the ocean, Abe's is a large, friendly family restaurant best known for its fresh fish and seafood and soul food buffet. Must-tries include a low-country smothered shrimp and crab dish, succulent stewed oysters, and a wonderful concoction of shrimp and okra over rice. Delish! • **$20+/AA**

✳Alice's Fine Foods & Southern Cooking
468–470 King St., 843/853-9366
Unlike many other cafeteria-style eateries, Alice's specializes in seafood platters. Well, what did you expect, you *are* in Charleston! Stuffed shrimp, fried oysters, deviled crabs, and stuffed fish filet are just a couple of the local favorites offered alongside a terrific soul food menu. The menu changes daily, but you're sure to find something you'll like at Alice's. • **$15/AA**

✳Caribe
652 St. Andrews Blvd., 843/571-7533
How do you like your lobster—jerked in a fiery marinade or curried in spicy, Caribbean seasonings? Caribe offers classic Caribbean fare, but nothing about Caribe's cuisine is traditional. Along with the luscious lobster, this neat little eatery offers a wonderful steak Caribe, escoveitch fish, oxtails, and jerk pork. • **$20+/AA**

Charleston Battery Sandwich Shop & Brew Pub
451 King St., 843/805-7799
Serving great hearty sandwiches piled high with deli meats and salads, Charleston Battery Sandwich Shop & Brew Pub is a casual stop where the bread is made on site and so is the beer. This is a good place to get a bite, grab a beer, and go. • **$10/AA**

Hyman's Seafood Co.
213–215 Meeting St., 843/723-6000
This local favorite is cheap and cheerful with *beaucoup* seafood to choose from, including the deviled crab dinner, fried oysters, shrimp

and grits, crispy whole flounder, and a raw bar. If you can't decide, go with the combination platter. Featuring up to seven different items, you can go wild and taste a little of everything on the menu. • **$15+**

✳Latasha's A Taste of New Orleans
43-A Cannon St., 843/723-3222
This quaint little bistro knows a thing or two about Creole cookin'. The roux in the crawfish étouffée has the right color—and the right taste. The po-boy sandwiches are well stuffed, and the Creole gumbo is thick and spicy. Just goes to show you, you *can* find good New Orleans fare outside of Orleans Parish! • **$15+/AA**

✳Ultimate Eating
859 Sea Island Pkwy., St. Helena Island, 843/838-1314
Steamed Frogmore Stew brimming with shrimp, scallops, crabs, and smoked sausage, fragrantly stewed shrimp and grits, and devil crabs seasoned Gullah-style are just a few of the gifts from the Gullah kitchen offered at Ultimate Eating. This charming cottage is St. Helena's favorite restaurant, bringing a little of that simple Gullah living to life. • **$15+/AA**

Festivals

Charleston takes its commitment to fine arts seriously, offering two of the country's largest cultural arts festivals: the Spoleto Festival USA and the Moja Arts Festival.

Native Islander Gullah Celebration
Hilton Head, 800/721-7120, www.gullahcelebration.com
The coastal regions of the South Carolina low country are home to one of the nation's most distinctive cultures, that of the Gullah people. With their unique dialect, simple God-fearing lifestyle, and delightful cuisine finally receiving the credit it deserves, the Gullah are the focus of this month-long festival. Art exhibits, storytelling, youth programs, gospel, blues and soul music performances, and lots of good food and fellowship round out the calendar of events. • **Every weekend in February/Admission charges**

Let The Good Times Roll

Annual Rhythm & Blues Festival, 843/254-2547—The music ranges from Motown to moldly-oldies and "doo-wah ditty." · Last weekend in June/Music charge varies

Charleston Jazz and Arts Festival, 843/849-1020—Ramsey Lewis, McCoy Tyner, Branford Marsalis, and David Sanborn are just a few of the jazz giants who have graced the stages at the Charleston Jazz Fest. Highlights of the weekend include a nightclub jazz crawl and a jazz brunch with the festival's headliner. · First weekend in October/Admission charge

Low Country Budweiser Blues Bash, various venues, 843/762-9125—Every day—well, at least of early February—Charleston has the blues, big-time, when the city's premier blues event of the year blows into town. More than 60 of the low country's brassiest blues artists perform at nearly 20 venues. · First and second weekend in February/Music charge varies

Spoleto Festival USA
Various venues, 843/577-4500
Widely praised as one of the country's most lively and scrumptious arts festivals, Spoleto is a 17-day feast for the senses, with an agenda so diverse it guarantees to satisfy even the most discriminating palate. More than 120 performances of opera, theater, jazz, dance, chamber, and contemporary music—even a circus!—fill the bill in Charleston's historic theaters, churches, and parks. Past productions have included the African American theatrical play *Running Man*, the seductive modern steps of the Bill T. Jones/Arnie Zane Dance Company, and the smooth sounds of Chick Corea and Gary Burton. Piccolo Spoleto brings the creative canvas to the streets with fine art exhibits scattered throughout downtown marketplaces and other venues city-wide. • **Third week in May through first weekend in June/Admission charge for some events**

Moja Arts Festival
Various venues, 843/724-7305
Charleston gets its "moja" working every fall when the Moja Arts

Rhythmic sounds abound at the Moja Art Festival.

Festival celebrates the many creative talents and achievements of the African American and Caribbean citizens of the low-country region. *Umoja* means "one" or "unity" in Swahili, and thousands of people come from all over the country for 10 days of too much fun and festivities. So many folks come out for the community block parties featured for this weekend celebration, or to tee up at the charity golf tournaments, or to bring the family picnic basket for an afternoon of free live music from some of the country's most prominent R&B acts, that it would be a shame to miss it. Charleston comes alive as visitors and locals alike shake their way through town in the Caribbean street parade, guided by colorfully garbed stilt walkers and dancers. Then there's the reggae block party, the gospel music and cool jazz performances, poetry readings, storytelling, award-winning theatrical presentations, and hundreds of exhibits from some of the country's finest artists and craftspeople. With such an extensive events calendar, it is imperative you call in advance to find out where and when these happenin's are taking place. Highlights include:

Caribbean Street Parade/Reggae Block Party—Celebrating the bond between the West Indies and the Carolinas

Dance Gala—Local and national dance troupes perform

Moja Gospel Fest—Say Amen, somebody! as local choirs and singers praise God in song

Palmetto Invitational Band Classic—The friendly battle between local high school bands guarantees high-steppin' theatrics and plenty of braggin' rights!

Last week in September through the first weekend in October/Many events are free

Museums

African American Heritage Museum
Avery Research Center for African American History and Culture, 125 Bull St., 843/727-2009

The museum represents a shared effort between the Avery Research Center and other historical institutions throughout Charleston, all of which are committed to the authentic telling of African American history. Related sites and exhibits include the Charleston Slave Market Museum, Aiken-Rhett House, and McLeod Plantation.

Avery Research Center for
African American History and Culture
125 Bull St., 843/727-2009

Formerly the site of Avery Normal Institute, one of the most prestigious African American private schools in the nation circa 1865, the Avery Center houses an extensive archive of Gullah culture and the Sea Islands. These collections today serve as the primary source for information on African Americans in South Carolina's low country. Ask Muima Maat, one of Avery's resourceful storytellers and historians, for the lowdown on the region and its people.

Charles Pinckney National Historic Site
1254 Long Point Rd., Mt. Pleasant, 843/881-5516

African American life during the colonial era is examined through

Gallery Hoppin'

African American Gallery, 43 John St., 843/722-8224—This is one of Charleston's premier African American art galleries, showcasing works by local, national, and international artists. · AA

Gallery Chuma, 43 John St., 843/722-7568—World-renowned Gullah artist Jonathan Green's vibrant color portraits depicting life in the low country and the work of the multi-talented John Jones and his warm watercolors of the Charleston landscape are just two of the celebrated African American artists whose original art and prints are on display and available at Gallery Chuma. · AA

various exhibits housed at the former country home of Charles Pinckney, Revolutionary War officer and four-term governor of South Carolina. • **Admission charge**

The Charleston Museum
360 Meeting St., 843/722-2996
The nation's first museum features, among other exhibits, an impressive permanent collection of African American artifacts and documents recounting the history of enslaved Africans from their arrival in Charleston through Emancipation. • **Admission charge**

Gibbes Museum of Art
135 Meeting St., 843/722-2706
The Gibbes Museum's permanent exhibits include, among other showings, an imposing collection of art, photography, and artifacts by some of yesterday's and today's most gifted African American artists. • **Admission charge**

Penn Center, Inc.
Martin Luther King Jr. Dr., St. Helena Island, 843/838-2432
Established early during the Civil War but before Emancipation, the Penn Center is considered one of the country's most important African American educational institutions. Located on a 50-acre

Outside the Slave Market, Portrait by John Jones

national historic landmark district covered with moss-draped weeping willows and offering majestic, panoramic views of the island seascape, the Center is the home of the first Freedman's School. Later renamed the Penn School, this school was one of 30 small learning institutions established in the 1860s by Northern abolitionists for the education of the newly freed slaves. Here, African American adults were prepared for life away from the plantations. Center exhibits tell the history of Penn School as well as relate the history of Sea Island and Gullah African Americans. • **Admission charge**

Slave Market Museum
6 Chalmers St., 843/727-2009
This building, once licensed for the auction of slaves, is now a museum that vividly illustrates the horror stories of Charleston's involvement in the importation of African slaves through its exhibits of authentic artifacts and documents from that period. Included in this assemblage is the private collection of one Walter Pantovic, featuring more than 100 items such as shackles, badges, anklets, and a neck collar used to restrain and control the enslaved, and a 1746 ship's document listing the cost of "a negro at 170 pounds sterling." And *who* claimed the treatment of slaves in the United States was civil and humane? • **Admission charge**

Churches

Emanuel AME Church
110 Calhoun St., 843/722-2561
Emanuel AME Church was organized in 1816 by Morris Brown and a group of free Negroes and slaves known as the Free African Society. After an ill-fated slave rebellion led by Denmark Vesey, a local Charleston clergyman, the church was forced to go underground in 1822. It later reorganized and reopened in 1865.

First Baptist Church
48 Meeting Place, 843/722-3896
Founded in 1682, First Baptist Church is the first and oldest Baptist church in the South.

Morris Brown AME Church
13 Morris St., 843/723-1961
Founded in 1867 under the leadership of Bishop Daniel A. Payne, this historically African American church is named for Morris Brown, founder of the first AME congregation in Charleston (Emanuel AME Church) in 1816. It is presently the largest congregation in the seventh Episcopal district, with a stated membership of 3,000 and an active membership of 1,000. The Honorable James E. Clyburn (D–SC), chairperson of the Congressional Black Caucus, is a member of Morris Brown.

Old Bethel Methodist Church
222 Calhoun St., 843/722-3470

Old Bethel Methodist Church was established in 1798, growing out of the rapidly expanding congregation of the Blue Meeting House. In 1852, construction began on a new building. When the new Old Bethel was completed in 1880, the original structure was donated to the church's Black members for worship services, classes, and meeting use. Behind Old Bethel rest the graves of many of Charleston's slaves and free Blacks.

St. Mark's Episcopal Church
16 Thomas St., 843/722-0267

During pre-Civil War days, free Black people in Charleston attended church services with Whites. But when Union occupation caused many White Episcopalian churches to close, a group of prominent black Episcopalians organized their own congregation. St. Mark's was formed on Easter Sunday, April 16, 1865. November 8, 1878, marked the completion of the church, an impressive Roman-temple-style building, one of the last of its kind built in the United States and one of Charleston's most extraordinary structures.

Recreation

Gullah Tours

Descendants of the enslaved Africans brought to Charleston from West Africa in the 18th and 19th centuries, South Carolina's Gullah people still live modestly, keeping mostly to themselves on the Sea Islands that have not been purchased for resort use, and retaining the language and customs brought over from the Motherland so many centuries ago. The only way to truly experience this unique and fascinating island culture is to tour them firsthand.

Gullah 'n' Geechie Mahn Tours
851 Sea Island Pkwy., St. Helena Island, 843/838-7516

Geechie Mahn tours can not only take you directly to the Sea Islands but can also introduce you to the local residents. Narrated by well-informed guides, this tour company offers perhaps the only route by which visitors will be welcomed without suspicion into this secluded community.

Gullah Tours Charleston
843/763-7551, www.gullahtours.com
Gullah historian Alphonzo Brown can introduce you to his native Charleston and Sea Island culture with highlights that include a tour of McCloud's Plantation, where members of the all-Black 54th and 55th Massachusetts Regiment of the Union Army were cared for during the Civil War; a talk with Charleston's number-one blacksmith and citizen, Philip Simmons; visits to the burial sites of former slaves; and stations on the Underground Railroad. All tours leave from Gallery Chuma at 43 John Street.

Resorts

Charleston is home to hundreds of beautiful beaches and resorts; however, you have to go up the coast a bit to Myrtle Beach to find a special stretch of sand African Americans can call all our own. In the 1930s, George Tyson acquired this beachfront property, one tract of which he renamed Atlantic Beach, the other the Black Pearl. Atlantic Beach became a major destination for African American vacationers from the 1940s to the 1960s; however, as with many urban communities, the resort lost its popularity in the 1970s when economic change and desegregation offered more choices for African American travelers.

Today Atlantic Beach is undergoing major renovation. The town is polishing up its slightly tarnished coastline, making efforts to court new businesses, residents, and visitors to its beautiful shores. For the town's largest event, the Atlantic Beach Bike Festival, more than 100,000 folks shine up their monster hogs and roar into town Memorial Day weekend. For three days, cycle enthusiasts and just plain party folks come on down to witness wild motorcycle races, gospel and R&B concerts featuring local and national artists, all-night beach parties, car and truck shows, and lots of showing off and trash talking. All in good fun, of course!

Chicago

Chicago. Back in 1779, African-Haitian explorer Jean Baptiste Point DuSable established a trading post on Lake Michigan. Well, look at his trading post now! From notorious gangsters, legendary blues artists, and boxing greats to disgruntled cows, Chicago has experienced it all.

Where else but in Chicago, after spending the day shopping on a street called the Magnificent Mile, could you hike just a few short blocks through the hustle and bustle of the busy business district to dip your poor, tired dogs in the sparkling cool waters of a Great Lake? An ear-popping ride to the top of the Sears Tower in the heart of downtown not only puts you closer to God, but offers a spectacular view of the city. Hey, and who cares if "the hawk" blows in the winter? Summertime in Chicago is sublime! Head outdoors to Grant Park for the annual "Taste of Chicago" food-tasting event and the city's star-studded Blues Festival. Then hightail it over to Hyde Park for a family reunion, or listen to revered jazz artists playing under the stars at Ravinia, or simply sail your cares away on Lake Michigan. If you absolutely *have* to be in Chicago in January, bring your heavy coat and take comfort in knowing that nearly every restaurant in town offers valet service.

With its sophisticated North Side, its legendary South Side, its notorious West Side, and its bustling Loop or downtown areas, the only way to see all of Chicago is by car. Take the Dan Ryan Expressway south and start your day with a hearty down-home breakfast and plenty of neighborhood gossip at Izola's Restaurant.

Tour the corridor from 75th through 79th Street for a peek at the day-to-day activities of one of the South Side's busiest communities. In the lush green meadows of Hyde Park, the DuSable Museum of African American History exhibits a remarkable collection of artifacts tracing the area's Black culture and achievements. A few blocks away is the sprawling compound of the Honorable Elijah Muhammad, leader of the Nation of Islam, as well as several homes currently occupied by Minister Louis Farrakhan.

As you drive toward downtown, you'll pass by the Victory Monument, located at 35th and Martin Luther King Jr. Drive, commemorating the accomplishments of the all-Black Eighth Illinois Regiment. Two historic Black churches, the Olivet Baptist Church and the Quinn Chapel AME Church, remain pillars of strength in the South Side community. Both served as stations on the Underground Railroad. Then take the stunning drive down Lake Shore Drive back to the Loop for a casual lunch at Chicago's favorite theme eatery, Heaven on Seven, and enjoy a classic American menu with a Big Easy twist.

And how can you *not* go shopping while in Chicago? Michigan Avenue is still a must-do shopping treat, even though today it's more like one big suburban mall rather than a downtown experience. The highlight of the strip: standing in line at Garrett's for a mixture of the best warm caramel and cheese popcorn ever! For those who go for something more exotic, check out Belmont Avenue for antiques and retro looks, or Oak Street for chic and pricey European fashions. Biba, an African American-owned boutique, caters to women who love body-conscious haute couture and who have a perfect size 8 figure. If too much white wall space is a problem, stop by the Bayo Gallery for brilliant, one-of-a-kind, monochromatic paintings by the African artist of the same name; or visit Nicole Gallery, where you'll find a likewise impressive collection of Haitian, African American, and African art.

Now, the big question remains, where to dine? If you want to make it a memorable evening, check out One Sixtyblue, where the menu is modern American and considered one of the city's best. Ready for a little night music? Jazz Showcase offers terrific local and national acts nightly. What, midnight and not ready to turn in yet? Kingston Mines and the Checkerboard Lounge are just starting to rock the house with Chicago's renowned blues. History, architecture, shopping, fine dining, and riveting music—that's what makes Chicago *our* kind of town!

Restaurants

To dine in Chicago, with its wealth of four-star restaurants and exotic ethnic eateries, is reason enough to schedule a Windy City weekend. Fantasizing the gastronomic orgy that awaits your palate can make one dizzy with anticipation—not to mention hungry! What to eat, where to start? How about delicious, deep-dish pizza topped with chunks of ripe tomatoes; succulent, spicy rib tips from the South Side; prime rib and artery-clogging steaks; tender grilled octopus from Greektown; or extra-crispy fried chicken with a splash of hot, saucy jazz on a Sunday afternoon? Mmm—lead the way!

Fine Dining

✳Charlie Trotter's
816 W. Armitage Ave., 773/248-6228
This is how it is at Charlie Trotter's: $100 gets you about nine courses, another $75 will pour the wine to go with your meal. The superb cuisine, with the Sample Grand menu changing daily, is a tantalizing fusion of French, Asian, and new American cuisines; the wine list is considered one of the best in the country. Is it worth it? No doubt. • **$100+**

✳Crofton's on Wells
535 N. Wells St., 312/755-1790
In a city full of great restaurants, Crofton's on Wells is one of the best. Reservations are a must at this must-do spot, where the decor is minimalist chic and the nouvelle American cuisine of wonderful grilled baby octopus, seared-rare ahi tuna, and tender grilled venison medallions is sublime. Outdoor seating available. • **$45+**

✳Le Colonial
937 N. Rush St., 312/255-0088
Le Colonial transports you back to romantic Saigon of the 1920s with natural rattan chairs, oversized palms, bamboo shades, outdoor

Steinkamp/Ballogg Photography

Elegant dining at Michael Jordan's new concern, One Sixtyblue in Chicago.

seating under cooling ceiling fans, and exquisite French Vietnamese cuisine. Wok-seared monkfish, shrimp wrapped around sugar-cane skewers, an abounding Bouillabaisse, and crispy ginger-marinated duck are just a few of the delights well worth discreetly licking one's fingers over, even in mixed company! • **$45+**

✳One Sixtyblue
160 N. Loomis, 312/850-0303
Yes, Michael Jordan is a silent partner in this wildly successful restaurant, and the dining room is always filled with luminaries, but that's not the reason to go to One Sixtyblue. Go because the decor is smart,

Army & Lou's

Arguably the most famous African American-owned restaurant in Chicago, Army & Lou's (422 E. 75th St., 773/483-3100, · $15/AA) was established in 1945 by William and Luvilla Armstrong. The restaurant has changed owners several times over the years and has weathered many storms, but in the capable hands of current owner Dolores Reynolds and her associates at In Good Taste, Inc., Army & Lou's is ready for the next 50 years. Since its beginnings, local politicians and business people have used Army & Lou's as a meeting place. Former mayor Harold Washington is said to have conducted much of the city's business in the banquet room next door.

Reputation aside, the cuisine at Army & Lou's is nothing fancy. According to Reynolds, it's "southern-style cooking—comfort food, good and well-prepared—like your mother or aunt would make." Nonetheless, she claims that a visit to Army & Lou's "will give you a look into the true flavor of what Chicago and its people are all about." Specialties of the house include Army & Lou's award-winning fried chicken, short ribs of beef, chitterlings, pork chops, and blackberry cobbler (the best!).

the wait-staff is commanding and competent, and the modern American cuisine featuring pan-roasted dry sea scallops with porcini mushroom and wood-roasted loin of veal with fingerling potatoes is just plain wonderful! Reservations suggested. • **$45+/AA-invested**

Casual Dining

Addis Abeba
3521 N. Clark St., 773/929-9383

Diners at Addis Abeba are seated around large, colorful woven baskets, upon which large plates of highly seasoned Ethiopian dishes are placed within easy reach of everyone's hands. Vegetarian meals are the specialty, so try some *inqoudai* (fresh mushrooms and yellow split peas seasoned with garlic and ginger) or *fosolia* (string beans, onions, and carrots cooked in tomato sauce). • **$20+/AA**

West Side Story

Dejoie, 731 W. Randolph, 312/382-9999—Its interior is as sleek as Chicago was "back in the day," but with a modern edge. Cool jazz on the weekends, a choice-but-narrow selection of entrées from a new American menu, and any imperfections are camouflaged by the attentive wait-staff. · $35+/AA

Flat Top Grill, 1000 W. Washington Blvd., 312/829-4800—Choose from some 30 exotic sauces like a fiery red hot chili paste to a milder ginger soy, toss in as many vegetables as you like, and add tofu or a couple of shrimp. Give it to the chef and in five minutes, your own Asian gourmet concoction is served. One low price, all you can eat... how can you go wrong? · $15

Millennium, 832 W. Randolph, 312/455-1400—Dry-aged steaks, charred lamb chops, classic martinis, cigars, sidewalk seating, contemporary music, and the best coconut lime sorbet for dessert! Sometimes the simplest of foods is all one needs. · $45+

Wishbone Restaurant, 1001 W. Washington Blvd., 312/850-2663—Across the street from Oprah's studio is a restaurant where, on Sunday mornings, patrons can wait up to 45 minutes for brunch. Best known for its hearty southern-style breakfasts including biscuits and gravy and fresh fruit juices. · $25+

✳Bistro 110
110 E. Pearson St., 312/527-2583
After a day of marathon shopping on Michigan Avenue, relax your feet and your nerves at Bistro 110. Great salads, sophisticated sandwiches, and a live jazz Sunday brunch makes this one of downtown Chicago's favorite spots. • 30+

✳Frontera Grill
445 N. Clark St., 312/661-1434
Without question, Frontera Grill is one of the best restaurants in Chicago, serving Mexican fare so authentic, you'd swear you were in Acapulco. Yet, could you find food in Mexico presented with the theatrics and panache of a four-star restaurant or margaritas that taste so divine? Spicy chipotle-marinated quail with avocado-chipotle salsa; chiles rellenos stuffed with cheese and minced-pork picadillo; and griddle-seared Florida pink shrimp are a few of the featured entrées. If

you don't have reservations, try to grab a seat at the bar, and be prepared to wait! • **$30+**

✳**Heaven on Seven on Rush**
600 N. Michigan Ave., 312/280-7774
Hurricane cocktails, zydeco music, every hot sauce known to man, oyster po-boys, and cast-iron-skillet-fried chicken are Heaven on Seven's ways of bringing a bit of the Big Easy to the Windy City. This place is fun, loud, and always packed, so be prepared to wait at least 20 minutes for a table on weekends. The bananas Foster French toast with toasted pecans for brunch is nothing short of nirvana! • **$20+**

Lem's
5914 S. State St., 773/684-5007
311 E. 75th St., 773/994-2428
People from all over the state come to this hole-in-the-wall takeout joint, and what brings them? William Lemons, the owner, says it's his grandmother's barbecue sauce, made from a recipe passed down to his uncle and father, who started Lem's 45 years ago. But the main attraction is the rib tips, which are thick and tender like nobody's business. Need we say more? • **$10/AA**

Oldies but Goodies

Gladys' Luncheonette, 4527 S. Indiana Ave., 773/548-4566—Gladys' is one of Chicago's oldest African American-owned diners, and it still serves original recipes dating back to 1945. Breakfast is a tradition at Gladys', and the biscuits are legendary. Lunch and dinner menus change daily, but you can count on Gladys' for smothered or fried chicken and short ribs of beef. · $10+/AA

Izola's, 522 E. 79th St., 773/846-1484—For more than 45 years, proprietor Izola White has served home-cooked meals, 24 hours a day, six days a week! And like Ms. Izola says, 'If you can't find anything on this menu, you weren't hungry when you came in!' The lunch and dinner menus seem to go on and on forever, but some of the house favorites include stewed chicken and dumplings, grilled liver and onions, and Ms. Izola's famous apple cobbler. · $10+/AA

Maxine's Caribbean Spice
1225 E. 87th St., 773/933-4714
This restaurant may be modest, but the food more than makes up for the lack of ambience. Classic Caribbean fare of oxtails, just-spicy-enough jerk chicken, curried goat, cabbage and codfish, and escovietch fish makes Maxine's a South Side favorite. • **$15/AA**

Salaam Restaurant & Bakery
700 W. 79th St., 773/874-8300
Owned and operated by the Nation of Islam, the service and organization at this multifaceted food establishment and banquet facility are most impressive. The first floor is shared by four different operations: the Salaam Bakery, the Blue Seas Take-Out Counter, Elijah's Garden Restaurant, and the Atrium Restaurant. The gem of the entire operation can be found upstairs in the Salaam Grand Ballroom, which is available for banquets, weddings, receptions, and business functions. • **$15+/AA**

Nightclubs

Chicago has more nightlife than most cities put together. But if you're in the mood for some down 'n' dirty blues, smooth straight-ahead jazz, or funky reggae, or you're ready to hit the dance floor to try out the latest steps, Chicago's nightlife aims to tease!

Back Room
1007 N. Rush St., 312/751-2434
Seven nights a week the Back Room showcases some of Chicago's finest local talent in an upscale environment. The crowd is a bit touristy, but the music is for real. • **Music and minimum drink charge**

Cotton Club
1710 S. Michigan Ave., 773/341-9787
Cool jazz up front and the hottest vibes out back are terms that aptly describe one of Chicago's hot nightspots: the Cotton Club. If you feel you're becoming a bit too mellow, pass through the double doors and enter the Cotton Club's "alter ego" dance room. Here,

Nothin' but the Blues

Blue Chicago, 736 N. Clark St., 312/642-6261; 536 N. Clark St., 312/661-0100—Big-Time Sarah and BTS Express, the Chicago Blues and Rhythm Kings, and Willie Kent and the Gents with Patricia Scott are just a few of the local talents who make Blue Chicago one of the hottest clubs in town. · Music charge

✳**Buddy Guy's Legends**, 754 S. Wabash Ave., 312/427-0333—Live blues seven nights a week, featuring some of Buddy's famous friends like King Floyd, Johnny Adams, Junior Wells, and Earl King, to name a few. This spacious, comfortable nightspot owned by legendary Chicago blues man Buddy Guy serves up a full dinner menu of Cajun Louisiana-style food including baby back ribs and hoppin' john. · Music charge/Dinner $20/AA-invested

Checkerboard Lounge, 423 E. 43rd St., 773/624-3240—If there was ever a neighborhood blues joint, this has got to be it! The Checkerboard Lounge has kept it real for more than 40 years, offering up nothin' but the blues. Muddy Waters and Junior Wells regularly played here, and Chuck Berry and Mick Jagger (he gets around, doesn't he?) have made guest appearances. · Music charge/AA

House of Blues, 329 N. Dearborn St., 312/755-1790—War, Ziggy Marley, Average White Band, the Radiators, Al Green, Roy Ayers, good southern food, silky smooth martinis … need I say more? · Music charge/Dinner $20

✳**Kingston Mines**, 2548 N. Halsted St., 773/477-4646—For the late-night crew, Kingston Mines is the place to be! The party doesn't get started until midnight, with two live stages of continuous music playing till 4 a.m. Mick Jagger sightings are frequent here, as are sightings of local and national talent in the market for a little late-night jammin'. · Music charge/Dinner $10–$20

High 'Steppin'

Fifty Yard Line, 69 E. 75th St., 773/846-0005—This is a casual neighborhood meet-and-greet spot, where the music is strictly old-school and steppin' is the only dance in town. · Cover charge/AA

New Dating Game Lounge, 8926 S. Stony Island Ave., 773/374-8883—Open nightly, this lounge has everyone steppin' on the weekends, and slow draggin' like in the old days on Sunday nights. · No cover charge/AA

the walls virtually sweat from dancers gettin' their grooves on! • **Cover charge/AA**

✳Green Dolphin Street
2200 N. Ashland, 773/395-0066
By the middle of the first set, it's standing room only at Green Dolphin Street. But that's OK, because with this club's showcase of terrific live talent egging the crowd on, it's just too hard to sit down and dance in those rickety little café chairs. If the smoke-filled room *full* of rowdy adults gets to be too much for you, Green Dolphin Street has an excellent and refined fine-dining restaurant in the room next door. Now if only they could *close* the door. • **Music charge/Dinner $35+**

✳Jazz Showcase
59 W. Grand Ave., 312/670-BIRD
Jazz Showcase dispels the myth that a nightclub has to be "smokin'" to serve up blisteringly hot music. Here, every seat is a non-smoking one, and Jazz Showcase only features the best. So any night you fall in is sure to be great! • **Music charge**

Narcisse
710 N. Clark St., 312/787-2675
A cool, swanky, champagne-drinkin', caviar-dippin', cigar-smokin', vodka-sippin', candle-meltin', black skimpy dress-wearin', young international clientele describes the scene at Narcisse. If you love

pretense, overpriced drinks, and stylin' and profilin', this hot spot lounge of the moment is the only place to be!

Wild Hare
3530 N. Clark, 773/327-4273
Wild Hare is where reggae reigns supreme, featuring national and international acts seven days a week. Leave your good clothes at home and come to party! • **Music charge**

Festivals

No other city offers more free outdoor music festivals than Chicago does. Originally organized to encourage unity and diversity among the locals, this good ol' time just could not be contained and limited to Chicagoans only. Folks come from all over the state and the country to hear the likes of none other than Ray Charles, Ruth Brown, and Tramaine Hawkins throw down in Grant Park—and it's all free! Now, that's *our* kind of town!

Chicago Blues Festival
Grant Park, 773/774-3370
How can anyone *not* love the blues? It can stir up the soul, take over the body, and transform any stick-in-the-mud, down-in-the-dumps person into a hip-grinding, knee-slappin', dancin', singin' fool! The Chicago Blues Festival knows full well the power of its magic, and some 600,000 devoted blues lovers who make the pilgrimage to Grant Park for four days and nights to hear the dirtiest blues around can't be wrong! Ray Charles, Taj Mahal, the Phantom Blues Band, Bobby Blue Bland, Ruth Brown, and local favorites like the Kim Wilson Blues Revue and Denise LaSalle are just a few past performers. It was a sight to see when some of the greatest harmonica players in the world gathered together on stage to give props to the late, great Junior Wells in their moving tribute, "Remembering Jr." Several blues pioneers are recognized each year so their legacies will not soon be forgotten. Then again, how could they be? For those who don't quite get enough from the park concerts, the local blues clubs offer after-parties filled with enthusiastic fans and performers jammin' till the wee hours. • **First Weekend in June/Free**

Enjoy the delicious grilled, jerked chiken at the African/Caribbean International Festival of Life

Chicago Gospel Festival
Grant Park, 773/774-3370

A true blessing takes place in Grant Park every year when spiritual performers like Tramaine Hawkins, Beverly Crawford, Melba Moore, Mavis Staples, and national, international, and local choirs raise the roof on the Petrillo Music Shell for the annual Chicago Gospel Festival. More than 250,000 people come out to put their hands together and praise God's name. • **Second weekend in June/Free**

Taste of Chicago
Grant Park, 312/744-3370

Where to start, where to start? First, buy at least two rolls of tickets—a real taste requires at least three—and get ready to do lots of eating! Begin at booth #1 and don't stop till you get enough! The Taste of

Taste of Chicago Tips

"The Taste"

Roasted corn-on-the-cob dipped in Cajun butter; barbecued turkey legs; classic Chicago beef hot dogs topped with pickles, tomatoes, sweet peppers, onions, and mustard; strawberry pierogies; coconut-lime sorbet; rainbow ice cream cones (with chocolate, strawberry, palmer, and pistachio ice cream, and orange sherbet); toasted ravioli; jerk chicken with red beans and rice and callaloo; chocolate-dipped frozen bananas; Haitian chicken stew; grilled lobster tails; and cheesecake on a stick.

What to Bring

A hat and sunscreen; a blanket for a picnic on the grass or for listening to the bands; Tums; elastic-waist pants or loose-fitting clothing and comfortable shoes

And Finally

Take public transportation; there's nowhere to park!

Chicago is the granddaddy of all taste fests, with more than 70 restaurants and caterers doing their best to satisfy the palates of discriminating Chicagoans and visitors. For 10 days, "the Taste" fills Grant Park with great food, live concerts, storytelling, cooking demonstrations, and amusement rides for the kids. The week climaxes with a spectacular Fourth of July fireworks show. Earth, Wind & Fire, the Isley Brothers, and Chicago (the band) have rocked the main Petrillo Music Shell in past years. • **Last weekend in June through July Fourth weekend/Free**

African/Caribbean International Festival of Life
Washington Park Sunken Garden

The great lawn in front of the DuSable Museum fills with the fragrant aroma of jerk chicken, the laughter of children, and the hip-swaying music of the global village. Thousands come out in 98-degree weather to "lime" the night away with international reggae stars like Third World and other artists performing gospel, calypso,

R&B, hip hop, and jazz. While the performances are worth the price of admission alone, the over-duplication of vendors selling the same jewelry, African print fabrics, and other Afrocentric items quickly becomes tiresome. Thank goodness, there's plenty of non-stop talent and good food to occupy the day. • **Fourth of July weekend/ Admission charge**

Bud Billiken Parade
39th and King Dr., 773/225-2400
Can you imagine your child celebrating the return of the school year? Hard to picture? Well, throw in a parade with all their school chums participating along with other kids from around the city, drill teams, high-kicking majorettes, a sprinkling of luminaries from the entertainment and political arenas, and culminating with the crowning of the young king and queen of the city. Add more than a million spectators and you have the Bud Billiken parade, one of the oldest and most celebrated parades in America. Sponsored by the *Chicago Defender* newspaper, the purpose of this event is to bring attention to young people's needs and to provide them the opportunity to celebrate their childhood. After the parade, everyone gathers in Washington Park for picnics, barbecues, and games. • **Second Saturday in August/Free**

Chicago Jazz Festival
Petrillo Music Shell, Grant Park, 312/427-1676
One would think that Chicagoans would be festivaled out by Labor Day, but instead, they save the best for last! The Chicago Jazz Festival is a weekend of non-stop all-day, all-night jazz. The party gets started right with the annual Jazz Club Crawl. The Wednesday before the fest, die-hard jazz buffs hop on buses that drop them off at some 14 different jazz clubs around the Loop. On Friday, things really get serious by dusk when giants like Horace Silver, vocal legends extraordinaire Houston Person and Etta Jones, the World Famous Count Basie Orchestra, and new bucks Joshua Redman and Terence Blanchard take to Pertrillo Music Shell. And what a sight it is. Thousands of folks sitting on blankets with picnic baskets filled with their favorite goodies, listening to great music under the stars. For jazz enthusiasts, it doesn't get any better than this! • **Labor Day weekend/Free**

Outside of the famed DuSable Museum in Chicago

Museums

A. Philip Randolph Pullman Porter Museum
10406 S. Maryland Ave., 773/928-3935

The A. Philip Randolph museum was established in February 1995 to recognize the accomplishments of the Brotherhood of Sleeping Car Porters, the first Black labor union admitted to the American Federation of Labor (of the AFL-CIO). A. Philip Randolph founded the Brotherhood in 1926. Photographs, memorabilia, clothing, documents, and exhibits tell the heroic history of the nation's Black Pullman porters, who for decades provided America's rail-traveling public with "miles of smiles" and extraordinary service despite pervasive racism and rampant employment discrimination. • **Admission charge**

Gallery Hoppin'

Akainyah Gallery, 357 W. Erie St., 312/654-0333—Owner Samuel Akainyah is known not only for his rare collection of contemporary African art but also for his own bold interpretations of life on canvas. · AA

Bayo Gallery, 60 E. Chicago Ave., 773/363-2700—Upon entering African artist Bayo Iribhogbe's small studio and gallery, you will be immediately captivated by his paintings. The artist is renowned for his distinctive use of the knife and for his vibrant color and monochromatic work. · AA

Nicole Gallery, 230 W. Huron St., 312/787-7716—This handsome gallery showcases one of the city's finest collections of Haitian art and Shona stone sculptures from Zimbabwe, as well as an assortment of impressive paintings and mixed-media pieces from artists representing the African Diaspora. · AA

Art Institute of Chicago
111 S. Michigan Ave., 312/443-3600
One of the most impressive collections of African American and African art is found at the majestic Art Institute of Chicago. In addition to a permanent and extensive presentation of African artifacts, the museum showcases collections from all over the world, dating from 3000 B.C. to the present day. Revolving exhibits, fine art paintings, drawings, sculpture, photography, textiles, and architectural works make up the museum's extensive holdings. • **Admission charge**

Chicago Children's Museum
Navy Pier, 700 E. Grand Ave., 312/527-1000
For children of all ages, the Chicago Children's Museum provides hours of entertainment in an exciting learning environment. The museum introduces kids to innovative technology and cyberspace tools and toys—there's an E.R. exhibit where they can experience the thrills and tensions emergency-room doctors face, and the Waterways room where they can get just plain wet. Special revolving exhibits like "The World of Dr. Seuss" keep young ones enthralled for hours. • **Admission charge**

DuSable Museum of African American History
740 E. 56th Pl., 773/947-0600
Presiding over picturesque Washington Park, the DuSable Museum of African American History (named after African-Haitian explorer Jean Baptiste DuSable) houses one of the most comprehensive collections of Black history and cultural artifacts in the United States. Established in 1961 in the private residence of art historian Dr. Margaret Burroughs, the museum moved in 1973 to its present location. Today, the DuSable Museum shares more than 10,000 pieces, including printed work, paintings, exhibits, sculptures, and photographs, with thousands of visitors each year. • **Admission charge**

Museum of Contemporary Art
220 E. Chicago, 312/280-2660
With more than 5,300 pieces in its permanent collection, its emphasis on minimalism, conceptualism, and surrealism, the Museum of Contemporary Art is one of the country's largest assemblages of modern art. The view of Lake Michigan from the sculpture garden is breathtaking. • **Admission charge**

Churches

First Church of Deliverance
4315 S. Wabash Ave., 773/373-7700
Designed by Walter Bailey, the first African American architect registered in Illinois, First Deliverance was the first African American church to broadcast its Sunday service over the radio.

Mosque Maryam
7351 S. Stony Island Ave., 773/324-6000
Mosque Maryam is the national headquarters of the Nation of Islam.

Mt. Olivet Baptist Church
3101 S. Martin L. King Dr., 773/737-1523
Considered one of the leading Black churches in the country, Mt. Olivet Baptist is best known for their congregation's 1850s protest against the Fugitive Slave Law.

Quinn Chapel AME Church
2401 S. Wabash Ave., 312/791-1846
Quinn Chapel AME is listed in the National Register of Historic Places and is the oldest Black church in Chicago. Quinn Chapel served as a station on the Underground Railroad and aided in the abolition movement.

Salem Baptist Church
11800 S. Indiana Ave., 773/821-4300
Reverend James T. Meeks received national acclaim when he accompanied Rev. Jesse Jackson Jr. on his famous rescue of the Kosovo POWs in 1999.

Trinity United Church of Christ
400 W. 95th St., 773/962-5650
With more than 7,000 members, Trinity United Church of Christ is one of the largest and most popular churches in the Chicago area. Six nationally recognized choirs light up its modern sanctuary weekly.

Recreation

Harpo Studios
1058 W. Washington Blvd., 312/633-1000
Don't even think that all you have to do to be part of the *Oprah Winfrey Show* audience is waltz right in and stand in line for tickets for that day's taping. It is "highly recommended" to call at least one month in advance. Yes, girlfriend, it's that fierce!

Navy Pier
600 E. Grand, 312/595-PIER
Start your day out right! Take the water taxi across Lake Michigan to Shedd Aquarium on the Navy Pier. It's a never-ending barrage of shops, eateries, theaters, exhibits, gardens, live music stages, and a very long boardwalk, perfect for rollerblading. The Chicago Children's Museum and the IMAX® 3-D theater will keep the kids entertained without realizing they're also learning. During the summer months, fireworks light up the night sky twice at week, and dancing under the stars requires only a little rhythm. The best time to go

Beachfront Property

How cool is it when a public sandy beach is only a short drive from downtown or across the street from your favorite department store? Only in Chicago.

Oak Street Beach: Lake Shore Drive and Oak Street

North Avenue Beach: Lincoln Park, North Side

57th Street Beach: Across from Hyde Park on the South Side and Lake Shore Drive

to the Navy Pier is at night, when you can view Chicago's greatest asset, its magnificent skyline, in all its glory. From the top of the giant Ferris wheel or from a bench on the edge of the pier, it's the most spectacular free show in town. (Call for a schedule of events.)

Golf

Family Golf Center
221 N. Columbus Dr., 312/616-1234
Located in the heart of the city, this facility boasts a nine-hole par three, 92 range stations, and a short game area.

Jackson Park Golf Course
6400 Richards Dr., 312/254-0909
Chicago Park District's premier 18-hole facility, Jackson Park also features tennis courts.

South Shore Golf Course
7059 S. Shore Dr., 312/245-0909
Once an exclusive private country club, this nine-hole course is now enjoyed by all South Side residents. The views of Lake Michigan are spectacular.

Cleveland

C leveland. No other city has been the butt of so many jokes. Considered at one time "the armpit of America," Cleveland is finally getting the last laugh. Its old theater district, Playhouse Square Center, has been transformed into the nation's second-largest performing arts center, making "the new Cleveland" a serious destination for premier stage productions and concerts. If your taste tends toward the more soulful, the Rock-and-Roll Hall of Fame and Museum dishes the dirt on every major rocker who has ever graced a stage and influenced the greatest musical revolution of the 20th century. The funky, newly developed entertainment district known as "the Flats" cradles the Cuyahoga River, attracting locals and tourists alike to its many restaurants, shops, and nightclubs.

A day in downtown Cleveland starts with a soulful breakfast of fluffy pancakes, scrambled eggs, and warm biscuits, courtesy of Loretta's Restaurant. After your morning meal, walk west on Euclid and pop into the Arcade, a walk-through shopping area filled with dress and gift shops and specialty stores. Rastus' Place is loaded with hard-to-find black art posters, memorabilia, books, and other stuff you don't need but *have* to have. For shopping on a trendier tip, continue two more blocks to Public Square. Tower City Center, located at the foot of this bustling business center, is a modern shopping complex filled with designer-line department stores and European-style boutiques.

If you didn't come to shop and brought too many clothes to begin with, then hop on the Waterfront Rail Line. This above-ground people-mover is a great way to see the downtown area. Get off at the Flats Entertainment District station and spend hours exploring the area's sprawling mall compound, filled with contemporary shops, restaurants, and nightclubs.

Across the river in Ohio City is the historic West Side Market, an indoor/outdoor emporium where every type of edible delicacy, fresh produce, seafood, and meat your heart desires can be purchased. Hop back on the train to the next stop: the Rock-and-Roll Hall of Fame. Resembling a tipsy Egyptian pyramid supported by lots of shiny metal scaffolding, the Hall is filled with more psychedelic guitars, sequined dresses and jackets, gold 45s, photographs, album covers, and live music to shake your booty to than the law allows! Too much fun, this music monument is Cleveland's pride and joy, and rockers of all ages enjoy the journey through time.

Later, head back to the hotel to pick up a rental car and take a tour of the local neighborhoods. Catch a quick lunch at The Lancer in midtown, where the delicious fried catfish is always the specialty of the house. Then visit University Circle, the site of a plethora of museums, performing arts stages, galleries, and gardens galore. Be sure to check out the African American Museum and the Crawford Auto-Aviation Museum in this area. Not far from University Circle is Shaker Heights, home to the second-oldest shopping center in the nation, and also graced by some of the most charming, stone-faced antique, gift, and clothing boutiques you'll find anywhere. Many of these businesses are African American-owned, including the Malcolm Brown Art Gallery, one of the premier galleries in the city showcasing contemporary works by the hottest Black artists.

Return downtown for a quick rest before heading out to dinner in the Flats. Among many excellent choices, the Watermark Restaurant is a good pick. Sample their signature fresh sea scallops, seared and served with sautéed oysters and mussels, and savor the scenic Cuyahoga River view. After a stroll around the waterfront, head over to the Warehouse District for a night of smooth, live jazz downstairs at Sixth Street Under. Still have energy to burn? Mirage on the Water promises to wear you out with its bumpin' hip hop and R&B. Hhhhmmmmm, looks like the "Mistake by the Lake" has learned its lessons well!

Restaurants

Between the opening of the Flats and the revitalization of the Warehouse District, downtown Cleveland abounds with first-class restaurants, many of which offer sidewalk alfresco dining on warm summer nights. However, if your taste buds crave a more soulful flavor, head to the suburbs where the fried catfish is the freshest, and the service the friendliest.

Fine Dining

Lu Cuisine
1228 Euclid Ave., 216/241-8488

Lu Cuisine features fine dining, courtesy of the Pacific Rim, in a seductive, sophisticated setting. Specialties of the house include seared sea scallops in black pepper sauce and delicate shrimp mixed with a medley of three different mushrooms in a spicy brown sauce. • **$30+**

*Moxie Restaurant
3355 Richmond Rd., Beachwood, 216/831-5992

Most restaurants earn notoriety for an eclectic menu, a stand-out signature dish, or impeccable service. Moxie is known for its extensive wine menu: more than 20 wines available by the glass and some 100 bottles to choose from, most from California vineyards. About 40 percent of the bottles are priced under $40. Translation: Don't leave home without the credit cards. Moxie's new American menu also serves up high prices, but the meal and the wine is often worth the drive. • **$35+**

*Sans Souci
Renaissance Cleveland Hotel, 24 Public Square,
216/696-5600

The days of terrible, overpriced hotel restaurants are over (except for breakfast—$8.50 for muffins, juice, and coffee is standard). Sans Souci's charming dining room, adorned with sunflowers and wall murals, transports diners to the French countryside of Provence. The restaurant's artistic menu features cuisine from the Italian, Spanish, French, and Moroccan rivieras. • **$35+**

The Flats

Watermark Restaurant, 1250 Old River Rd., 216/241-1600—Folks argue over which is the prettier sight: the view of the Cuyahoga River bend from a patio dining table at the Watermark or the grilled salmon kissed with vanilla maple Veloute and sprinkled with spiced pecans. This restaurant's sophisticated menu features innovative seafood dishes with Asian influences. · $35+

Dick's Last Resort, 1096 Old River Rd., 216/241-1234—If you have a hankering for a big ol' bucket of barbecued ribs, fried chicken, shrimp, or catfish, this delightful link in a nationwide chain of restaurants is the place for you! Lots of napkins are needed after every messy bite. Live music nightly including Sunday gospel buffet brunch. · $15+

Max & Erma's, 1106 Old River Rd., 216/771-8338—Classic American fare is served up nightly in this favorite local dining spot. How can you go wrong with a place known for its gourmet, extra thick hamburgers, homemade onion rings, and hot apple pie?! · $20+

Casual Dining

✻Diamond Back Brewery
724 Prospect Ave., 216/771-1988
Diamond Back Brewery has got it going *on* with seven different dining and entertainment areas including a pub and sports bar, a champagne bar, a dance club, and a game room complete with pool tables. The international menu welcomes visitors to a tempting selection of hot and cold tapas, foccacia-crusted crab cakes, tabouleh, couscous with blackened chicken, and mushroom rellenos stuffed with spinach and manchengo cheese. Main dishes of barbecued Atlantic salmon, handmade barley raviolis, and a flour tortilla lasagna with a mix of spicy Chihuahua cheese and marinated chicken. Live music ranges from Latin music to straight-ahead jazz.
• **$30+/AA-invested**

CVB of Greater Cleveland

Chillin' out in Cleveland's warehouse district.

✳Ella Wee's Carnegie Deli & Soul Fixin's Restaurant
7719 Carnegie Ave., 216/391-5460

Ella Wee's should be in the "Cruddy But So Good!" Hall of Fame.
"Cruddy" means the restaurant's interior is plain, and "so good"
means the food is just that! Local politicians meet weekly in Ella's rear

Cheap and Cheerful

Everything and Then Some, 16405 Euclid Ave., 216/531-2000—Classic soul food served cafeteria-style. · $10/AA

Island Style Jamaican Cuisine, 2144 Noble Rd., 216/851-4500—Take out traditional Caribbean fare like jerk chicken, stewed chicken, and oxtails. · $10/AA

conference room. The *Phil Donahue Show* fixed national attention on this modest spot. Open from 7 a.m. for a hearty breakfast to 8 p.m. for dinner, Ella Wee's serves up the best in home cooking. Chicken and dumplings, neck bones, chitlins, short ribs of beef, and a side of Ella's famous fried corn are a few of the specialties. • **$10/AA**

Fat Fish Blue
21 Prospect, 216/875-6000
Fat Fish Blue tries hard to bring a little of the Crescent City (New Orleans) up north, and they do a good job on most of the menu items. For a memorable meal, it's best to stick with the nontraditional items like pecan chicken with Jack Daniels sauce served with creamy grits, blackened steak with baked sweet potatoes, or broiled red snapper brushed with sherry. Live blues nightly. • **$20**

✳The Lancer
7707 Carnegie Ave., 216/881-0080
The Lancer, the oldest Black-owned restaurant in Cleveland, attracts the city's top who's-who clientele and is a favorite with out-of-towners. No doubt the allure is the house specialty: whole catfish, deep-fried a golden brown yet served with not a trace of grease, well seasoned, and all *good*! Other must-tries include Brandon's Belly Buster 24-ounce porterhouse steak, a combo of Australian lobster tails and filet mignon, and the fried shrimp and frog legs platter. Save room for a slice of seven-layer or luscious rum cake. • **$20+/AA**

Nightclubs

Café Isabella
2025 Abington Rd., 216/229-1177
This *très* upscale restaurant is best known for its great late-night crowd, who come to Café Isabella to enjoy the cocktail hour and to listen to some of the best local jazz around.

Cleveland Bop Stop
1216 W. Sixth St., 216/664-6610
Offering straight-ahead jazz for veteran and novice alike, the Bop Stop is *the* place for serious music lovers in Cleveland. Seats are arranged so everyone can see the musicians, and the intensity on their faces. Open seven nights a week. • **Cover charge**

Improv Comedy Club
2000 Sycamore St., 216/696-4677
Tommy Davidson, Paul Mooney, Dave Chappelle, and Jamie Foxx are just a few of the top comedians who have performed at the Improv, located in the newest complex in the Flats. This is where superstars Jerry Seinfeld and Roseanne got their start. • **Cover charge**

Mirage on the Water
2510 Elm St., 216/348-1135
The party is here! Located in the Flats, Mirage on the Water is a spacious upscale dance club that caters to young urban professionals. Inside dance to R&B, hip hop, and urban contemporary music; from the patio deck watch the boats sail by. The Mirage features plenty of plush banquettes for those who prefer to see and be seen from a seated position. • **Cover charge/AA**

Sixth Street Under
1266 W. Sixth St.,
216/589-9313
One of Cleveland's premier jazz spots, this unpretentious downtown club features local artists Tuesdays through Saturdays. Soak up local flavor on Thursday nights, when the jam sessions last till 2:30 a.m. • **Cover charge/AA**

Festivals

Cleveland's neighborhoods come alive each spring with street festivals that celebrate the city's changing and diverse neighborhoods.

Tri-C Jazz Fest
Cuyahoga Community College, Metro Campus, 216/987-4444
Lou Rawls, Dee Dee Bridgewater, Spyro Gyra, Art Blakey's Jazz Messengers, Latin jazzman Eddie Palmieri, and Flora Purim are just a few of the jazz greats who have performed at the Tri-C Jazz Fest, which annually attracts more than 40,000 people. When the musicians aren't performing, they take time to teach, enlighten, and entertain area high school and college students about America's jazz heritage. Cuyahoga Community College created this festival to educate more people about jazz and to develop and inspire local talent. The artists invited each year represent the gamut of American jazz, from traditional to Latin, bebop to fusion. Concerts are held on the Tri-C's metropolitan campus and in venues like Playhouse Square, Severance Hall, and Reinberger Chamber Hall. • **Last week in April, first week in May/Admission charge**

Great American Rib Cook-Off and Music Festival
Burke Lakefront Airport, 440/247-2722
In five days, 55,000 pounds of ribs are devoured, 444,600 rib bones are sucked on and tossed, and 7,500 pounds of cole slaw, 3,600 gallons of baked beans, and 23,400 ears of corn are consumed by some 125,000 people at this annual food and music fest. That's a whole lotta eatin'—so bring extra napkins to wipe the barbecue sauce off your chin! Two stages keep the party goin' all day long with live music from top headliners in the rock 'n' roll, blues, and country arenas. • **Memorial Day weekend/Admission charge**

Taste of Cleveland
Nautica Stage, west bank of the Flats, 800/489-8444
More than 30 local restaurants put their best dishes forward at the annual Taste of Cleveland festival. Sample-sized portions of ethnic delicacies are served (the better to taste even more goodies, my dear!), ranging from barbecue, fried chicken, fries, and onion rings, to Thai *satay*. Vendors from local microbreweries and vineyards are

University Circle's Annual Parade the Circle Celebration, recognizing the vibrant diversity of Cleveland's community.

also on hand to quench revelers' thirst. Other delights include live rock 'n' roll, R&B, and jazz performed by big-name artists like the O'Jays; cooking demonstrations; waiters racing for charity; and a good-natured competition among the mayors of area townships as they vie for bragging rights in the Mayor's Best Dessert Cup Challenge. • **Labor Day weekend/Admission charge**

Museums

African American Archive Collection of the Western Reserve Historical Society
10825 East Blvd., 216/721-5722
Everything you wanted to know about African Americans' role in the settlement of Cleveland can be found at the African American Archive Collection. Housing a fascinating and extensive collection of photographs, records, and memories of prominent Black Clevelanders, the archives also host lecture series on "the social, religious, and cultural history of African Americans."

African American Heritage Trail
Various sites, 216/921-2726
Who knew that the city of Cleveland was filled with so much fascinating African American history? Fifteen stops along the African American Heritage Trail take you to Central High School, which graduated literary giant Langston Hughes and former U.S. Representative Louis Stokes, as well as to St. John's Episcopal Church, known as the "Station Hope" on the Underground Railroad, and League Park, once the home of the Cleveland Buckeyes, winners of the 1945 Negro World Series.

Rock-and-Roll Hall of Fame and Museum
1 Key Plaza, 888/764-ROCK
Tina Turner, Little Richard, Mick Jagger, Eric Clapton, Aretha Franklin, the Supremes, Stevie Wonder, Jimi Hendrix, and Smoky Robinson are just a few of the rock 'n' roll legends illuminated by this absolutely fabulous repository of music memorabilia. In addition to showcasing psychedelic guitars, sequined jackets, hand-painted platform shoes, and leopard fabric-covered cars, the R&R Hall of Fame and Museum features more than 50 exhibits, 1,000 original artifacts, 20 films, and several interactive musical kiosks. Great fun for the entire family! • **Admission charge**

University Circle

Only four miles from downtown, University Circle encompasses the nation's largest collection of museums, performing arts centers, art galleries, and lush gardens assembled on one campus. Every year on the second Saturday in June, University Circle presents Parade the Circle, a daylong festival celebrating the artistic expression and creativity of Cleveland's African American, Caribbean, and Hispanic communities. When you're in the area, look for these attractions:

African American Museum, 1765 Crawford Rd., 216/791-1700—This was one of the first museums in the country to celebrate African American heritage.

Cleveland Center for Contemporary Art, 8501 Carnegie Ave., 216/421-8671—Warhol, Johns, Calder, and Bearden are just a few of the contemporary artists whose works are displayed here.

Cleveland Museum of Art, 11150 East Blvd., 216/421-7340—This museum houses more than 34,000 works of art spanning some 5,000 years, from ancient Egypt to the present. · Free

Crawford Auto-Aviation Museum, 10825 East Blvd., 216/721-5722—Operated under the direction of the Western Reserve Historical Society, the museum takes visitors back to an era when cars were gas-guzzling, chrome-and-glass behemoths and air travel was just getting off the ground.

Karamu Performing Arts Theater, 2355 E. 89th St., 216/795-7070—Cleveland's Karamu Theater is the country's first multicultural arts center devoted to stage productions depicting modern-day African American life and culture. Its annual performance of Black Nativity is world-renowned.

Churches

Antioch Baptist Church
8869 Cedar Ave., 216/421-1516
This gorgeous historical landmark was founded in 1893.

Old Stone Church
91 Public Square, 216/241-6145
Built in 1834 of pale Berea sandstone, the Old Stone Church is one of the oldest places of worship in Cleveland.

Olivet Institutional Baptist Church
14 Quincy Ave., 216/721-3585
The Olivet Institutional Baptist Church was Dr. Martin Luther King Jr.'s base of operations when he visited Cleveland to campaign for Carl Stokes, who later became Cleveland's first Black mayor.

St. John's African Methodist Church
2261 E. 40th St., 216/431-2560
St. John's, the oldest African American church in the state of Ohio, was established in 1830.

St. John's Episcopal Church
2600 Church St. 216/781-5546
The last station and stop on the Underground Railroad before entering Canada was St. John's Episcopal Church. Its bell tower served as a lookout point for signals from boats transporting runaway slaves across Lake Erie to freedom.

Recreation

Amusement Parks

Cedar Point Amusement Park
1 Causeway Dr., Sandusky, 419/627-2350
With a lucky 13 "scream machines" on one sprawling campus, Cedar Point houses the largest collection of roller coasters anywhere.

Tee Time

Big Met Golf Course, 4811 Valley Pkwy., Fairview Park, 440/331-1070

Boston Hills Country Club, 105 E. Hines Hill Rd., Hudson, 330/656-2438

Fowler's Mill Golf Course, 13095 Rockhaven Rd., Chesterland, 440/729-7569

Geauga Lake
1060 N. Aurora Rd., Aurora, 330/562-8303
Big fun for those with a strong stomach, Geauga Lake's giant 12-story Ferris wheel, called the "Time Warp," and countless other rides and attractions will entertain the whole family all day long.

SeaWorld Cleveland
1100 Sea World Dr., Aurora, 330/562-8101
You know the deal—Shamu, dolphins, water splashing all over the spectators. Great fun for everyone.

Beaches

Fairport Harbor
Lakefront Park, 301 Huntington Beach Dr., Fairport Harbor, 440/639-9972
A beach in Cleveland? Oh, yeah! And while it may not be Miami Beach, you'll have plenty of room to catch some rays. Recreational facilities nearby.

Parks

Cleveland Metroparks Zoo and Rainforest
3900 Brookside Park Dr., 216/661-7511
Stare down a 12-foot crocodile, spy on a busy ant colony up-close-and-personal through a view camera, cringe over creepy tarantulas, scorpions, and centipedes, and marvel as a blinding thunderstorm drenches the indoor lobby of this zoo's rainforest exhibit every few minutes. More than 300 scaly reptiles, 10,000 plants, lots of large

cats, scores of swingin' primates, and more insects than you would ever want to see in your life are on display in this very cool, tropical jungle complex. Spread out over a 165-acre campus, the Cleveland Metroparks Zoo is the seventh-oldest zoo in the country.

Dallas

allas. Who would believe that a city best known for bow-legged cowpokes and a cheesy TV show would boast more restaurants than San Francisco and Manhattan? Who knew that a city renowned for big-as-Texas rib-eye steaks and in-famous as the site of JFK's horribly public assassination would offer diners nearly 6,500 restaurants to choose from? Dallas lays claim to all these fames, as well as the invention of the almighty computer chip and the even grander frozen margarita!

Today, Dallas truly lives up to the state's notorious "everything is bigger in Texas" attitude. Women with big "jew-ahls" and even bigger hair make daily raids on the outlandishly opulent, larger-than-life shopping malls, in search of more stuff to shove into their already overstuffed closets. The "Big D" is also home to the Texas State Fair—the largest hog-callin', pie-eatin', family get-together in the nation.

What else? Oh, yeah, Dallas also boasts the largest urban arts district in America. The nation's largest collection of African American folk art is on proud display at the African American Museum. Now that's *big*, Texas-sized news!

Plan to start your morning on a solemn, poignant note with a visit to the Sixth Floor Museum at Dealey Plaza, where Lee Harvey Oswald allegedly shot and killed President John F. Kennedy. Around the corner from Dealey Plaza is the massive JFK Memorial, a 50-square-foot open-roofed monument.

The Southwest Black Arts Festival celebrates the culture of African Americans with live music, food and art booths.

Dealey Plaza is located in the West End Historic District, the spot where the city was established back in 1841. Today the West End is home to renovated warehouses that encompass a quaint shopping emporium. As if the denizens of Dallas needed another place to drop those retail dollars!

Head northeast on Ross Avenue to the Dallas Arts District, where tranquil gardens are punctuated by graceful waterfalls and priceless sculptures. Next, take I-75 north two exits to Lemmon Avenue to visit Freedman's Memorial Cemetery, a pre-Civil War African American burial ground. Desecrated in the 1930s when railroad tracks were laid across it, then again in the 1940s when the Central Expressway/Highway was constructed, this sacred land has at long last been reclaimed and restored as a true final resting place. Today more a testament to life than a tribute to the deceased, the cemetery honors those who crossed over with the dream of freedom burning in their hearts.

Traveling further north to the crossroads of I-75 and Northwest Highway, you'll reach NorthPark Center, offering some of the best shopping in Dallas. But before you wear out your credit card, stop off at DC's Café opposite the mall for a super soul food lunch of tasty fried catfish, macaroni and cheese, greens, and to-die-for fried sweet potato pie.

After a day of power shopping and touring, slide back toward downtown and head over to Fair Park. Home to eight museums, the one not to miss is the African American Museum. It is filled with fascinating artifacts from the old Wild West.

Then comes the biggest question of the day: where to go for dinner? As Dallas is home to literally thousands of restaurants, it's gonna be hard, but more than likely, it's gonna be good wherever you go! For a real Texas-sized meal (and a similarly sized check), Del Frisco's can't be beat; splurge on the filet mignon and succulent lobster. The too-trendy set flocks to Sipango for jazz and after-dinner cocktails. If the vibes up front are too mellow for you, Sipango's Rio Room can light your fire with 1970s disco and R&B. Now, if all of this nice-nice partyin' is *still* too tame, shoot over to the Park Avenue Nightclub, where you and 500 of your nearest and dearest friends can get your groove on to the tunes of hip hop, R&B, and old school.

Restaurants

With 6,500 eateries offering every variety of cuisine known to man, Dallas boasts four times more restaurants than Manhattan. Yet, truth be told, most visitors come to Dallas to eat (1) steaks, (2) Mexican food, (3) Tex-Mex cuisine, and (4) barbecue. Tex-Mex (Mexican food with a Texas flair) is the local favorite bar none—and a national obsession, to boot. Dallas also lays claim to the invention of two widely celebrated taste treats: the chicken fajita and the frozen margarita. If you're not sure what you're in the mood for, scope out one of Dallas's many restaurant rows. The too-trendy Greenville Avenue, McKinney Avenue, and Deep Ellum Avenue corridors will not fail to inspire you. If you can't find a restaurant that arouses your appetite along one of these strips, you just weren't hungry to begin with!

Cow Palaces

Al Biernat's, 4217 Oak Lawn Ave., 214/219-2201—Aged New York Strip steaks, fall-off-the-bone osso buco, and four-pound lobsters almost steal the spotlight from Biernat's eclectic and colorful interior. · $45+

Chamberland's Prime Chop House, 5330 Belt Line Rd., Addison, 972/934-2467—Beef, aged to perfection, kissed with a glorious cognac peppercorn sauce and served with garlic mashed potatoes, fresh asparagus, or tender corn hand-cut off the cob is just one of the temptations from Chamberland's Texas-style menu. · $40+

✳**Del Frisco's Double Eagle Steak House**, 5251 Spring Alley Rd., 972/490-9000—The 16-ounce prime rib eye and 24-ounce porterhouse cut steaks served here are all well and good, but if you're going to do Del Frisco's right, order the medium-rare filet mignon and luscious three-pound lobster tail. Well worth any consequences that may arise the following day! · $45+

Fine Dining

Bizú
2504 McKinney Ave., 214/303-1002
Somehow, among the barrage of Thai, Italian, Tex-Mex, and Nouvelle this and that, classic French cuisine has gotten lost in the cream sauce. Bizú's menu is wonderfully refined, with dishes that put dining Français on the map, but the gorgeous dining room gets all the attention. • **$40+**

Casual Dining

✳**Caribbean Grill**
3068 Forest Ln., 972/241-9113
This cheap and cheerful spot stands out from the bevy of neighboring ethnic eateries. Caribbean Grill features the obligatory colorful decor, reggae blasting from the stereo, and jerk chicken on the

Tex-Mex

✳Javier's, 4912 Cole, 214/521-4211—A long-time local favorite, Javier's serves up a mean margarita and a tangy seafood ceviche. This Mexican cantina is also known for its salsas and mole sauce—fresh, fiery, and flavorful! · $15+

Monica's Aca y Alla, 2914 Main St., 214/748-7140—This is no sleepy road-side cantina. Monica's gives up mucho attitude with it's smart decor and even sassier menu including familiar Mexican dishes cleverly modernized with influences from Italy and the Far East. Weekend Brunch is always a crowd-pleaser, but it's the great live Latin jazz that really spices up those warm Texas nights. · $20+

Nuevo Leon, 2013 Greenville, 214/887-8148—Nuevo Leon is known city-wide for its fun, whimsical ambience, its killer salsas and chips, and its slightly unusual menu selection. After all, when was the last time you had beef tongue? · $20+

✳Taco Diner, 4011 Villanova, 214/696-4944—This cute upscale eatery serves great Mexican favorites like nachos, fajitas, and flautas. Must haves: fresh seared tilapia tacos and moist pork tacos topped with jalapeños, cilantro, and sweet onions. Muy bueno! · $15+

menu, but the food sure is good. Highly recommended: the jumbo shrimp in coconut milk and the rum punch.• **$20+/AA**

✳DC's Café
8224 Park Lane, 214/363-4348
"When God made man, He created only a few things that were absolutely necessary. You may not have to have clothes, but you *have* to eat!" So says owner Damon Crow. This straightforward thinking—along with a powerful spiritual faith and his momma's fried sweet potato turnovers—accounts for the success of DC's Café. Pork chops, fried catfish, and daily down-home specials are featured items on the mouth-watering menu. Take out; limited seating.• **$10/AA**

✳Elaine's Kitchen
1912 Martin Luther King Jr. Blvd., 214/565-1008

The menu at Elaine's Kitchen is arranged by entrée size (small, medium, or large) and priced accordingly. Oxtails, curried goat, curried chicken, jerk chicken, stew peas, cow foot, ackee, and red snapper are a few of the selections coming from this small take-out spot, hailed "Best Caribbean Place" and "Best for $5" by the local press. If these testimonies aren't enough to convince you to stop by, notice that the long line for lunch starts forming early in the morning. That many people can't be wrong!• **$10/AA**

✳Famous Smokey John's Bar-B-Q & Home Cooking Depot
1820 W. Mockingbird, 214/352-2752

This is the kind of place you expect to see in Dallas. Straight out of the wild, wild West, Smokey John's casual, rustic decor showcases authentic western antiques. The place is known for its barbecued beef, ribs, ham, hot links, and chicken, but there are plenty of other home-style specials on the menu. A plethora of vegetable sides and other salads round out the feast.• **$10+/AA**

Hardeman's BBQ
2901 S. Lancaster Rd., 214/371-7627

Featuring family recipes passed down from generations of great pit men, Hardeman's has served delish BBQ since 1955. The beef brisket is slow smoked for eight hours. As Hardeman puts it, "We take the time to prepare our food as if we were eating it ourselves!" The tender barbecued pork ribs, links, and chicken are just a few of the reasons people keep coming back. Amen!• **$10/AA**

Henderson's Chicken Shack
4837 Gaston, 214/827-2191

OK, so the neighborhood is a little rough—one o'clock in the morning might not be the best time to cruise by Henderson's for a snack. All the more reason to check it out for dinner so you don't miss out on the wonderfully tasty cholesterol-drenched fried chicken livers. Henderson's fried chicken is considered by many to be some of the best in the city: not too greasy and best when eaten with fluffy white bread, pickles, and jalapeño peppers. Take-out only.• **$10/AA**

✴Queen of Sheba Café and Restaurant
3527 McKinney, 214/521-0491
Texas's oldest Ethiopian restaurant and certainly one of its best, Queen of Sheba provides customers with a most enjoyable dining experience. The owners' motto: "Hospitality is our way of life. It is our family tradition to serve you any way we can!" Actor Danny Glover stops by whenever he's in town to sample from the award-winning menu, replete with tantalizing dishes that encourage sharing. The lunch buffet provides an excellent way to sample many authentic Eritrean foods; the Queen's Dinner is a complete meal from appetizer to dessert, and including an aperitif, a glass of wine, and coffee or tea.• **$20/AA**

Nightclubs

Along with its plethora of restaurants, Dallas serves up nightlife. Most of it is country western and rock 'n' roll. Underground clubs like the Bomb Factory, a hip hop club, and Dred and Irie, the reggae club where Erika Badu debuted, are deeply nestled in Deep Ellum; find them through local channels. The more sophisticated lounges and bars offer live jazz but, overall, this is a young folks' town where dance clubs rule and tequila Jello shots are the dessert of choice.

✴GG's Jazz
5915 E. Northwest Hwy., 214/692-7088
Nancy Wilson, Howard Hewitt, and lots of great local talent have appeared at GG's Jazz. This upscale nightclub's dance floor is packed on the weekends, hosting "T.J.'s Open Mike Night" for the talented and nervy, ladies' nights, live bands, dancing, specially priced drinks, and a complimentary buffet on certain evenings. Call for a schedule. • **Cover charge/AA**

Lakeside
3100 W. Northwest Hwy., 214/904-1770
The Bar-Kays, Lakeside, and other great local groups regularly pack the house at Lakeside. Featuring urban contemporary, rap, hip hop, and R&B, this club caters to a crowd that *knows* how to party! Laid-back and dress code-free, Lakeside can hold up to 1,800 folks on a Saturday night.• **Cover charge/AA**

*Park Avenue Nightclub
9100 N. Central Expressway, 214/739-5548

This sexy establishment was designed by Charles Bush, nightclub designer/owner extraordinaire. With capacity for 1,500 souls, the club features three bars (complete with animal-print bar stools), a huge dance floor, an area for private parties, and a sound system that cranks out R&B and old-school favorites. Additionally, big-name bands such as Morris Day, Solo, and Groove Theory have performed at the Park Avenue.• **Cover Charge/AA**

Reciprocity
210 S. Tyler, Oak Cliffs, 214/941-4428

Disclaimer: Reciprocity is not a nightclub, it is a cultural community center committed to local artists, businesses, and families. So, why is it in the nightclub section, you ask? Because on Friday nights the mic is open to anyone brave enough to read their poetry aloud to a crowd. The stage is also open to musical and dance performances, and musical groups perform most Saturday and Sunday nights. The center also displays and sells original local artwork, artifacts, and creatively designed clothing. In the nutrition department, this healthy environment peddles all-natural vegan foods, juices, and vitamins in their co-op.• **AA**

*Samba Room
4514 Travis St., 214/522-4137

America's love affair with pre-Cold War Havana shows no sign of ending at the Samba Room, where Dallas's beautiful people indulge the Hollywood version of Cuba, not the impoverished reality. But that's OK. Restaurants will be the new century's amusement parks, and the Samba Room sizzles in that role, offering exotic island-fusion dishes, lots of tropical foliage, and a cigar-friendly lounge filled with the intoxicating sounds of Afro-Cuban music. The Samba Room's Sunday brunch is dee-*lish*!• **Cover charge/$30+**

*Sambuca
2618 Elm, 214/744-0820

This jazz/supper club chain establishment marries the "Harlem Nights" attitudes of the '30s and '40s with cool, funky modernism. The result? This is just what a jazz club should be: splashy, sleek, and *très* sophisticated. Sambuca features a wonderful (though pricey) Mediterranean dinner menu and offers live jazz nightly.• **Music charge/Dinner $30+**

✴Sipango
4513 Travis St., 214/522-2411
This playground for adults offers contemporary dining, live jazz six nights a week, and dancing to '70s disco and '80s funk Thursday through Saturday nights. The Italian-influenced menu features such stand-outs as mussels steamed with roasted chiles and garlic; grilled artichoke, asparagus, and gorgonzola pizza; double-crown pork chops with sweet potatoes; and creamy risotto with Maine lobster.• **$30+**

Festivals

Just because you stage the country's largest fair doesn't mean you can't also host small annual multicultural celebrations. Dallas can, and does, all throughout the city. It's a welcome, vibrant reminder that the Big D is no longer just another dusty cow town.

African American Heritage Festival
Old City Park, 214/421-5141
Every year, the African American Heritage Festival gathers everyone together for a community celebration of history, accomplishment, and pride. Past activities include African American quilt displays and expert demonstrations, a Texas Buffalo Soldiers exhibit, and dramatic storytelling about our most heroic Black leaders. Of course, with any African American festival, best believe there will be plenty of soul stirring music, spoken word stage performances, and lots of good food.• **Third Saturday in February/Admission charge**

Annette Strauss Artists' Square
1800 Leonard St., 214/953-1977
Downtown Dallas comes alive during state fair days with the sounds of gospel, jazz, blues, and tejano, accompanied by lots of tapping, leaping, pounding, and pirouetting of feet. Located in the Dallas Arts District, the Annette Strauss Artists' Square hosts free multicultural outdoor events all year round. Annual activities include:

Catherine Whiteman portrays Sojourner Truth at the African American Heritage Festival.

Juneteenth Celebration, first weekend in June
Southwest Black Arts Festival, third weekend in June (214/827-7110)
Praise in the Park Gospel Festival, last Saturday in June
Taste of African America Dallas, July Fourth weekend
Heritage Taste of Dallas, last weekend in September
Dallas Jazz Festival, third weekend in October (214/520-7789)

State Fair of Texas
Fair Park, 214/565-9931
Texans sure like to show off—and they do such a good job of it! Case in point: the State Fair of Texas. Hosting more than 3.5 million folks over 24 days, the fair is without question the largest

At the State Fair, Don't Miss:

African American Museum, Fair Park, 214/565-9026—Past special exhibits have focused on Black Texans' folk art.

Al Lipscomb Classic Football Game, Cotton Bowl, Fair Park, 214/421-8716—Just in case you don't think there's enough going on, one of the South's favorite football rivalries, Grambling State versus Prairie View, battles annually at the Cotton Bowl. · First Saturday in October

World Music Stages, various venues—Lou Rawls, War, and other gifted musical artists have brought a little soul to the Lone Star state during the State Fair in previous years.

annual event of its kind in the country. It features North America's largest Ferris wheel—a dizzying 212 feet tall—as well as a corny 52-foot robot, appropriately named "Big Tex," which, by some miracle, waves its arms *without* creating hurricane-strength winds. And what state fair would be complete without livestock contests for best Angus beef cattle (note: alive and *not* pre-cooked), Holstein cows, poultry, pigeons, swine, llamas, and Nigerian dwarf goats. Yes, that's what I said: Nigerian dwarf goats. There are also countless cooking competitions and a showcase of some 400 automobiles—and that's just the short list! But probably what's most impressive about the State Fair of Texas is the lineup of international and multicultural acts, including Spanish flamenco dancers, African drummers, Caribbean steel drum bands, and Peruvian pipers. In conjunction with the fair, the neighboring African American Museum typically displays special exhibits focusing on Black Texans's contributions to Lone Star history and culture. Oh, and how could it be a true state fair without some serious Texas food? We're talkin' beef brisket sandwiches, sausage on a stick, corn dogs, barbecued turkey legs, and juicy roasted corn on the cob here, festival favorites all!• **Late September through mid-October**

Museums and Attractions

Dallas Arts District

Covering a staggering 60 acres, the Dallas Arts District encompasses lovely gardens, water sculptures, priceless European art, and two stunning examples of modern architecture: the Morton H. Meyerson Symphony Center, designed by I. M. Pei, and the Dallas Museum of Art, charted by Edward Larabee Barnes. The district claims to be the largest of its kind in the country. Adding to its distinction are the Cathedral Guadalupe, home to the Catholic Diocese of Dallas (built in 1898), the esteemed Booker T. Washington High School for the Performing and Visual Arts, historically Black St. Paul United Methodist Church (founded in 1873), and the lovely Belo mansion. Highlights include:

Annette Strauss Artists' Square, 1800 Leonard St., 214/953-1977—This year-round outdoor arts center is home to many multicultural outdoor musical events.

Dallas Museum of Art, 1717 N. Harwood St., 214/922-1200—The first museum in Dallas to feature the art and culture of the Western Hemisphere, it also houses a premier collection of pre-Columbian art.

Morton H. Meyerson Symphony Center, 2301 Flora St., 214/670-3600—The center hosts the annual African American Festival Concert, among other events.

Trammell Crow Center Sculpture Garden, 2001 Ross Ave., 214/979-6100—More than 20 works by French masters, lovely, waterfalls, and gorgeous landscaped gardens grace these grounds.

Fair Park

Fair Park features eight museums nestled on a 277-acre national historical landmark site, scenic gardens and fountains, the Cotton Bowl stadium, the nation's largest collection of 1930s art deco architecture, and the Texas Star Ferris wheel—the largest of its kind in North America and the second largest in the world. Fair Park is also home to the State Fair of Texas, the granddaddy of them all!

African American Museum, 3536 Grand Ave., 214/565-9026—Home to the nation's largest collection of African American folk art.

"Sculp-Tour"

Downtown Dallas is filled with an impressive array of sculpture. More than 30 significant pieces decorate the downtown area, as do the following noteworthy artworks:

Mustang Sculpture Exhibit, Williams Square, O'Conner Rd., 972/869-9047—Nine bronze mustangs appear to gallop across a stream in this majestic tribute to Texans' most beloved wild creature.

Pioneer Plaza, Young and Griffin Sts.—This plaza, which marks the location of the 1850s Shawnee Trail, is the site of the largest bronze monument of its kind: a realistic depiction of a cattle drive, 4.2 acres long, that features 56 life-sized longhorn steers.

Dallas Museum of Natural History, 3535 Grand Ave., 214/421-3466—Here, visitors go face-to-face with the likes of such prehistoric beasts as the Texas tenontosaurus and a 90-million-year-old protostega sea turtle.

Dallas Aquarium, 1300 Robert B. Cullum Blvd., 214/670-8443—Some 5,000 aquatic creatures from around the world make this their home.

Dallas Horticulture Center, 3601 Martin Luther King Jr. Blvd., 214/428-7476—This center displays plants from Africa and Texas as well as a collection of antique roses.

Other Museums and Attractions

Conspiracy Museum
110 S. Market St., 214/741-3040

Skeptical, are you? Don't quite see things in black and white? For those who seek answers to questions often dodged by the "official story," a stop at the Conspiracy Museum is a must. This museum challenges popular conceptions about nearly every alleged assassination plot in U.S. history. After you study these thought-provoking exhibits, you may never view the past in the same way again.• **Admission charge**

Freedman's Memorial
Lemmon Ave. and I-75

The Freedman's Memorial is a moving tribute to the thousands of souls whose eternal peace was disrupted in the 1930s and 1940s when modern transportation displaced the graves of some 7,000 enslaved and free African Americans. Only 1,500 bodies were recovered and reinterred. Today, the Freedman's Memorial celebrates these lives on beautifully landscaped grounds that feature five magnificent bronze statues. The rear interior wall displays 10 poems written by area schoolchildren, and the names of many of those buried at the site are engraved on the entrance steps.• **Free**

Sixth Floor Museum at Dealey Plaza
John F. Kennedy Memorial
411 Elm St., 214/747-6660

Dallas turned a national tragedy into a celebration of life with the creation of the Sixth Floor Museum at Dealey Plaza and the John F. Kennedy Memorial. The museum is housed on the sixth floor of the building from which Lee Harvey Oswald allegedly shot JFK. The window from which the fatal shot supposedly was fired is now sealed off by glass and surrounded by photographs, video footage, and documents commemorating the life and times of the late president. Around the corner is the John F. Kennedy Memorial, a massive walled monument symbolizing an open tomb.• **Admission charge**

Churches

Elizabeth Chapel CME Church
1028 E. Tenth St., 214/375-6462

A Dallas Historic Landmark since 1980, Elizabeth Chapel CME was one of the earliest CME churches in the state of Texas.

New Hope Baptist Church
5002 S. Central Expwy., 214/421-5296

Since 1873 New Hope Baptist has been committed to furthering the development of the African American community. New Hope organized the first school for African American children. Between 1934 and 1954, under the leadership of Rev. Maynard Jackson, grandfather of former Atlanta mayor Maynard Jackson, New Hope organized the first progressive voters' league in Dallas and encouraged the government to hire the first African American postal clerks and mail carriers.

St. Luke Community United Methodist Church
5710 E.R.L. Thornton Fwy., 214/821-2970
Established in 1933, St. Luke's Community is best known for its spectacular stained-glass windows. Each panel represents a significant event in African American history, from the migration era to the Civil Rights movement. Depicting such leaders as Bishop Desmond Tutu, Malcolm X, Rev. Martin Luther King Jr., this Texas National Registered Landmark immortalizes the strength, courage, faith, and determination of a strong race and invincible community.

St. Paul United Methodist Church
1816 Routh St., 214/922-0000
Founded in 1873, St. Paul's is the only African American congregation in downtown Dallas. Housed in an historic landmark building designed by African American architect William Sydney Pittman, the church was also the site of one of the city's earliest schools for Black children.

Recreation

Amusement Parks
Six Flags Over Texas,
2201 Road to Six Flags, Arlington, 817/640-8900
Six Flags Hurricane Harbor,
1800 E. Lamar Blvd., Arlington, 817/265-3356

Golf
Cedar Crest Golf Course,
1800 Southerland, 214/670-7615
Stevens Park Golf Course,
1005 N. Montclair, 214/670-7506

Tenison Park Golf Course,
3501 Samuell Blvd., 214/670-1402

Tennis

Fair Oaks Tennis Center, 7501 Merriman Pkwy., 214/670-1495
Fretz, 14700 Hillcrest Rd., 214/670-6622
Kiest, 2324 W. Kiest Blvd., 214/670-7618

Denver

Denver. There is something about the air here. And it has nothing to do with its thinness, although nosebleeds are a hazard in a city that sits a mile high. No, it has more to do with its freshness. Denver exudes a cleanliness that can transform a savvy, martini-sipping urbanite into a Timberland-touting, flannel shirted lover of the outdoors ready to scale the highest mountain, even without the help of an SUV.

The Rocky Mountains, all 150 miles of them, stretch from the Wyoming border to glorious Pikes Peak. Along the way they protectively wrap their majestic, jagged arms around the lovely Mile-High City. Combine all that crisp air with elevation and 300-plus days of sunshine, and you'll understand why Denver gleams like the clearest and most multifaceted of diamonds. One glance at this awesome sight and you'll know what that famed "high" is all about!

Before you head for the hills, give downtown Denver a good going over; it deserves it. Start your morning with a steaming cup of herbal tea at BG's Joe House, located in the historic African American community of Five Points. One of Denver's oldest neighborhoods, Five Points was once the West's most progressive and prosperous Black community. Today, Five Points is regaining its luster with an influx of restaurants, offices, and trendy boutiques. Up and down Welton Avenue and California Street, you'll find such intriguing stores as Akente Express, purveyor of upscale African-inspired clothing and artifacts, and the Hue-Man Experience bookstore, which stocks every book by a Black author known to man. The Black West Museum and Heritage Center offers a fascinating look at African Americans' contributions to the development of the Wild West. Around the corner, if it's near noon, join the line forming for lunch at M&D's Café, where you can get a fried catfish sandwich, a side of potato salad, and the best peach cobbler à la mode this side of the Colorado River.

Though surrounded by mountains, Denver itself is flat as a pancake, so you have to seek more elevation to appreciate the spectacular vistas. The rotunda in the State Capitol offers visitors a panoramic view of the city and the breathtaking Rockies. But why just look when you can be a part of all that splendor? Take I-70 west to Red Rocks Amphitheatre, a 9,000-seat natural outdoor arena carved out of huge, 500-foot-high red sandstone cliffs. Luther Vandross's lilting baritone voice echoed throughout the foothills the last time he performed here. Just down the road a piece is Buffalo Bill's grave and Lookout Mountain, which affords incredible views of Denver and the natural splendor surrounding it.

After an invigorating day in the hills, head back down to the mile-high mark. Call the Denver Performance Arts hotline to see if the renowned Cleo Parker Robinson Dance Ensemble is staging one of its masterful modern ballets this evening. Then head on over to Lodo, the hot, trendy section of lower downtown, and Jax Fish House, where the microbrewed beer is frosty and the Rocky Mountain raw oysters are plump and cold. After appetizers, the hip crowd goes to Vesta's Dipping Grill to dine on pan-seared filet of sole with curried udon noodles dipped in coconut mango lime sauce. Your whirlwind day begs to end on a mellow note. If for no other reason than to give yourself a chance to get your head out of the clouds, head over to the York Street Café to groove on some of the city's best local jazz musicians.

Restaurants

When the air is as thin as it is here, relief should never be but a stone's throw away. Maybe that's why Denver boasts more microbreweries than any other city in the United States! To flatter a tall, cold one, try grilled mountain rattlesnake, buffalo steak, or a plate of

Rocky Mountain oysters. If these dishes are just a bit too exotic, never fear: Denver has thousands of restaurants of all ethnic distinctions, including some noteworthy African American eateries, just in case you're homesick for some good ol' soul food.

Fine Dining

✴Radex
100 E. Ninth Ave., 303/861-7999
Chic, sexy, and damned-if-the-food-isn't-just-great, Radex is *the* spot in Denver for those weary of all those "brew ha-ha's" and hungry for a slice of sophistication. The restaurant's washed salmon-colored walls can warm even the bitterest of cold winter days. Radex's plush setting provides the perfect complement to its New American cuisine. Perfectly grilled meats and Radex's famous mounds of mashed potatoes are the stars of this show. • **$35+**

Strings Restaurant
1700 Humboldt St., 303/831-7310
One of Denver's favorite places to celebrate special occasions (then, again, who needs a reason to eat out?), Strings always delights with its terrific, ever-changing menu of modern American classics. The fish is always a sure bet, as are such signature dishes as the wonderfully thin carpaccio and tasty, tender sautéed calves' liver. • **$35+**

Casual Dining

✴Bocaza Mexican Grille
1740 E. 17th Ave., 303/393-7545
8101 E. Belleview Ave., 303/740-8330
1 Broadway, Unit B-108, 303/282-0022
How to build a restaurant empire: Step one—Find out what the people want. Step two—Use only the freshest ingredients in your homemade salsas and burritos. Step three—Create a vibrant and stylish dining area. Step four—Give patrons plenty of flash for their cash. The result: Bocaza! This upscale and contemporary Mexican fast-food restaurant, the brainchild of two African American visionaries, is on the verge of revolutionizing the restaurant industry. Be on the lookout for one opening near you. • **$10/AA**

Sidewalk dining in Larimer Square.

Cheesy George's Burgers & Bones
313 Havana St., Aurora, 303/363-7939
Cheesy George's serves great "semi-fast" food, like its "Andi Burger" topped with green peppers and fried onions and its "Cheesy George Burger" topped with chili and cheese. Then there's something called the "Crack Brown," a spicy Polish sausage topped with chili, and the "El Cheapo," a grilled cheese-and-that's-it sandwich. Oh, and don't forget the ribs, which are sold by the bone—but you won't be able to eat just one! • **$10/AA**

✳Ethel's House of Soul
2622 Welton Ave., 303/295-2125
In the heart of Denver's predominantly Black Five Points neighborhood sits Ethel's House of Soul, a modest spot where the food isn't

fancy but it's always good. The mural on the wall is a classic, featuring an old-time caricature of a seasoned cook surrounded by a few of his favorite dishes, from bacon and eggs to fried chicken. House specialties include pork chops, smothered steak, neck bones, chitterlings, hog maws, chicken and dressing, and, of course, peach cobbler. • **$10/AA**

Horne's Catering Restaurant
2861 Colorado Blvd., 303/320-8571
This hole-in-the-wall serves good soul food to go, like fried catfish, barbecue ribs, roast duck, neck bones, liver and onions, pigs' feet, and oxtails—just to name a few. But Horne's biggest seller is the chitterlings. The kitchen goes through about 180 pounds a week! Lawd, that's a lot of pig! • **$10/AA**

Jax Fish House
1539 17th St., 303/292-5767
If you desire a quiet, intimate meal for two, go somewhere else. Jax is Lodo's most popular haunt, and, on a good night, noise levels vie with those at Mile High Stadium after a Broncos touchdown. Now, we're not mad at 'em, just know that folks go to Jax to have a good time. In addition to the buoyant atmosphere, Jax serves some of the best seafood around, and there's a serious raw bar for oyster lovers. • **$35+**

Kapre Fried Chicken
2729 Welton Ave., 303/295-9207
Kapre Fried Chicken has been around since 1957, serving what many consider "the best fried chicken in town." It's good, too—just spicy enough, with a nice, crispy skin. Other specialties include fried shrimp, whiting, catfish, hot links, and gizzard, liver, and giblet dinners. Actually, that's the whole menu at Kapre Fried Chicken, but with chicken this finger lickin', what else do you need? • **$10/AA**

✳M & D's Café
2004 E. 28th Ave., 303/296-1760
Since 1977 M & D's has wowed Denver with its award-winning barbecue and fried fish. Not only is M & D's known for serious barbecue ribs, chicken, sliced meats, and hot links, but the fish, whether it's catfish or buffalo, is thick and crispy. But the line tumbling out the front door is there for the killer "wear your elastic-waist pants

and get ready" peach cobbler à la mode. Start that diet tomorrow…unless, of course, you come back to M & D's the next night for more! • **$15+/AA**

✴**Painted Bench**
404 E. 20th Ave., 303/863-7473
The Painted Bench restaurant is a wonderful addition to the resurgent Five Points corridor. Its quaint appointments and home-dining-room-like furnishings bring new life to the refurbished 100-year-old structure. The New American menu includes a few delicious surprises like tender buffalo brisket and seared elk burger. • **$25+**

✴**Sam Taylor's Bar-B-Q**
435 S. Cherry St., 303/388-9300
"The best barbecue ribs in town"? How does one live up to such praise? Well, if you're Sam Taylor's, it ain't hard to do! This award-winning spot is known citywide not only for its barbecue and sausage "sammiches," but also for its "BBQ Poke," hot links, and 25-plus brews, including Sam's own. • **$10+/AA**

✴**Santino's**
1939 Blake St., 303/298-1939
Family-style Italian dining, where the portions are so large you know what you're having for lunch the next day, made a major comeback in the 1990s. At Santino's, the portions are not only ample enough to feed everyone and his or her grandmother, but what reads as a traditional Italian menu tastes anything *but*! Suggested favorites: anything you order, 'cause it's *all* good! • **$20+**

✴**Vesta's Dipping Grill**
1822 Blake St., 303/296-1970
You may think if you create a dining area as visually spectacular as the one at Vesta's Dipping Grill (and what's with that name, anyway?), the food can play second fiddle. But not at Vesta's. The meats and seafood, seemingly casual fare, are grilled over an open flame, then served with a variety of salsas and dips just as delicious as the sexy decor. As for the curious name, the restaurant is named after Vesta, the Roman goddess of the hearth, who was just doin' her grillin' thing. • **$30+**

✳York Street Café
2239 E. Colfax Ave., 303/331-7727
Colorado lamb chops with a smoked Gouda and avocado risotto, blackened catfish with dirty rice and potato frites, and Southwestern shrimp fettucine and crawfish étouffée are just a few of the tasty items on York's from-all-over-the-place menu. Night time is the right time to stop by York Street on Tuesdays through Saturdays, when the joint jumps with live jazz, blues, and DJ music. The good vibes continue on Sunday with a live jazz brunch. • **$20+/AA**

Coffee Houses

✳BG's Joe House & Corporate
2747 Welton Ave., 303/308-0811
More than just a pleasant stop for a sandwich and a cup of joe, BG's offers an early morning menu of gourmet coffees, cappuccino, steamy espresso, more than 50 varieties of herbal teas, and heart-smart sandwiches, soups, and salads. For those who like to slurp and surf the Net, BG's recently installed personal computers, turning this neighborhood spot into a high-tech cybercafé! • **$5+/AA**

Sweet Surprise Bakery & Café
1514 17th St., 303/572-7772
Sweet Surprise is a cute little coffee bar serving espresso and cappuccino and delicious baked goods such as dense, fruity scones, tart lemon bars, bagels, donuts, and muffins. Health-conscious sandwiches like cashew chicken or turkey prepared with low-fat mayo and served on multigrain bread are great for those on the go. • **$5+/AA**

Nightclubs

El Chapultepec
1962 Market St., 303/295-9126
"Cold Beer, Hot Jazz" is the mantra here, and truer words were never written. You'll find the slogan painted on the side of "The Pec," Denver's premier jazz club. None other than President Bill Clinton and Wynton Marsalis have been seen on stage here, gettin' down with local musicians during impromptu jam sessions. • **Music charge**

Vartan's Jazz Club & Restaurant
1800 Glenarm Pl., 303/399-1111
This place is all about, and only about, one thing: jazz. Don't expect fancy decor, a bevy of supermodels lined up at the bar, or a fine dining menu. However, if like your jazz straight-ahead and to the point, you've come to the right place! • **Music charge most nights**

✻York Street Café
2239 E. Colfax Ave., 303/331-7727
Tuesday and Thursday nights, it's DJ jazz jams at the York Street Café, blues on hump night, and live jazz weekends. • **Music charge some evenings/AA**

Festivals

When it comes to festivals, Denver likes to put major emphasis on the great outdoors, good food, good music, and good beer.

Juneteenth Celebration
Five Points District, 303/399-7138
Although Juneteenth celebrations started in the Denver area in the early 1950s, the community of Five Points didn't organize its annual four-day celebration until 1966, and the partyin' hasn't stopped since! Commemorating the end of slavery in Texas, Juneteenth in Denver turns Welton Avenue into a crowded parade route filled with jubilant revelers. Excitement swells as celebrants welcome the newly crowned Mr. and Mrs. Juneteenth and jam to high-steppin' high school bands while chompin' on some great soul food. Continuous live musical and other entertainment, along with a Sunday raise-the-roof-and-praise-God gospel extravaganza, keep the festivities going all weekend long. • **Third weekend in June/Free (donations welcome)**

Festival of Mountain and Plain: A Taste of Denver
Civic Center Park, 303/534-6161
Sure there's music, arts and crafts, and activities for kids, but the real reason more than 350,000 people pack the Civic Center Park every Labor Day weekend is to get their "eat" on at the Taste of Denver, one of the country's best tasting festivals. More than 50 Colorado

*Hand-stitched dolls are just some of the unique items found at the Watu
Sokoni Marketplace at the annual Black Arts Festival.*

Bill Picket Invitational Rodeo

Originated in Denver, the Bill Picket Invitational Rodeo (877/MO-RODEO) rounds out its eight-city tour in the Mile High City. The only Black traveling rodeo, BPIR showcases the country's best ropers, riders, and all-around skills of the American cowboy and cowgirl. Actor and accomplished cowboy Glynn Turman serves annually as grand marshall.

restaurants fork out everything from spicy barbecued lamb ribs to deep-fried pickles. Your must-try list must include: Cajun turkey legs, buffalo bratwurst, lobster, crab-and-cheese-stuffed portobella mushrooms, catfish nuggets, and sliced apples with caramel sauce. But the gorging isn't over yet! In the Greek Theater, the city's fine-dining restaurants get into the act, serving fancy-schmancy goodies like four-cheese tortellone bolognese, barbecued shrimp-and-mango soft tacos, basil-crusted salmon, and watermelon sorbet. Now *that's* a food festival! • **Labor Day weekend/Free**

Black Arts Festival
East High School, 303/860-7747
Denver's Black Arts Festival is more than just a showing of fine art by a talented few: It embraces a culture so gifted it takes three days and several venues to display. Three stages showcase some of the most explosive local musical talent, offering everything from jazz, blues, soul, salsa, hip hop, and gospel to traditional Caribbean and African-influenced drumming. Spoken word and dance performances as well as poetry readings round out this multifaceted exposition. At the festival's Watu Sokoni Marketplace you'll find gorgeous printed fabric from Senegal and unusual Gambian artifacts. The Joda Village recreates the exhilarating sights, sounds, and smells of a Nigerian village, complete with traditional huts whose residents wear native African garments and present live drumming and dance performances. And of course, arts and crafts by local and nationally known African American artists abound at the festival, displayed for purchase or simply admiration. • **Second weekend in July/Free**

Theater and Dance

Cleo Parker Robinson Dance, Denver Center for the Performing Arts—One of the country's premier dance troupes, Cleo Parker Robinson Dance electrifies audiences with original performances during the fall and spring months at the Denver Performing Arts complex. · AA

Eulipions, Inc., 1770 Sherman St., 303/863-0019—The Eulipions theater group's celebrated production of Langston Hughes's Black Nativity is an annual holiday tradition. Eulipions produces other urban stage productions in its 500-seat theater and cabaret space. · AA

Museums and Galleries

Black American West Museum & Heritage Center
3091 California St., 303/292-2566

Did you know that nearly a third of the cowboys who helped build the American West were Black? Did you know there were Black cowboys, period? Well, neither did Paul Stewart, until he met a Black cowboy, who told him stories of how he helped tame the West when the country was still young. This inspired Stewart to learn more about these unsung Western settlers and to pay tribute to their heroism. The Black American West Museum & Heritage Center uncovers the truths about the West's African American pioneers through documents, artifacts, and other fascinating historical memorabilia. What started as the seed of one man's inquisitive nature has grown into the country's most sweeping collection focusing on the African American presence in the West. • **Admission charge**

Mosadi's Collections
2200 Kearney St., 303/331-0700

Mosadi's Collections is Denver's premier African American-owned art gallery. More than a hundred artists are on exhibit with an extensive assortment of paintings, serigraphs, lithographs, sculptures, and artifacts. • **AA**

Churches

Campbell Memorial Church in Christ
2828 Fairfax St., 303/329-8184
One of the fastest growing churches in the Five Points community, Campbell Memorial is applauded for its many outreach programs and ministries.

House of Joy Miracle Deliverance Church
3082 Leyden St., 303/388-9060
Established in 1965 by the late Pastor Ruben Beechum, the House of Joy is a ministry whose outreach not only touches the community but also reaches around the world. In 1989 the House of Joy of South Africa was established.

Shorter Community African Methodist Episcopal Church
3100 Richard Allen Ct., 303/320-1712
In 1863, Mary E. Smith and Mary Randolph instituted the first Colored Methodist Church in Colorado. Using unorthodox fundraising methods parishioners raised enough money to move the church into a square brick building in 1866. In 1886, after two moves and a name change (to St. John's AME), delegates at the Annual Conference voted to honor then-presiding Bishop James A. Shorter by renaming the church Shorter Chapel.

Zion Baptist Church
933 E. 24th Ave., 303/861-4958
Zion Baptist was the first Black church in Colorado. It was founded in 1865 by freed slaves who had headed west, searching for their own piece of the American dream.

Recreation

Skiing

National Brotherhood of Skiers
1525 E. 53rd St. Suite 402, Chicago, Ill., 773/955-4100, www.nbs.org
Since 1973 the National Brotherhood of Skiers (NBS)—or "Black

Ski," as it has come to be known—has successfully dispeled the myth that Black folks stay inside during the winter and know nothing about skiing. With more than 7,000 members in 48 states, the NBS and its affiliates plan several major ski jamborees annually, including national summits and mini-summits, some as far away as Austria and Italy. Vail, Copper Mountain, Winter Park, and Aspen are some of the popular Colorado resorts Black Ski members frequent.

Black Enterprise & AXA/Equitable Ski Challenge
Keystone Resort, Keystone, 800/209-7229
You don't have to be a ski fanatic to enjoy the BE weekend ski challenge. There's also ice skating, sleighing, picnicking, shopping at the many quaint and très expensive boutiques, and sitting in front of a roaring fire, sipping hot cider (a personal favorite!). At night, corporate-sponsored theme galas and plenty of parties offer opportunities galore to meet and greet some of the country's most prominent African American executives. Just be sure to bring long-johns, sun block, and plenty of business cards! (Martin Luther King Jr. holiday weekend)

Golf

City Park, E. 25th Ave. and York St., 303/295-4420
Wellshire Golf Course, 3333 S. Colorado Blvd., 303/692-5636

Detroit

Detroit. Not only did this city share with the world its two greatest gifts—the Model T Ford and the vocal cords of Aretha Franklin—it lays claim to numerous other famous firsts and achievements. The "Motor City" was the site of the first paved concrete road and the first electrical power plant. Detroit hosts the largest free jazz festival in the United States, the Ford Montreux-Detroit Jazz Festival. And it is a city in which many African Americans have made their marks. African American inventor Garrett Morgan developed the first traffic light, which was installed in Detroit. Detroit has the largest NAACP membership in the nation, and each year it hosts the organization's largest sit-down fundraising dinner. And thanks to the genius of Berry Gordy, founder of Motown Records and the brains behind the "Motown Sound," nearly every American can sing (or attempt to sing) the first stanza of the Temptations' early hit, "My Girl." And as if that's not enough to distinguish the city, Detroit is also the potato chip capital of the world! Who knew?

A perfect day in Detroit starts with fresh-squeezed juice, wonderful homemade bread, and the sweetest fruits and berries in town, courtesy of the Russia Street Café in the famous Eastern Market district. After breakfast, wander through the market, encompassing the largest flower mart in the world, to smell the roses and other blossoms. Relish the rainbow of produce and spices on sale—and try to avoid being hit by a side of beef hoisted high on the shoulders of a strong-armed butcher en route to a nearby restaurant.

If you swoon over incredible views, don't miss the Summit Observation Deck on top of the cylindrical Renaissance Center. Across from the Renaissance Center, at the corner of Woodward and Jefferson Avenues, is a 24-foot statue called *The Fist*, dedicated to Detroit's number-one son, boxer Joe Louis. Take the People Mover, Detroit's version of the subway, to Greektown, a two-block strip in the heart of the city filled with terrific restaurants, bakeries, and shops. To the north is the historic Second Baptist Church, best known as a major station on the Underground Railroad. If you're not in the mood for *spanakopita* (too bad—Greektown's is the best!), walk a couple of blocks to Absolute Tiffany's, where you can get a less exotic but still-terrific lunch of almond chicken salad, jerk wings, and cornbread, or a beer-blackened catfish sandwich on sundried-tomato bread.

Later, drive up Woodward Avenue, the first concrete road in the United States (which, in some spots, looks like it hasn't been paved since!). Woodward was once the main thoroughfare for Detroit's thriving African American business community. After desegregation and the riots of the 1960s, many of the enterprises closed. Today a museum district, Woodward is undergoing revitalization, the focus of local efforts to transform the avenue into a hotbed of arts and entertainment venues.

While on Woodward Avenue, visit the impressive Charles H. Wright Museum of African American History. The museum's permanent exhibit, "Of the People: The African American Experience," is a stunning tribute to Black culture—and not to be missed. Next, put on your red dress and high-heeled sneakers and shimmy on over to the Motown Historical Museum to see where it all began! Across the street you'll find the Institute of African American Arts, where some of Detroit's finest artists display their masterpieces.

If it's after-five entertainment you're looking for, head to Flood's, one of Detroit's favorite watering holes and a great place to meet some prominent local professionals. For a unique dining experience, bring your appetite and clean hands to the Blue Nile, an absolutely delightful Ethiopian restaurant in Greektown, for a flavorful feast of lamb, chicken, beef, and vegetable dishes. For late-night cocktails and sweet live jazz guaranteed to leave you on a high note, cop a squat at Duet's clef-shaped bar. Still not ready to go home? The MGM Grand Casino, open until 4 a.m., offers dancing, late-night shows, and plenty of exciting entertainment—perfect relaxation after the slot machines have cleaned all the change out of your pockets! As the saying goes, Detroit is the "real McCoy"—and native Elijah McCoy was a 19th-century African American inventor the phrase was coined for, you know!

Restaurants

When it comes to range, breadth, and sophistication, few other metropolitan areas boast African American restaurants that rival Detroit's. From a bohemian-inspired coffeehouse to a dining room graced by piano music and one of the largest selections of champagnes in the city, Detroit's Black-owned eateries have got it goin' on! Although 75 percent of the city's residents are African American, Detroit is also known for its diverse ethnic neighborhoods, each eager to share its wonderful recipes and traditions with diners.

Casual Dining

✳Absolute Tiffany's
440 Clinton St., 313/964-8900
Like the multicolored stained glass of the many Tiffany lamps that hang throughout the dining room, this restaurant's menu is also kaleidoscopic, featuring Cajun, Oriental, Italian, and southern cuisines. The absolute winners coming from the renowned kitchen include a luscious mélange of shrimp, sundried tomatoes, spinach, mushrooms, and fettuccine called Shrimp Angelena and a thick New York Strip steak sprinkled with cayenne pepper and prepared Bayou-style. Absolutely wonderful! Live jazz Friday and Saturday nights. • **$30+/AA**

✳Beans & Cornbread
29508 Northwestern Hwy., Southfield, 248/208-1680
Whenever Mick Jagger and the boys hit the Motor City, they get a serious craving for some real down-home soul food. And if Aretha's not in town to cook it herself (as Keith Richards often requests), the Stones call Beans & Cornbread to throw down on some serious smothered pork chops, fried catfish, and mean greens. Located about 20 minutes from downtown, this upscale eatery has become *the* destination for those seeking both the traditional and the nouvelle. Harlem burritos,

Cheap and Cheerful

Brown Bag and Eatery, 15070 Hamilton, Highland Park, 313/869-6668—
Located in Highland Park, about 20 minutes north of the city, the
Brown Bag and Eatery has become a favorite of savvy locals. Daily spe-
cials include smothered pork chops, fried catfish, chili macaroni, baked
chicken, po-boy sandwiches, vegetable stir-fry with rice shrimp, and
Creole gumbo. Closed on Saturday. · $10+/AA

✳**Bush's Garden of Eating**, 3955 Woodward Ave., 313/831-6711—Open for
breakfast, lunch, and early dinner, this modest eatery offers favorites
such as short ribs and dressing, pork chops, porterhouse steak, and
fried chicken. Cash only. · $10/AA

Mr. FoFo's, 8902 Second, 313/873-4450—Mr. FoFo's deli counter serves up
huge corned beef, roast beef, turkey, and hot pastrami sandwiches; fried
fish dinners; barbecued ribs and chicken; and short ribs of beef. Mr. FoFo's
bakery will satisfy your sweet tooth with delicious deep-dish cobblers,
pineapple upside-down cake, donuts, and banana pudding. · $10+/AA

Steve's Soul Food, 8443-47 Grand River Ave., 313/894-7978—Steve's has
cafeteria-style service and a large, pleasant dining area, and it wouldn't
be a soul food joint if they didn't serve chicken (baked, fried, or barbecued), fried fish, collard greens, macaroni and cheese, and sweet potato
pie, now would it? · $10/AA

✳**Turkey Grill**, 8290 Woodward Ave., 313/872-4624—A turkey take-out?
Oh, yeah! Especially when you're talking Cajun-fried turkey wings,
turkey burgers, and turkey kabobs. Along with sandwiches, whole
turkeys—either smoked or fried—are also available. Cash only. · $10/AA

shrimp and wild mushroom fritters, escargot in puff pastry, and potato
leek soup—this is soul food? If it's good to ya, it is! • **$20+/AA**

✳Blue Nile Restaurant
508 Monroe St., 313/964-6699

Ethiopian dining is too much fun for just two, so bring the gang!
Once you're seated on low, ornamental chairs, you'll be greeted by a
hostess offering warm, moist towels. Wash your hands—you'll be

eating with them! According to owner Seifu Lessanework, "Eating with one's hands and feeding each other is a custom of Ethiopia. It shows caring and loving." Try the Ethiopian Feast, made up of almost a dozen chicken, beef, lamb, and vegetable dishes, served on a colorful round platter and scooped up with a spongelike bread called *injera*. It's great fun and very sensuous, so dig in and don't be shy! After all, what's a little finger lickin' among friends? • **$20+/AA**

Café Mahogany
1465 Centre, 313/963-6886
By day, Café Mahogany serves up cappuccinos, lattes, deli sandwiches, and fresh-baked bagels. By night, it offers even more: acid jazz and poetry on Tuesdays, a comedy showcase on Thursdays, live jazz on Fridays and Saturdays, and, on Friday nights, hip hop from 2 a.m. until they throw you out. • **$10/AA**

Courthouse Brasserie
1436 Bush, 313/963-8887
Once inside this cute tiny bistro filled with antiques and bric-a-brac, you'll understand why area patrons call it a "rose in a field of thorns." The narrow menu features simple, delicious, and classic American dishes like Philadelphia chowder, shrimp scampi, whitefish with capers, and tender rack of lamb. • **$30+**

✳Duet
3663 Woodward Ave., 313/831-3838
Located in Orchestra Place, Duet sings a high note when it comes to theatrical ambience, eloquent international clientele, and symphonic new American cuisine. Standing ovations go to the Maine lobster over angel hair pasta, paper-wrapped shrimp, pan-roasted veal chops, and chicken breast stuffed with chorizo and manchego cheese. The clef-note-shaped bar is *the* hot after-work "see-and-be-seen" spot in Detroit. Live jazz nightly. • **$35+**

East Franklin Restaurant
1440 Franklin, 313/393-0018
Located in the up-and-coming Detroit neighborhood of Rivertown, East Franklin offers a reasonably priced menu in an antique red-brick upscale environment. Fried chicken and fried catfish are the house

specialties—recipes for both are closely guarded family secrets. Other favorites include orange roughy, smothered steak, baby back ribs, and fancy chops. • **$20+/AA**

Edmund Place Restaurant
69 Edmund, 313/831-5757
Edmund Place is a lovely Victorian-style restaurant that boasts an extensive international menu featuring salads, pastas, stir-fry dishes, and southern specialties. Beef *satay* in honey soy sauce, seafood pasta, chicken and pinched dumplings, orange roughy, smothered New York sirloin, and baby back ribs are just a sampling of some of the restaurant's savory offerings. Sunday brunch is served. • **$25/AA**

✱Harlequin Café
8047 Agnes, 313/331-0922
To hear proprietor Sherman Sharpe recite the evening's menu, complete with glowing descriptions of each dish and elaborate hand gestures, is to experience nothing short of grand theater! Harlequin Café specializes in French-inspired cuisine, served in a lovely dining room with live piano music and one of the most extensive champagne lists in Detroit. Recommended entrées include shrimp pesto, tilapia with citrus madeira sauce, lamp chops, Wilshire sweetbreads, veal Marsala "Don Corleone," and whiskey peppercorn steak. And each dessert is an artistic creation unto itself! • **$30+/AA**

✱Intermezzo
1435 Randolph St., 313/961-0707
In the heart of Detroit's theater district is a chic corridor called Harmonie Park, home to trendy boutiques, wonderful restaurants, and a great place to celebrity-spot: Intermezzo. (The Artist has been sighted here on several occasions.) Outside, under Intermezzo's large parchment umbrellas, is the perfect spot to enjoy terrific Italian cuisine and some serious people watching. Fall-off-the-bone osso buco, grilled lobster on scrumptious fettucine, and Sunday brunch are favorites among the locals. • **$35+**

✱Ja·Da
546 East Larned, 313/965-1700
Named after a jazz tune performed by saxophonist Sydney Bechet

"back in the day," Ja•Da presents a spicy melody of barbecue and other soul favorites in a modern, loftlike setting. Aside from terrific sweet-and-savory barbecue dishes, Ja•Da serves up crispy fried catfish, a whole lotta shrimp, chicken and waffles, barbecued veggies, combination plates, and macaroni and cheese made with four gourmet cheeses. Straight-ahead jazz turns the place out on most nights.
• **$15+/AA**

✳Milt's Gourmet Bar "B" Que
10223 Whittier, 313/521-5959
Milt's Gourmet specializes in ribs, fish dinners, hickory-smoked turkey breast, and homemade soup, but the real reason to visit is the homemade cakes and pies. We're talkin' about luscious German chocolate cake, dense pound cake, and gooey caramel turtle cake. Proprietor Milt Goodman continues in the tradition of his mother, whom he claims baked a cake or pie every evening when he was a child. *No way* you can leave without at least *one* slice! Take-out only.
• **$10+/AA**

Nightclubs

Detroit is strictly old school when it comes to nightclubs. Places like the Bo Mac's and Flood's have been around for years; Baker's Keyboard Lounge is the oldest continuously operating jazz club in the country. After 50-plus years, Baker's continues to attract new enthusiasts while keeping die-hard jazz lovers happy. Just goes to show, good music is good music, no matter what its age.

Baker's Keyboard Lounge
20150 Livernois, 313/345-6300
The world's oldest jazz club, with its signature piano-shaped bar, is now a historic musical landmark. Every jazz great, from John Coltrane to Thelonius Monk to Earl Klugh, has performed at Baker's Keyboard Lounge. In keeping with years of tradition, the club showcases great local talent, offering live jazz Saturday through Wednesday evenings, blues on Thursdays, and R&B dance nights on Fridays. Most amazing of all, most nights you can hear great music without paying a cover charge. • **Usually no cover charge/Dinner $10/AA**

Bert's Marketplace
2727 Russell, 313/567-2030
Bert's Marketplace (located near the Eastern Market) provides great live music and good soul food with selections like Satchmo's fried whiting, Bird's fried chicken wings, John Coltrane's corned beef, and Billie Holiday's turkey burgers. Local and nationally known acts take center stage most evenings; call for a current list of entertainers. • **Cover charge/Dinner $15/AA**

Bo Mac's Lounge
281 Gratiot, 313/961-5152
Bo Mac's motto is "Come by, be yourself, relax, and let your hair down!" Whether it's live jazz on Thursday evenings or jumpin' to the juke box Tuesdays, there's always a party going on at Bo Mac's. The club caters to a mature crowd (35 and up) and features live vocalists, R&B, and jazz acts Thursday through Sunday. • **Cover charge/AA**

✻Flood's Bar & Grill
731 St. Antoine, 313/963-1090
Happy hour at Flood's, Detroit's premier see-and-be-seen spot, is *the* time to work the floor. Flood's offers a full menu, but the real reason to come here is the positive social scene—desperately missing in most cities, badly needed, and very much in demand everywhere. Enjoy live entertainment ranging from jazz to R&B most evenings. • **Cover charge/Dinner $10–$15/AA**

The Limit
15535 W. Eight Mile Rd., 313/341-8000
The Limit's success lies in the fact that it caters to a preferred crowd: the 35-and-older set. The club features live music most nights; karaoke on Monday; dancing on Wednesday, Friday, and Saturday; and great soul food. • **Cover charge/Dinner $10–$15/AA**

Festivals

Detroit's distinction as a "city of firsts" continues in the festival arena, with the Michigan State Fair, the country's first; the Ford Montreux-Detroit Jazz Festival, the largest free jazz event in North

America; and the International Freedom Festival, the world's largest annual display of pyrotechnics.

International Freedom Festival
Hart Plaza, 313/923-7400

You ain't seen fireworks until you've seen the show Detroit puts on every year to celebrate the relationship between the United States and its northern neighbor. Two weeks of festivities mark the two nations' birthdays: Canada Day on July 1 and Independence Day on July 4. The festival's highlight is 35 awesome minutes of more than 8,000 pyrotechnic explosions. More than 3 million people from both sides of the border enjoy such free events as local bands performing, chili cookoffs, reenactments of historical events linking the two countries, and lots of children's activities. • **Two weeks leading to the Fourth of July/Free**

Michigan TasteFest
New Center (off Woodward Ave.), 313/202-1952

Roasted sweet corn in the husk dipped in melted butter, tangy rib tips, fried catfish nuggets, spicy lamb gyros, Thai chicken *satay* in peanut sauce, creamy macaroni and cheese, moist butter pecan pound cake, and bite-sized sweet potato pies are just some of the delicious taste treats offered at the Michigan TasteFest. The best way to sample from the 40-plus booths tempting your taste buds is to try them all for a buck a taste. Unless you have an iron-clad stomach, bring a roll of Tums! • **Fourth of July weekend/Free**

Afro-American Music Festival
Hart Plaza, 313/863-5554

Three days of entertainment spanning traditional and contemporary African American musical forms—jazz, blues, gospel, and hip hop—comprise this lively event sponsored by the Metropolitan Arts Complex, Inc. The festival features food and an array of Afrocentric items. • **Third weekend in July/Admission charge**

African World Festival
Hart Plaza, 313/494-5800

Reggae superstars Maxi Priest, Third World, and Steel Pulse, jazz vocalist Regina Carter, and the Gambian National Dance Troupe are just a sampling of the internationally acclaimed artists who have rocked the stages of the annual African World Festival. Sponsored by the Charles H. Wright Museum of African American History, this weekend festival showcases the talents of the African Diaspora, with outdoor venues set up along the waterfront. In addition to free top-notch concerts, revelers enjoy amusing and educational children's performances, crafts demonstrations, unique Afrocentric merchandise for sale, and African, Caribbean, Creole, soul, and other international foods. With more than 1 million folks expected to partake in this year's festivities, this is one event *not* to be missed! • **Third weekend in August/Free**

Ford Montreux-Detroit Jazz Festival
Hart Plaza, 313/963-7622
For more than 20 years, almost a million jazz enthusiasts have descended on Detroit's Hart Plaza to groove to the mellow sounds of the Ford Montreux-Detroit Jazz Festival, the largest free jazz festival in North America. Internationally acclaimed artists like Dave Brubeck and Bob James, who have performed at the festival's sister event in Switzerland, along with such local-boys-done-good as Kenny Garrett, Elvin Jones, and Marcus Belgrave, get down with other renowned artists for more than 120 jazz events on five stages. Regional high school and college bands have a chance to strut their stuff at this event, which awards cash scholarships to top student performers. And what's an outdoor concert without food? Chow down on every type of cuisine known to man at the Montreux Grille Pavilion. So bring a blanket and an air cushion to soften your seat, because once you get to the festival, you won't want to leave. • **Labor Day weekend/Free**

Museums

Charles H. Wright Museum of African American History
315 E. Warren, 313/494-5800
The Charles H. Wright Museum offers a beautiful tribute to the struggles, perseverance, and achievements of African Americans. "Of the People: The African American Experience" is a powerful interactive exhibit covering 600 years of history, from the Middle

The spectacular rotunda inside the Museum of African American History.

Passage to the present day. Incorporating video footage, still photos, priceless memorabilia, and flip tiles with fun facts, this exhibit is especially entertaining for kids. In addition to its galleries, state-of-the-art theater, research library, and classrooms for educational programs, the museum hosts several special events throughout the year. Black History Month, Women's History Month, Black Music Month, Children's Day, African World Festival, Ancestor's Night, and Kwanzaa events enrich the minds of the community and enlighten those who wish to learn more. • **Admission charge**

Detroit Historical Museum
5401 Woodward Ave., 313/833-1805
The Detroit Historical Museum tells the fascinating history of southeastern Michigan through artifacts, multimedia exhibits,

Susan Stewart for the Detroit CVB

Where it all started—Hitsville USA, outside the Motown Museum.

photographs, and recreational activities. One of the museum's permanent exhibits, "Doorway to Freedom," tells the story of Detroit's role as a stop on the Underground Railroad, through which fugitive slaves moved toward freedom and solace in Canada. Pick up the free brochure outlining a walking tour of Underground Railroad sites around the city. The brochure also lists places that have shaped the history of Detroit's African American community. • **Admission charge**

Detroit Institute of Arts
5200 Woodward Avenue, 313/833-7900

Considered one of the finest fine art institutions in the United States and the fifth largest of its kind, the Detroit Institute of Arts houses some of the most famous and priceless paintings in the world. African, Egyptian, Native American, Asian, and 20th-century art are among the more popular permanent exhibits. Activities within the compound include children's workshops and art classes, gallery discussions, and after-work networking parties. • **Admission charge**

Henry Ford Museum and Greenfield Village
20900 Oakwood Blvd., Dearborn, 313/271-1620

With more than 160 vehicles in its permanent collection, the Henry Ford Museum is the ultimate car show. Its main exhibit, "The Automobile in American Life," features a veritable highway of 100 cars and trucks, including the first mass-produced motor vehicle (the Model T), the limousine in which President John F. Kennedy was assassinated, and several one-of-a-kind concept cars.

Greenfield Village is a lush, 81-acre outdoor museum that curates exhibits on significant places and events in American history. In summer, it hosts outdoor concerts and historical festivals, including the annual Celebration of Emancipation. Music, storytelling, and historical reenactments let visitors experience the lives of enslaved 19th-century African Americans.

A visit to the Henry Ford Museum and Greenfield Village is an all-day affair, so wear comfortable shoes. Attractions are spread out all over the place, and you won't want to miss a thing! • **Admission charge**

Motown Historical Museum
2648 W. Grand Blvd., 313/875-2264

Detroit *is* Motown, and America's love affair with it is forty years old and counting. The Motown Historical Museum is located in the original white-and-blue "Hitsville USA" house where the likes of Marvin Gaye, Smokey Robinson, the Temptations, and the Jackson 5 recorded their million-record sellers. Exhibits fall into three categories: the Man, the Business, and the Music. The Studio A exhibit showcases where the mega-hits were cut, Gordy's upstairs apartment, scores of gold records earned by Motown stars, and those outrageous 1960s costumes. While the Motown Museum is an interesting experience, the ultimate exhibit has yet to be realized—when is Diana Ross going to share with the world her 200-plus wigs, hundreds of false eyelashes, and thousands of costumes? Girlfriend, think it over! • **Admission charge**

Churches

Bethel AME Church
5050 St. Antoine St., 313/831-8810
Bethel AME is the site of one of Detroit's first public school classes organized for the education of Black children.

New Bethel Church
8430 C. L. Franklin Blvd., 313/894-5788
New Bethel Church grew from a Christian women's prayer band whose sole purpose was to praise God. In 1932 the power of their song inspired the development of the church. New Bethel has been led by many different pastors over the years, C. L. Franklin one of the more celebrated. His daughter, Aretha Franklin, made her singing debut here, praising God in her father's church. New Bethel's present choir is nationally known for its strong voices.

Second Baptist Church of Detroit
441–461 Monroe Ave., 313/961-0920
Second Baptist Church was established when African American Detroiters were denied entrance to the First Baptist Church. Detroit's first African American church, Second Baptist served for 30 years as the leading Underground Railroad station in the region.

Shrine of the Black Madonna Pan-African Orthodox Christian Church
7625 Linwood St., 313/898-0360
Founded in 1967 by the Rev. Albert B. Cleage, Shrine of the Black Madonna is the first church of the Black Christian Nationalist movement.

Recreation

Belle Isle Park
Detroit River (access from E. Jefferson Ave.), 313/852-4075
Sitting in the middle of the Detroit River, Belle Isle Park is a real jewel. Indeed, a visit to this amusement park is like a short vacation. Belle Isle's facilities include racquetball and tennis courts, baseball

fields, a golf course, beach and fishing areas, and picnic grounds. Attractions include the Belle Isle Aquarium, the nation's oldest freshwater aquarium, along with a nature center, conservatory, and zoo. Catch the annual Tenneco Automotive Grand Prix of Detroit, held the first weekend in August.

Windsor, Ontario
800/265-3633
Located across the Detroit River in Canada, Windsor is a short ride through the Windsor-Detroit Tunnel. Visit this city known for its china and glassware, chic boutiques, fine dining, and quaint Victorian houses. Casino Windsor might take any money you don't spend shopping, and several award-winning wineries are nearby.

Windsor was also a final stop on the Underground Railroad; numerous historical markers throughout the city and surrounding Essex County identify significant sites. The John Freeman Walls Historic Site and Underground Railroad Museum, 519/727-6555, located eight miles east of the Detroit-Windsor border, recreates the enslaved traveler's trip to freedom.

Casinos

The casinos listed below are located in temporary digs until their permanent homes, on the banks of the Detroit River, open in 2003.

Greektown Casino
400 Monroe St., 313/963-3357
Here you'll find 2,200 slot machines, 90 gambling tables, and nightclubs, shops, and live entertainment.

MGM Grand Detroit
1300 John C. Lodge Frwy., 313/393-7777
The casino features 2,100 slot machines, 80 tables, five dining rooms, and a relax-your-nerves spa.

Motor City Casino
1922 Cass at Grand River Ave., 313/237-7711
Located in the old Wonder Bread Bakery, the Motor City casino has 1,950 slot machines, 100 gambling tables, and two restaurants.

Houston

Houston. Far from the dusty cow town it once was, today's Houston shines brightly. Its crown jewel? An impressive and much-celebrated 17-block performing arts district, home to eight major performing arts organizations, and second in size only to New York City's. Houston's multicultural arts offerings are even more impressive; they include the acclaimed Kuumba House Dance Theatre and its soul-stirring African American dance and contemporary stage productions, and the Ensemble Theatre Company, the Southwest's oldest and, to many, most brilliant professional theater troupe dedicated to representing the African American experience.

When in Houston, start your day local style: with a Texas-sized breakfast of grits and gravy, smothered pork chops, fried eggs, and buttermilk biscuits from the city's most celebrated Black-owned restaurant. Located just south of I-45/75, This Is It! sits at the edge of Houston's African American neighborhood, Third Ward, near Dowling Street. Back in the day, Dowling Street was the district's main drag, best remembered as the site of many Civil Rights activities during the 1950s, '60s, and '70s. Today, Dowling preserves its history with such structures as the Wesley Chapel AME Church, designed by William Sidney Pittman, one of the nation's earliest African American architects. At the corner of Dowling and Elgrin is Emancipation Park, where the neighborhood recreation center sits on land originally purchased in 1872 by a coalition of ex-slaves led by the Reverend John Henry "Jack" Yates, Houston's most beloved African American philanthropist.

Hang a left on Wheeler Street to head to the Traditional African Art Gallery on the campus of Texas Southern University. Here, check out intriguing African masks and other artifacts, as well as modern bronze sculptures. Just a couple of blocks away, on Holman Street, you can view an ambitious restoration undertaking. Called "Project Row Houses," this effort seeks to renovate 22 "shotgun"-style dwellings that are being reclaimed for use as, among other things, a community gallery to showcase the talent of local African American artists.

Hungry, but can't decide what to eat? Stop by the Fusion Café and choose between fiery Caribbean-style curried goat or the Creole-inspired pork chop po-boy sandwiches. After lunch, head on over to the museum district and Hermann Park, where a number of Houston's most festive summer outdoor events take place. Then swing down to South Main Street to view the fabled Astrodome, the world's first domed arena. Before going in to check out the ol' Astroturf, however, stop by Hank's Ice Cream parlor for a cone of the creamiest butter pecan this side of heaven!

Later, head back downtown to Sam Houston Park in Houston's Fourth Ward, where you can tour the Greek Revival-style home of the Reverend Jack Yates, the first residence built by and for an African American in the city of Houston. Down the street, nestled in the shadows of Houston's impressive skyline, is the quaint but stately Antioch Baptist Church, also founded and pastored by Yates back in 1868.

As the clock inches toward happy hour, stop by Harlon's Bayou Blues to mix and mingle with the local after-work cocktail crowd. But before you settle down for a drink and some conversation, make sure you've made those eight o'clock dinner reservations for Mark's. Mark's serves some of the finest "new Texas" cuisine in Houston, and everybody knows it, so make that call! However, if you prefer a more casual environment, Café Noche is the place to go. The soft fish tacos and margaritas there are *muy bueno!*

If you've been blessed by the enjoyment of a fine meal and a stirring play, don't stop: It's time to party! Houston is known for its late-night activities. Head over to the Swank Lounge for dancing and shameless flirting, or swing by Ambiance, where the heat is on all night long!

Restaurants

How could it be that Houstonians eat out even more than New Yorkers, where most apartments barely have a functioning kitchen? It's true: The average adult resident in Houston dines out almost five nights a week. Must mean the city's restaurants serve up some really good eats! And while the top three favorite cuisines in the Houston area are Mexican, Cajun, and barbecue—this *is* Texas, after all!—palates in this still-evolving southwestern metropolis have eagerly accepted a wide variety of ethnic cuisines from French, Italian, and Japanese to Indian and Vietnamese. Anything to keep Houston's frequent diners from getting bored with rib-eye and potatoes!

Fine Dining

✳Café Annie
1728 Post Oak Blvd., 713/840-1111
Don't let this restaurant's casual name fool you: Café Annie's southwestern menu is what fine dining in Houston is all about. Grilled shrimp tostadas, semolina cakes, coffee-crusted filet mignon, lamb chops piled high on a white bean purée, and lush creme caramel are just a few teasers from Café Annie's extensive, deftly perfected menu. Reservations are a must.• **$40+**

✳Mark's
1658 Westeimer St., 713/523-3800
Eggplant drizzled with mascarpone sauce, zebra linguine with sautéed and fried calamari, portobella-crusted roasted halibut, roast duck with caramelized mango and summer cherry sauce, and bourbon-glazed pork tenderloin are just a few of the tantalizing dishes so exquisitely prepared and beautifully presented at Mark's. Located in a restored old church, Mark's offers a menu worthy of worship. • **$40+**

Casual Dining

✳Café Noche
2409 Montrose Blvd., 713/529-2409
Where can you find the best margaritas in Houston? Ask anyone and their response may very well be Café Noche, where the quality

You've Got to Have Soul—Food, That Is!

Alfreda's Cafeteria, 5101 Alameda St., 713/523-6462—Alfreda's serves "real old-fashioned soul food" and delicious "American home-cooked meals"—cafeteria style. House specialties include baked chicken, smothered steak, macaroni and cheese, greens, homemade biscuits, peach cobbler, and Alfreda's famous lemon ice-box pie with vanilla wafer crust. · $10/AA

Family Café, 2712 Blodgett St., 713/520-8444—The menu here changes daily, based on the quality and availability of fresh produce and meats. Breakfast starts at 7 a.m. The lunch/dinner cafeteria lineup typically features barbecued beef and ribs, liver with onions, ham hocks, yams, and "million dollar pie" (made with cream cheese, pineapple, pecans, and Cool Whip). · $10/AA

Houston's This Is It!, 207 Gray St., 713/659-1608—While enjoying your meal in the large dining room, check out the walls covered with photos of famous celebrity diners. And keep an eye open for others who may come walking through the front door! This Is It! is Houston's most popular casual soul food restaurant. Its menu changes daily, but rest assured you'll always be able to order the restaurant's signature baked chicken, oxtails, pork chops, chitterlings, and turkey wings. Opens for breakfast at 6:30 a.m. · $10/AA

Mama's Oven, 9295 S. Main St., 713/661-3656—Located just two blocks from the Astrodome, Mama's Oven features, like the menu says, "old-fashioned country cooking." Oxtails, Cornish hens, pork chops, honey glazed ham, turkey wings, and meatloaf are just some of the tasty favorites. Breakfast is served all day long. · $10/AA

of the frosty concoctions keeps the bar area packed nightly. Café Noche is also famous for its unique Mexican menu, especially the appetizers called "little boats," filled with spicy fish and pork and shaped like—that's right, you guessed it! The weekend brunch buffet is a favorite because it allows patrons to sample a mélange of the best Café Noche has to offer. • **$20+**

Cajun Comes to Houston

Creole's Louisiana Cuisine, 2933 Walnut Bend, 713/785-2340—The entrées at this take-out eatery change daily, but the specialties of the house include the stuffed bread (actually, a tasty sandwich filled with meat, sausage, cheese, and jalapeño peppers), chicken fricassee, and red beans and sausage. · $10/AA

Frenchy's Chicken, 3919 Scott St., 713/748-2233—The biggest seller at Frenchy's is the spicy chicken wings—so good, you'll be ordering more before you even finish licking the first batch off your fingers! This fast-food take-out stop also serves up a mean oyster po-boy sandwich, spicy gumbo, and sweet potato pie with praline pecan topping. Enuf said! · $10/AA

Magnolia Café, 6000 Richmond Hwy., 713/781-6207—You'll swear you're in Opelousas (that's Louisiana, y'all!) once inside this lovely restaurant, where the decor is as delightful as the overstuffed red snapper with crabmeat and the crawfish bisque. Sunday brunch is legendary. · $30+

Pappadeaux Seafood Kitchen, 12711 Southwest Frwy., 713/782-6310; 2525 South Loop W., 713/665-3155; 10499 Katy Frwy., 713/722-0221—One of the most popular Cajun chain restaurants in the country, Pappadeaux is always good for its seafood gumbo and its oyster-and-crabmeat foundeaux. · $25

*Café Noir
2606 Fannin, 713/659-5409
Track star Carl Lewis (one of several owners) is the newest *celeb de jour* to lend his name to the restaurant race. Café Noir's New American menu draws from Asian and Caribbean cuisines to offer an eclectic dining experience that matches its international crowd. The upstairs lounge is perfect for cigar enthusiasts and cognac sippers. • **$30+/AA-invested**

*Fusion Café
3722 Main, 713/874-1116
Lots of classic, good food comes out of the Fusion Café, a funky little

place where the decor all but sings "The Age of Aquarius." The menu is not just Caribbean but a "fusion" of island, soul, and Creole cookin'. Curried goat, oxtails, smothered pork chops, red beans and rice, and delicious bread pudding are just a few of the dishes served up fusion-style at the Fusion Café. • **$15+/AA**

✳Hank's Ice Cream
9291 S. Main St., 713/665-5103

Located just two blocks from the Astrodome, Hank's Ice Cream serves up some of the best and most imaginative frozen dairy goodness in all of Houston. Even so, flavors like cinnanna (a combo of bananas and cinnamon), soursop (a Caribbean-inspired delight), Irish cream, and mango are no match for Hank's number-one flavor: butter pecan. What's so great about it? Well, Hank uses whole pecan halves, roasted with a special secret something; then the nuts are folded, not blended, into the mix. Ice cream heaven! • **AA**

✳Harlon's Bar-B-Q House
11403 Martin Luther King Jr. Blvd., 713/738-2737
6930 Martin Luther King Jr. Blvd., 713/733-5687
Houston Intercontinental Airport, Terminal C
William P. Hobby Airport

According to owner Harlon Brooks, his take-out barbecue is "prepared with time and patience on the best pits, with hickory wood, using the same recipes we used over 20 years ago." The sauce, Brooks claims, is "spicy and sweet." And then there's Harlon's famous stuffed baked potato: A meal in itself, it is piled high with chopped barbecue and weighs about two pounds! • **$10+/AA**

✳Reggae Hut
4814 Almeda Blvd., 713/524-2905

As its menu proclaims, the Reggae Hut serves "authentic Jamaican food and vibes." This bohemian-style café is known for its great curried goat, brown stew chicken, curried shrimp, oxtails, garlic crab, and jerk chicken dishes. Fresh fruit smoothies, Irish moss, peanut punch, and Jamaican colas add to the Hut's "home-style island flava." Poetry readings are frequent happenings here, and local artists are welcomed to display their work in a setting punctuated by funky, handpainted tabletops depicting reggae greats. • **$10/AA**

Finger Lickin' Good

C. Davis Bar-B-Que, 4833 Reed Rd., 713/734-9051—Talk about a hole in the wall! But referring to C. Davis's as such doesn't seem to bother either the proprietor or his customers, who swear that Davis serves the best barbecue in Houston. A soul food lunch is featured daily, and live down-and-dirty blues turn the joint out on Sunday and Tuesday evenings. · $10/AA

Drexler's Bar-B-Q, 2020 Dowling St., 713/752-0008—Although the decor in this popular Houston restaurant pays tribute to basketball superstar Clyde "the Glide" Drexler, he has nothing to do with the great-smelling barbecue coming from the kitchen. Those props go to his relatives, who boast surviving in the barbecue business for 75 years. Barbecued ribs, hot links, chopped beef, and chicken are what's on the menu at this clean, family-oriented spot. · $10/AA

Harlon's Bayou Blues, 530 Texas Ave., 713/230-0111—Take a plate of serious beef brisket, ribs, and links. Add a stuffed baked potato piled high with barbecued pork. Throw in a professional after-work crowd of folks who love to relax and unwind at the upscale bar. Top it all off with live jazz on the weekends, and you've got, you guessed it, Harlon's Bayou Blues! The Sunday gospel brunch is another treat not to be missed. · $15/AA

RJ's Rib Joint
2515 Riverside Dr., 713/521-9601

Hardly a "joint" and located in an upscale residential neighborhood, RJ's is actually a cozy wood-paneled bistro complete with Tiffany lamps and comfortable high-back bar stools. What's more, the extensive menu offers far more than ribs. Entrées include the snapper royale with shrimp cream sauce, flounder stuffed with shrimp and crabmeat, chicken-fried steak, rib-eye steak, and grilled shrimp, just to mention a few. • **$15/AA**

✳Solero
910 Prairie St., 713/227-2665 or 713/227-0459 (Swank Lounge)

More than just an "in" spot for Houston's beautiful people, who

Harlon's Bar-B-Q House

Harlon Brooks and his family proudly shows off his wares at Harlon's Bar-B-Q House.

come to meet and greet and sip the great margaritas, Solero serves up deliciously innovative Spanish tapas and entrées. Upstairs in the Swank Lounge, strangers get better acquainted with the help of the lounge's serious martinis and their naughty, conversation-starting names. Themed music nights featuring salsa, jazz, hip hop, and R&B add to the sensuous vibes and keep the party going all week long. • **$25+**

Nightclubs

Houston is a club town. The following is merely a short list from a seemingly endless selection of night spots. The majority of Houston clubs are mixed, the most popular ones located downtown around the Main and Travis corridor.

*Ambiance
5851 Southwest Frwy., 713/661-6829

This is where the party's at in Houston! On Friday nights, you'll find wall-to-wall people, several birthday parties going on at once, plenty of major networking happening at the bar, and lots of stylin' and profilin' all over the place while urban contemporary, R&B, funk, and old-school music pumps the crowd. • **Cover charge/AA**

Crystal Niteclub
6680 Southwest Frwy., 713/784-7743

This Latin club rocks to a serious salsa/ merengue beat every weekend and is large enough to host spicy dance competitions in one wing and down-and-dirty hip hop in the other. • **Cover charge**

Groovy Grill
2619 Calumet St., 713/526-6464

You've heard of First Fridays? Well Houston has First Thursdays, and they happen every month at the Groovy Grill. • **Cover charge some nights/AA**

Jamaica Jamaica
2631 Richmond Ave., 713/529-8800

This laid-back reggae club is one of Houston's longstanding favorites, proving that less is often more. • **Cover charge/AA**

Jones Bar
410 Main St., 713/225-6637

Don't even think about showing up unless you're dressed to impress—at least dressed well enough to impress the doorman, or you might not get in. Upstairs at the 410 Club, the party is all about the sounds of contemporary pop music. • **Cover charge**

Mercury Room
1008 Prairie St., 713/225-6372
For those looking to hang with the "young and pretentious," the
Mercury Room is the place to go. This gorgeous club boasts a spectacular cherry wood-accented interior, a well-stocked bar, and fancy
hors d'oeuvres. Downstairs you can dance all night long to live jazz,
blues, and swing music. • **Cover charge**

The Phoenix
9600 Westheimer, 713/977-0100
Like its namesake, The Phoenix rises to the occasion every weekend with a throw-down old school, hip hop, and R&B music party.
Local and nationally known acts are showcased in this slick, high-
profile nightclub. • **Cover charge/AA**

✴Sambuca Jazz Café
909 Texas, 713/224-5299
This jazz/supper club chain marries the "Harlem Nights" attitudes
of the '30s and '40s with cool, funky modernism. This is just what a
jazz club should be: splashy, sleek, and *très* sophisticated. Sambuca
features a wonderful (though pricey) Mediterranean dinner menu
and offers live jazz nightly. • **Music charge/$30+**

✴Skybox
3911 Fondren Rd., 713/782-4040
Great views of downtown Houston provide a spectacular backdrop
to the jazzy sound of the Scott Gertner band as they ease you into
the weekend with their contemporary sounds. • **Music charge**

Festivals

Beautiful Sam Houston Park, a grassy oasis surrounded by the modern steel towers of the financial district, hosts outdoor concerts and
multicultural festivals almost every weekend.

Dine Around Houston
Various restaurants, 713/437-5207
Get ready for a gastronomic adventure of mouthwatering proportions!

A Little Local Flava

Afrika Fest 2000, Hermann Square, 713/524-2200—The two-day festival features a unique marketplace, a parade, lots of great food, entertainment, and African cultural expressions. · Second weekend in September

Creole/Cajun Heritage Festival, Sam Houston Park—713/655-1912—Zydeco music, crawfish étouffée, two-step dancing and "sho'nuf plenty a good eatin'" characterize this festival. A portion of the proceeds go to Houston's inner-city Catholic schools for much-needed supplies. · Third weekend in August

Harambee African American Arts Festival, 713/524-1079—Sponsored by Kuumba House Dance Theater, Houston's premier African and African American dance and stage production company, this two-day festival celebrates the contributions of the African Diaspora to American culture via dance, music, visual arts, crafts, and food. · Third weekend in July

Houston Caribbean Festival, 713/263-5767—A carnival and parade kick off this fall festival. Held in downtown Houston, the vibrant salute to the Caribbean experience features steel drums, colorful dancers, and delicious island food. · September/free

Pan-African Cultural Festival, 713/521-0629—Sponsored by the Shape Community Center, this festival celebrates the arts, culture, food, and music of the African Diaspora. · Memorial Day Weekend/Free

Every month, Dine Around Houston takes epicurean Houstonians to places where the dim sum is always fresh and the barbecue is always tender. Depending on the program, be prepared to taste a minimum of five different types of cuisines in one evening or to sample several variations on a food theme, such as beef brisket smoked five different ways! This tour is not just for gourmands, but also for those interested in learning about food preparation methods, for people who enjoy talking with chefs about the foods they prepare, and for folks who simply delight in meeting other folks who like to eat! • **Monthly/Reservations required/Price includes transportation**

Sam Houston Parks

The home of Jack Yates, Houston's first African American landowner.

Houston International Festival
Downtown Houston, 713/654-8808

More than a million people descend on downtown Houston for this festival, the city's largest cultural event. Twenty blocks are packed with adventuresome art, music, and food lovers eager to experience the seven multicultural markets, which together showcase some 400 exhibitors. Each marketplace, festooned with distinctive colors and decorations, features specially themed art, music, culture, and food:
African Market—Afropop music, African dancers, and treasures such as printed cotton fabric and stoic-faced ebony statues
Asian Silk Road Market—A taste of the Far East, with exotic artifacts and foods
Bayou Market—Local flavor, Texas music, barbecue for days!
Caribbean Market—Steel drums, stilt walkers, great island food, colorful Haitian paintings, and pungent curried goat
Children's Pavilion—Games, pony rides, petting zoo, theater, and face painting

Gypsy Market—Zydeco, country, gospel and blues performances, southern food favorites

International Market—Unique items from around the world

Latin Market—A recreated Mexican town square filled with great shopping and lots of good eats

The festival also features a juried arts fair, showcasing more than 200 of the country's most talented artists and their award-winning pieces. • **Third and fourth weekends in April**

Juneteenth Freedom Festival
Miller Outdoor Theater, Hermann Park, 713/529-4195
June 19 is recognized as the date when the last slaves in America were freed. Although President Lincoln issued the Emancipation Proclamation on September 22, 1862, the news did not reach the Lone Star State until years after the Civil War ended. On June 19, 1865, Major General Gordon Granger rode into Galveston, Texas, to declare that slavery, which had continued uninterrupted in Texas until that blessed day, had been abolished. Although Granger's announcement is the most widely recognized version of the delivery of these good tidings, legend has it that a lone Black rider spread the news from town to town.

Regardless of how the message was delivered, "Juneteenth," as it came to be called, became a day of great celebration among African Americans throughout Texas, and over the years the observance has spread across the country. Today, more than 600 cities and communities nationwide celebrate Juneteenth to commemorate the freedom and triumph of a brave people who overcame years of oppression and ultimately claimed victory.

The city of Houston celebrates Juneteenth annually with a parade and more than 100 groups including live bands, stage performers, dancers, and other entertainers at various sites throughout the city. Live music and stage performers entertain crowds into the late evening hours, and storytellers regale children and adults alike with tales from the African American past so the whole community will continue to understand the importance of the day. • **June 19/Free**

Houston International Jazz Festival
Hermann Square Plaza, 713/839-7000
The Houston International Jazz Festival is considered the only

event of its kind to spotlight jazz musicians from around the world. Let's set the stage: On Friday, several thousand of your nearest and dearest friends gather poolside to kick off a weekend of jazz, food, and fun. First up is a lunchtime concert followed by a meet-and-greet happy hour and a poolside jam session. Saturday, the main stage heats up in the late afternoon, with performances from half a dozen internationally known artists. Past performers have included Alex Bugnon from Switzerland, Jonathan Butler from South Africa, Sacbe from Mexico, and Tania Maria from Brazil. On Sunday, the Mayor's Jazz Brunch ends the weekend right, as attendees get the opportunity to meet the preceding day's headliners, hear more great music, and toast the success of another year's event. • **First weekend in August/Admission charge**

Museums and Attractions

Museum District Sites

Eleven museums grace this stunning oak-covered campus, which exhibits some of the country's most important works of art. Highlights include:

Children's Museum of Houston—This interactive museum is perfect for inquisitive minds and can keep kids entertained for hours.

Contemporary Arts Museum—Creative, ingenious works from the country's most compelling contemporary artists are showcased here.

Menil Collection—This museum houses a private collection that includes a stunning assemblage of artifacts from Africa, Oceania, and the Pacific Northwest.

Museum of Fine Arts—This museum encompasses more than 40,000 pieces of art and a glorious sculpture garden. Past exhibits have focused on contemporary works by African American women artists.

Other Sites

American Cowboy Museum
Taylor-Stevenson Ranch, 11822 Alameda, 713/433-4441
This ranch was established in the mid-1800s by E. R. Taylor and his slave, Ann, who raised six children together. A scheduled tour of

their sprawling homestead includes horseback riding, visits to a petting zoo, and detailed retellings of the history of the Black cowboy. • **Admission charge/AA**

Art Car Museum
140 Heights Blvd., 713/861-5526
The shiny chrome exterior of this futuristic garage sets the tone for what visitors will witness inside. Quirkily decorated cars, odd sculptures, photographs, and other unusual items make the Art Car Museum a got-to-see-it-to-believe-it stop. • **Free**

Jack Yates House
Sam Houston Park, 1100 Bagby, 713/655-1912
Rev. John Henry "Jack" Yates is recognized as Houston's most influential African American native son. Although Yates spent most of his life as a slave, when freed in 1865 he acquired the ability to read and write. Yates possessed leadership skills that helped him guide the development of a thriving community called Freedmen's Town. Among his other numerous accomplishments, Yates organized and helped build the Antioch Baptist Church; he also pastored the Bethel Baptist Church, established the Houston Baptist Academy, and encouraged parishioners to purchase land. His own home, built in 1870, was the first house erected by a freed slave. It has been preserved as a national historic landmark. • **Admission charge**

Project Row Houses
2500 Holman St., 713/526-7662
An ambitious undertaking that started with the refurbishing of a stretch of shotgun-style row houses, this project was initiated by a group of local artists intent on enriching the surrounding community with African American culture and art. Ten of the 22 houses serve as revolving galleries, while the balance provide temporary housing for young single mothers and their children. Through the Project's Young Mothers Residential Program, the young women not only benefit from a cheery living environment but also, under the supervision of a live-in mentor, prepare for life on their own. The success of this program has inspired the planning of other, similar housing developments in Houston.

Shrine of the Black Madonna Center and Bookstore
5309 Martin Luther King Jr. Blvd., 713/645-1071
This intriguing center displays a unique collection of original art, prints, rare and current books, historical documents, and other artifacts documenting the influence and impact of Africans and people of African heritage on the Americas. • **AA**

Traditional African Art Gallery
Carol H. Simms Sculpture Garden
Texas Southern University, 3100 Cleburne St., 713/313-7149
The gallery and garden here house an impressive collection of paintings, sculpture, statues, prints, and musical instruments from West, Central, and East Africa. Sculptor Carol Simms's three bronze pieces sit in the center of the TSU campus. • **Free**

Churches

Antioch Baptist Church
500 Clay St., 713/652-0738
Located amidst the congestion and skyscrapers of downtown this historical landmark was founded in 1868 by Rev. Jack Yates. The Antioch Baptist Church is the oldest Black Baptist congregation in Houston. It was built in 1879 by Black master builder Richard Allen.

Bethel Baptist Church
25 Tidwell Rd., 713/694-2381
Originally pastored by Rev. Jack Yates, Bethel Baptist Church is considered one of Houston's most treasured religious institutions.

Trinity United Methodist Church
2600 Holman St., 713/528-2356
Trinity is the oldest African American church in Houston, founded in 1848 as a mission church that helped many slaves escape to freedom.

Wesley Chapel AME Church
2209 Dowling St., 713/659-6682
The Wesley Chapel AME Church was designed by one of the country's first African American architects, William Sidney Pittman.

Wheeler Avenue Baptist Church
Wheeler Ave. and Ruth St., 713/748-5240
Located in the center of the African American Third Ward community, Wheeler is best known as the former gathering place for activists and church leaders during the Civil Rights movement.

Recreation

Amusement Parks

Six Flags AstroWorld and Water World
Kirby at Loop 610 S., 713/799-8404
This superlative amusement park features a suspended, looping roller coaster and a neighboring water park for those who like their adventures wet. • **Admission charge**

SplashTown Waterpark
Louetta Rd. at I-45 N., Spring, 281/355-3300
Bring your bathing suit and get ready to make a big splash in a park filled with super slides, waterfalls, and geysers. • **Admission charge**

NASA Space Center
1601 NASA Rd. 1, 281/244-2100
The NASA Space Center is a spectacular moonwalk through space and time, offering hands-on simulators, a Kids Space Place, tours of actual spacecrafts, and a chance to experience anti-gravity—too much fun! Check out the wall along the Astronaut Gallery to see, among others: Guion S. Bluford, the first African American in space; the late Ronald E. McNair from the ill-fated *Challenger* mission; and Mae C. Jamison, the first African American woman in space. • **Admission charge**

Golf

Bear Creek Golf World
Bear Creek Park, 281/859-8188
Located west of downtown, this course was ranked as one of America's top 50 public courses by *Golf Digest* magazine.

Hermann Park Golf Course
Hermann Park, 713/526-0077
This 18-hole public course is located next to the city's first major public park.

Melrose Golf Course
Melrose Park, 713/847-1214
Located north of downtown, this public course features a driving range.

Memorial Park Golf Course
Memorial Park, 713/862-4033
Located in the heart of the city, this 18-hole course boasts a beautiful Spanish-style clubhouse.

Parks

Emancipation Recreation Center and Park
3018 Dowling St., 713/528-2500
The land on which this historical park sits was purchased in 1872 by a coalition of ex-slaves led by Rev. Jack Yates, Houston's most renowned African American philanthropist. The original purpose of the purchase was to acquire a site for Juneteenth celebrations. Today, the park encompasses a swimming pool, softball field, children's playground, basketball courts, and lighted tennis courts.

Sam Houston Park
1100 Bagby St., 713/655-1912
The city's oldest park, Sam Houston not only hosts many outdoor festivals and special events, but also is home to seven historical structures. These include the first house built by a freed slave, that of Rev. Jack Yates, and the Kellum-Noble House, Houston's oldest standing home.

Kansas City

Kansas City. Oh sure, Kansas City boasts an impressive skyline, is home to the Negro Leagues Baseball and Jazz Museums, offers exciting dinner/gambling cruises on the Missouri River, and incites visitors to "ooh" and "ahh" at the hundreds of beautiful fountains sprinkled around the city. But let's face it, the real reason to make the pilgrimage to K.C. is for...the barbecue. Yes, the barbecue, and we're not talking about beef ribs, either! When people talk barbecued pig, they're talkin' about Kansas City!

Now, before savoring the main meal of the day, start off with a little breakfast. That means stopping at Maxine's Fine Foods for pork chops, hot cakes, and homemade biscuits. Maxine's is located near Prospect Avenue, famous back in the day as the main drag through the city's African American community, today an area that time forgot; only a few successful businesses remain. One section of Prospect rich in African American heritage, around 18th and Vine, has undergone a major facelift. Here the stunning new Negro Leagues Museum, the Kansas City Jazz Museum, and the Historic Gem Theater pay tribute to African American greats who played on the segregated stages and sports fields, and in infamous speakeasies, not so long ago.

What, lunchtime already? (Time flies when all you can think about is food!) Thank goodness, there's a Gates Bar-B-Q around the corner when you need one! After a succulent short end of pork ribs, cole slaw, and barbecue beans, walk that lunch off in the historic Westport area, a lively destination for shopping, dining, and

CVB/Greater Kansas City

Outside the Phoenix Piano Bar & Grill.

nightlife. Westport is known as the site of the last major Civil War battle west of the Mississippi River. A couple of blocks north of Westport, 39th Street attracts a hip crowd who meets to dine and shop for the same lime-green-and-orange daisy bellbottoms their parents wore and threw away 25 years ago.

It's dinnertime and the big question remains: paper or cloth napkins to wipe those barbecue-drenched fingers? If you like your ribs and blues down and dirty, head on over to the Grand Emporium, where Grace Harris will serve up whatever she happens to feel like fixing to go with the barbecue that evening. For those who like to dress for dinner, KC Masterpiece is the place for tender baby backs. Nighttime is the right time to jam to the sultry sounds of down-home K.C.-style jazz, and the Blue Room nightclub will take you there. If midnight is too early to turn in, stop by the Station Casino Kansas City; they won't throw you out until 6 a.m.!

Restaurants

Kansas City may not be the birthplace of barbecue, but arguably it's the place where it was perfected, offering more than 90 BBQ spots to choose from. Can you think of a more delicious way to get your fingers dirty? Slabs of pork ribs (beef ribs? forget about it!), rib tips, sliced smoked beef, barbecued chicken, and anything else you can think of that can be thrown on the grill—you'll find it in K.C. Of course, barbecue is not the only dish served here, but "when in Kansas City," as they say, take a seat and pass the wet naps!

Casual Dining

✳Arthur Bryant's
1727 Brooklyn, 816/231-1123
After "Barbecue King" Arthur Bryant passed away in 1982, the Brooklyn Barbecue Company acquired the leasing rights to his business. The company pledged to uphold the tradition established by the Bryant brothers so long ago. Indeed, the management guarantees your dining experience will be memorable as well as delicious. The menu offers, of course, ribs (by the slab or pulled), big messy sandwiches of sliced beef, turkey, or ham, and all the pickles you want. Fries and baked beans round out the menu. • **$10/Slabs of ribs slightly more**

G's Jamaican Quisine Restaurant and Bar
7940 Troost Ave., 816/333-9566
G's Jamaican Quisine is a casual, come-as-you-are kind of place that, on weekends, hosts local DJs spinning R&B oldies and reggae until 1:30 a.m. G's dinner menu features Caribbean favorites like jerk chicken, curried chicken and goat, cow's feet, escoveitch fish, and brown stewed chicken. Pour it all down with popular Jamaican drinks like Irish moss, sorrel, and ginger beer. • **$15+/AA**

✳Gates Bar-B-Q
47th and the Paseo, 816/923-0900
Linwood and Main, 816/753-0828
1221 Brooklyn, 816/483-3880
10440 E. 40 Hwy., Independence, 816/353-5880
10th and State, Kansas City, Kansas, 913/621-1134

K.C. Barbecue History

According to local barbecue legend, Henry Perry was K.C.'s first "master of the grill." Perry opened his eatery right after the turn of the century, on the corner of 19th and Highland. From an old trolley barn, he sold ribs wrapped in newspaper for 25¢ a slab. As his citywide reputation grew, people came from all over to sample his fare. Perry also shared his culinary secrets with two young apprentices: Charlie Bryant and George Gates. Bryant eventually bought Perry's place and recruited his brother Arthur to help run it. In 1945, Charlie retired and Arthur took over, adding his own personal touches to the business. Former presidents Harry S. Truman and Jimmy Carter, big-name celebrities, and grateful locals have all enjoyed Arthur Bryant's legendary barbecue.

While Arthur and Charlie were setting up shop, George Gates and his wife, Arzelia, opened their own barbecue stand at 19th and Vine. Business was so good, they opened a second location on 12th and Brooklyn. In 1960, George Gates passed away and his son Ollie took over the family business. Today, Gates Bar-B-Q has seven locations in the Kansas City area.

103rd and State Line Rd., Leawood, Kansas, 913/383-1752
Gates is arguably the most famous African American-owned barbecue restaurant in the United States. Its mild barbecue sauce is thick and just sweet enough not to overpower the well-smoked and tender pork ribs, beef sausage, mutton, chicken, and sliced beef, ham, or turkey—just a few of the meats the restaurant's able staff work their magic on. Barbecue beans and the yummy "yammer" (sweet potato) pie are must-have orders to complete the Gates experience. • **$10+/AA**

Hayward's Pit Bar-B-Que
11051 S. Antioch, Overland Park, Kansas, 913/451-8080
Since 1972, Hayward's Pit Bar-B-Que has received national acclaim. As the restaurant claims, "The name Hayward's is synonymous with barbecue in Kansas City." Hayward's prepares nine tons of barbecued

When You Tire of Barbecue

Blue Nile Cafe, 1715 W. 39th St., 816/931-7171—Classic, fiery Ethiopian cuisine is eaten with one's hands and the help of a little piece of *ingera*, a spongy flatbread. · $20/AA

Club 427, 427 Main St., 816/21-2582—A trilevel dining emporium complete with a sophisticated menu including a wonderful white-and-black sesame-seed encrusted yellow fin tuna. This upscale and pricey (for Kansas City) spot also serves up great live jazz nightly. · $35

✳**Japéngo**, 600 Ward Parkway, 816/931-6600—Beautifully presented Pacific Rim cuisine is served in an even more impressive upscale setting. · $25+

meats, smoked and sauced to perfection, for 10,000-plus patrons *each week*! The award-winning menu consists of ribs, burnt ends, rib tips, sliced beef, ham, pork, turkey, smoked sausage, and chicken. Pass on the cole slaw; Hayward's oversized fries and onion rings are the way to go! • **$15/AA**

Hot Tamale Brown's Cajun Express Restaurant
10 W. 39th St., 816/561-2020
Festooned in Mardi Gras colors and posters, Hot Tamale Brown's offers Bourbon Street hot tamales, crawfish étouffée, red beans and rice, jambalaya, chili, filé (pronounced "fee-lay") gumbo, mint lemonade, and sweet Cajun coffee. This small, casual spot does mostly take-out business, although indoor and outdoor seating is available. • **$10/AA**

Madry's Dash of Flavor
26 E. 39th St., 816/753-3274
Madry's Dash of Flavor is a simple family restaurant serving down-home food with a healthy twist. The all-you-can-eat lunch and dinner buffet is offered seven days a week. Fried chicken, turkey and dressing, macaroni and cheese, fresh greens, cabbage, yams, the prettiest home-made rolls ever, and fresh-squeezed lemonade are just a few of the items on the buffet line. • **$10+/AA**

✳Maxine's Fine Foods
3041 Benton Blvd., 816/924-2004
In her more than 35 years in business, Maxine Byrd has served nearly everyone in Kansas City, from members of the Chiefs professional football team to local politicians to hometown celebrities—they've all eaten at her modest little restaurant dozens of times! Breakfast is *the* time to meet and greet at Maxine's, when the kitchen serves up hearty combinations to get your day going: T-bone steak and eggs, pork chops and hot cakes, Polish sausage and grits, homemade biscuits and bacon, hash browns, and more. •
$10–$15/AA

Finger Lickin' Good!

✳Grand Emporium, 3832 Main St., 816/531-1504—With sister "Amazing" Grace Harris doing all the cooking herself, one never knows what goodies will be available—Grace fixes what she feels like! Late-night diners and jazz enthusiasts make their way to Grand Emporium for both the music and the ribs. · $10+

✳KC Masterpiece, 4747 Wyandotte St., 816/531-3332—For those who wish to eat barbecue in a civilized manner—that is, on something other than paper plates—KC Masterpiece offers very good baby backs. Prices are slightly higher, but ambiance costs, right? · $20+

✳L.C.'s Bar B-Q, 5800 Blue Pkwy., 816/923-4484—Not only is the barbecue here great, the beans smothered in brisket trimmings and pit drippings are slammin'! So are the fries! · $10+/AA

Papa Lew's Barbecue & Soul Food, 1504 Prospect Ave., 816/231-2800—Papa Lew's restaurant offers each and every patron something no other restaurant can: a sincere, heartfelt hug from owner Dorriss Lyman. This simple, family-style cafeteria serves soul food and barbecued ribs. · $10+/AA

✳Rosedale Bar-B-Q, 600 Southwest Blvd., Kansas City, Kansas, 913/262-0343—Opened in 1934, Rosedale Bar-B-Q is K.C.'s oldest continuously operating barbecue restaurant. And the good ribs are why! · $10+

Niecie's Restaurant
6902 Prospect Ave., 816/333-1206
Talk about a family affair! "Big Perry" Ward's wife manages the restaurant that, like the nightclub he runs, bears her name. And believe me, Niecie Ward should be named Businessperson of the Year for the tremendous stamina she displays in keeping her home and professional life together. After a long day at the restaurant, she somehow finds the energy to spin records at the family's nightclub until the wee hours! Niecie's Restaurant serves down-home food in a comfortable, luncheonette-style atmosphere. • **$10/AA**

Nightclubs

From the late 1920s until the mid-1940s, Kansas City was a mecca for jazz clubs and speakeasies—and for the notorious gangsters who ran them. Duke Ellington and Ella Fitzgerald are just two jazz greats who gained national fame playing K.C. clubs. Today's jazz spots uphold a cherished tradition of yesteryear, showcasing great local talent to heat up most K.C. nights. Remember that sax player's name; you just might be listening to the next Charlie Parker!

Jazz It Up!

B.B.'s Lawnside BBQ, 1205 E. 85th, 816/822-7427—Best known as a blues club, B.B.'s also dishes out some straight-ahead jazz along with a mean plate of ribs.

✳Grand Emporium, 3832 Main St., 816/531-7557—Offering great barbecue as well as great live music, Grand Emporium is considered one of K.C.'s best venues for live jazz and blues. · Cover charge some nights

Jardine's, 4536 Main St., 816/561-6480—Several of K.C.'s top musicians play six nights a week in this intimate bistro.

Phoenix Piano Bar & Grill, Eighth and Central, 816/472-0001—Here you'll find live music six nights a week along with a choice dinner menu.

That legendary Kansas City nightlife lives on.

The Blue Room
Kansas City Jazz Museum, 1616 E. 18th St., 816/474-2929
Thursday through Blue Monday, the Blue Room takes you back to the days of bootlegged liquor and juke joints jumping with K.C.-style jazz all night long. Seventy years later, the liquor is legal and the jazz is still red hot. The club pays tribute to the "age of sass" with a wall mural featuring jazz greats and a Wall of Fame that gives the nod to local jazz pioneers. • **Cover charge**

Epicurean: Phase II
8625 Troost, 816/363-6910
The Epicurean Lounge features live jazz on weekends in the early evenings and a DJ spinning R&B, top 40s, and urban contemporary sounds during the week. Plenty of good bar food like chicken wings, catfish, and club sandwiches is available. • **Cover charge/$10 bar menu/AA**

Mardi Gras Lounge
1600 E. 19th St., 816/842-VINE
Located in the historic 18th and Vine district, Kansas City's Mardi
Gras Lounge has become a local landmark. This club, around since
the 1940s, is one of the oldest in town. During the week, it hosts a
mature crowd who enjoys groovin' to the juke box and playing elec-
tronic darts. Many evenings, the club offers live music. • **AA**

Niecie's Lounge & Grill
6201 Blue Pkwy., 816/921-5990
Niecie's Lounge & Grill is *the* Kansas City night spot! After 6 p.m.
on Friday the parking lot is packed because the city's who's who are
"in the house." The atmosphere at Niecie's is upscale, lively, and unpretentious. The kitchen offers a complete down-home dinner
menu. • **No cover charge/AA**

Festivals
Barbecue and jazz, jazz and barbecue—in K.C. there's little else.

Kansas City International Jazz Festival
Crown City Square, 2405 Grand, 816/444-4558
This new-kid-on-the-block jazz fest starts the weekend out right with
a jazz pub crawl. Revelers visit some 15 clubs for a fierce combination
of great music and tasty barbecue. Thousands of jazz fans flood the
Crown City Square to hear the great sounds of Chick Corea, Bobby
McFerrin, Maynard Ferguson, and David Sanchez. Bring your
portable chairs, picnic baskets, and blankets, but leave the beer at
home. Alcoholic beverages can be purchased only on the festival
grounds. For information on the Jazz Lovers Pub Crawl, Thursday
before the Jazz Festival, call 816/967-6767. • **Last weekend in June**

Kansas City Blues and Jazz Festival
Penn Valley Park, 800/530-KCMO, www.kcbluesjazz.org
Check out this lineup: Pat Metheny, Wilson Pickett, David
Sanborn, David "Fathead" Newman, Etta James, Bobby Womack,
Boney James, Staple Singers, Michael Franks... Only the best per-
formers in the United States are asked to take center stage at the

Kansas City Blues and Jazz Festival. More than 50,000 disciples show up to catch the soulful spirit soundings known as jazz and the blues. Harrah's Jazz Stage and the Blues Stage showcase big-name talents; the players on the Heritage Stage, though perhaps not household names, are considered to be among the originators of Kansas City jazz. The Heritage Stage also features local gospel, musical, and high school acts. In addition to playing great music, jazz masters participate in the festival's "Soul School," offering storytelling and instruction on how to make your saxophone cry in pain. Of course, it wouldn't be a K.C. festival without a little barbecue to go with all that good music. Nearly 20 food vendors "pull out the pig" and plenty of napkins to make this festive annual event a real down-home affair. • **Third weekend in July/Admission charge**

Ethnic Enrichment Festival
Swope Park, Meyer Blvd. and Swope Pkwy., 816/871-5771
More than 50 countries participate in this three-day event that celebrates cultural diversity through elaborate stage performances, distinctive musical concerts, and food delicacies from around the world. • **Third weekend in August/Free**

Spirit Fest
Liberty Memorial Grounds, 816/471-3378
Three main musical and performance art stages, a lively children's pavilion, a Christian rock pavilion, and lots of good vibes is what the Spirit Fest is all about. Past nationally known artists have included B.B. King, Bob Dylan, James Brown, the Beach Boys, the Neville Brothers, and Santana. Needless to say, the three-day Spirit Fest evokes the essence of brotherhood and family. • **Labor Day weekend/Admission charge**

Livin' on the Vine: Festival of Favorites
1616 E. 18th St., 816/474-8763
The festival celebrated 15 years in 1997. This culturally diverse, family-oriented event, sponsored by the Black Economic Union of Greater Kansas City, is free to the public. In addition to great jazz, blues, and gospel, the festival hosts an art auction, youth and heritage activities, creative art workshops, and a highly diverse vendorship for visitor shopping and eating. Year 2000 performers will

include George Benson, the Manhattan Transfer, James Ingram, Patti Austin, Oleta Adams, Bobby Watson, Mike Metheny, and the George Duke Orchestra. • **Second weekend in September/Free**

American Royal Barbecue
American Royal Complex, Kemper Arena, 816/221-9800
Oh, to be a judge at the American Royal Barbecue! By weekend's end, 20,000 pounds of meat will have been smoked and tasted, and one lucky grillmaster's entry will have been crowned "Best Barbecue on the Planet." More than 350 grill teams have competed for that favored title, with 50-plus judges poised to hand out awards for best ribs, bone carving, sausage, sauce, brisket, and sides. Actually, when you think about it, being a judge requires too much thinking; maybe it's better to simply join the other 35,000-plus barbecue lovers who come out every year to stuff themselves with the best food the country has to offer. • **First weekend in October/Admission charge**

Museums and Attractions

18th & Vine

Historic Gem Theater Cultural and Performing Arts Center
1615 E. 18th St., 816/842-4538
Built in 1912 as a movie house within the African American community, the Gem Theater today is enjoying a revival. Today "the Gem," which recently received a facelift, is Kansas City's premier state-of-the-art entertainment and performance theater. And it's not hard to find. Just look for the striking yellow, red, and white neon marquee—you can't miss it!

Kansas City Jazz Museum
1616 E. 18th St., 816/474-8463
No other museum in the country is devoted solely to the original American art form known as jazz. The Kansas City Jazz Museum is big fun, too! With lots of interactive exhibits, this historical musical showcase is sure to please even diehard enthusiasts, with displays on Count Basie, Ella Fitzgerald, and Charlie Parker. Photographs, musical instruments, and artifacts tell the story of this musical form's

Back in the day—an exhibit inside the Negro Leagues Baseball Museum.

tempestuous journey from rejection to adoration. • **Admission charge**

Negro Leagues Baseball Museum
1616 E. 18th St., 816/474-8463
The opening of the Negro Leagues Baseball Museum was one of the proudest moments of museum board chairman Buck O'Neal's life. The same was true for the other surviving members of the Kansas City Monarchs team. Their lives in baseball and those of their colleagues are chronicled through photographs, mementoes, and video storytelling. Among the memorabilia displayed here are a

Tee Time

Kansas City has a plethora of lush golf courses to challenge both experienced and beginning golfers. Below is just a short list of some of the more popular 18-hole courses near the downtown area. Call 800/767-7700 for a free guide.

Royal Meadows Golf Course, 10501 E. 47th, 816/353-1323

Tiffany Greens 10111 N. Helena Ave., 816/505-4653

Swope Memorial, Swope Pkwy. and Meyer Blvd., 816/523-9081

baseball thrown by Satchel Paige, bats cracked by Josh Gibson, and uniforms worn by Jackie Robinson. The exhibits authentically portray the heroism and athleticism of those who made Negro Leagues history, and bring into public view the impact they had on desegregation and the Civil Rights movement. • **Admission charge**

Other Attractions

Bruce R. Watkins Cultural Heritage Center
3700 Blue Pkwy., 816/923-6226
The dream of former county circuit court clerk and political advocate Bruce R. Watkins, to establish a community cultural center, was not realized until nine years after his death. The Bruce R. Watkins Cultural Heritage Center showcases area historical and art exhibits, spoken word and dance performances, a library, and tributes to local heroes. Call for a schedule of events. • **Admission charge**

Kemper Museum of Contemporary Art
4420 Warwick Blvd., 816/561-3737, www.kemperart.org
Distinctive and celebrated pieces of contemporary art are included in the permanent collection here. Jasper Johns, Frank Stella, Georgia O'Keeffe, Christopher Brown, Willem de Kooning, and Robert Mapplethorpe are just a few of the famous artists whose work hangs at the Kemper. • **Admission charge**

Nelson-Atkins Museum of Art
4525 Oak, 816/751-1227
Famous for the two giant shuttlecocks sitting on the lawn out front
and noted for its gorgeous Chinese art, the Nelson-Atkins Museum
is home to an impressive collection of Asian and African art, including sculptures and artifacts from West and Central Africa. • **Admission charge**

Churches

Allen Chapel AME Church
3421 N. 29th St., 816/921-2151
The Allen Chapel AME and the Second Baptist Church share the
same beginnings. Each church was established in October 1863,
evolving from the Stragglers' Camp, a group of free Black migrants
led by the Reverend Clark Moore. Allen Chapel is the Mother
Church in the Kansas City area and one of the oldest Black churches
in Kansas City.

Ebenezer AME Church
3808 Brush Creek Blvd., 816/861-6614
In the mid-1880s, 19 people with letters from the Allen AME
Church organized the Ebenezer AME Church in the home of
Fannie Moore.

Second Baptist Church
3620 E. 39th St., 816/921-2326
Just before the end of the Civil War, in a shantytown called
Stragglers' Camp, a small group organized the Second Baptist
Church, the oldest Black church in the Kansas City area.

St. Stephen's Baptist Church
1414 E. Truman, 816/842-6311
The Reverend J. W. Hurse was a street paver by day and a preacher
by night, conducting revival meetings in tents and collecting fol-
lowers. He was called to pastor the Pilgrim Baptist Church in 1902,
but his differences with church deacons forced the breakup of
Pilgrim Baptist and the creation of St. Stephen's.

Casinos

Argosy Riverside Casino
I-635 and Hwy. 9, 816/746-3100
The area's first riverboat casino is its prettiest, with a Mediterranean seaport theme and a three-story, glass-domed rotunda.

Flamingo Hilton Casino Kansas City
I-35 and Front St., 800/946-8711
You can't miss the Flamingo: Its cheesy pink-neon flashing lights beckon drivers from the road into the bilevel game room, which features 1,000-plus slot machines.

Harrah's North Kansas City Casino
Hwy. 210 and Chouteau Trafficway, 800/HARRAHS
Harrah's runs two riverboats: the *North Star Casino*, a duplicate of an 1800s sternwheeler, and the *Mardi Gras*.

Station Casino Kansas City
I-435 and Hwy. 210, 888/440-7700
The sheer size of this place will make your head spin. More like a convention center than a casino, Station boasts a hotel, concert arena, megaplex theater, and two casinos with more slot machines than you care to know about.

Los Angeles

os Angeles. Once the "land of milk and honey," today the headquarters for Apathy Anonymous, Los Angeles has changed over the years. It's true L.A. has more cars per person than the law allows—most of them stuck bumper-to-bumper on the 405 Expressway—but if you drive anything less than a BMW 325I, they might not let you enter the city. New Yorkers hate L.A. because walking is de rigeur unless you're training for a marathon, wearing black is simply not a daytime option, a sense of urgency was outlawed in the 1980s, and public smoking prohibited in the 1990s. (OK, so no smoking is a good thing!)

L.A. should consider hiring a new P.R. agent. Despite the lousy press, the City of Angels is still the perfect place to find that quirky gift for your slightly eccentric sister-in-law or to test your coordination as you dodge pedestrians while in-line skating at Venice Beach. And where else does the sun take a brilliant bow by casting rose and gold shadows on the nearby mountains? Just a show biz-y reminder that tomorrow's weather will be a glorious repeat of today's. Ahhhh, that's why we love L.A.!

You've already heard: Los Angeles is *very* spread out, with countless sections to explore and highways to travel. So gas up the car and make sure the AC is working. First, head out to Hollywood for a breakfast of fried chicken wings, scrambled eggs, and waffles at Roscoe's Chicken & Waffles. Don't waste your money on a map of the stars' homes. Most likely, you won't catch Eddie Murphy mowing his lawn. You can, however, see if your feet are the same size as

Mr. Murphy's, or other stars', in front of Mann's Chinese Theater. In front of the theater, up and down Hollywood Boulevard, is the famous Hollywood Walk of Fame, where a galaxy of movie and musical stars from Paul Robeson to Tina Turner are honored with individual plaques.

Down the street is one of the world's most famous intersections: Hollywood and Vine. This spot is home to Capital Records, whose success is credited to musical giants such as Nat King Cole, Ella Fitzgerald, Miles Davis, and Duke Ellington. A stunning mural by African American artist Richard Wyatt on the side of the building pays homage to these jazz greats. Jump on the 101 Freeway to the 110 and head southwest to downtown to take in the California Afro-American Museum. For a little "sub-culture," jump back on the 101 and head west to infamous Venice Beach, where thong-clad beauties whiz by on in-line skates, and tanned, muscle-strained men vie to see who can exude the most testosterone between sweaty bench presses.

Enjoy a down-home lunch of Uncle Wade's baked beef short ribs, fresh collard greens, and Aunt June's fresh candied yams at the legendary Aunt Kizzy's Back Porch in Marina Del Ray. To avoid traffic, take Manchester all the way across and make a left onto Crenshaw Avenue. Within the heart of this predominantly African American locale lie the communities of Baldwin Hills, Inglewood, Crenshaw, the infamous South Central, and the Sugar Hill District, once home to Hattie McDaniel and Ethel Waters. The First AME Church, founded by freed slave and wealthy landowner Biddy Mason, anchors the area. In the heart of the Crenshaw community is Leimert Park, a tiny triangle of land that has grown into a bustling haven of Black commerce. Stop by the Museum in Black for a walk down Jim Crow lane and to view other memorabilia relating to Black history and culture. Then visit the exquisite Elephant Walk restaurant for a wonderful dinner of southern specialties. Across the street is the Comedy Act Theater, where outrageous laughter is on the playbill Thursday through Saturday nights. After the show, catch the late-night jazz set upstairs at 5th Street Dick's, where some of the finest local talent jam into the wee hours. While the music inside gets fired up, so do the serious chess matches at the sidewalk tables out front. This is L.A. nightlife? Oh, yeah! When Los Angeles locals party, they say "enough, already" to the false Hollywood glamour. However, if you came to L.A. for that scene (and tell the truth, who doesn't?), stop by the Voodoo

Lounge for major star sightings and plastic-fantastic guessing. Did she or didn't she? In Los Angeles, only her surgeon knows for sure!

Restaurants

Over the years, the West Coast dining scene has spawned a number of influential and tasty food trends as well as high profile chefs whose tantalizing recipes have sent bored home cooks back to their kitchens. Recent mouthwatering concoctions include barbecue chicken and garlic mashed potato wrap sandwiches, banana and blueberry smoothies, and tofu and sprouts pizza. The phenomenon known as "New California" cuisine refers to the mixing of French cooking with fresh West Coast seasonings, blended with Asian or Mexican influences—no surprise, given the growth of those communities in the Golden State.

Fine Dining

✳Elephant Walk
4336 Degnan, 323/299-1765
With its mahogany appointments, English lace tablecloths, antique light fixtures, and an eloquent, full-size zebra positioned on the sidewalk to greet diners, Elephant Walk is without question L.A.'s most charming restaurant. The menu, which changes daily, features sophisticated southern cuisine. • **$30+/AA**

✳Hal's Bar & Grill
1349 Abbot Kinney Blvd., Venice, 310/396-3105
Hal's Bar & Grill is located just down the street from Venice Beach and, as a result, attracts a chic international crowd of artists, actors, and neighborhood regulars to its richly decorated dining room and Monday-night sets of live jazz. The menu, which features New American cuisine with an emphasis on natural, fresh ingredients, changes weekly, but the following is a sampling of what you can expect: grilled half chicken basted with Thai spices and served with Hal's fries (the best!), pan-roasted duck in spicy passionfruit glaze, grilled ahi tuna in vegetable coulis, and roasted king salmon on a bed of risotto. • **$35+/AA**

✳Reign
180 N. Robertson Blvd., 310/273-4463
Keyshawn Johnson, wide-receiver for the New York Jets, is the newest
celebrity to throw his hat—or in this case, helmet—into the compet-
itive restaurant arena. What will make his restaurant succeed? Well,
his name, for one. The type of diners Johnson attracts are from the
beautiful PYT, Gucci-wearing set. If your name conjures pop culture
and big cash, you're all but guaranteed to reel 'em in. Reign's prices
are high enough to pay the steep rent, but, as good as the "southern
cooking with inspired California cuisine" is, $6 for a side of mac and
cheese is out of control. Even so, the food is quite good. • **$40+/AA**

Casual Dining

Art's Wings & Things
4213 Crenshaw Blvd., 323/294-9464
You can't miss Art's Wings & Things—just look for the sign with
the shapely chicken inviting passersby to "Let My Wings Do Their
Thing to Your Taste Buds." Art's take-out chicken wings come several ways: buffalo style, mild, hot, sweet-and-sour, teriyaki style, and
laden with mumbo sauce. Philly cheesesteak sandwiches, fried vegetables, and burgers round out the menu. • **$10**

✳Aunt Kizzy's Back Porch
4325 Glencoe Ave., **Marina del Rey**, 310/578-1005
When you walk inside Aunt Kizzy's Back Porch restaurant, you are
greeted by Magic Johnson, Oprah Winfrey, Bill Cosby, and Whoo-
pie Goldberg—well, at least in cardboard cut-out form and spirit!
From its cozy log-cabin interior to its lively walls that feature Dulan
family photos and memorabilia along with more famous faces, to
proprietor Adolph Dulan himself, who strolls from table to table
greeting patrons with his dazzling smile—Aunt Kizzy's exudes per-
sonality plus. The menu features authentic down-home cuisine, and
it's a "relative" affair: Aunt Johnnie's fried chicken, Uncle Wade's
baked beef short ribs, Cousin Willie Mae's smothered pork chops,
and Sister Zethel's meatloaf. There are lots of sides to choose from
and old-time country desserts like Aunt Kizzy's sweet potato pie,
"sock-it-to-me" cake, and pineapple coconut cake. Sunday brunch is
served. • **$15+/AA**

Are We in LA or La (Louisiana)?

Gagnier's of New Orleans, 1315 Third St. Promenade, Santa Monica, 310/319-9981—The Gagniers, Louisiana natives, bring a little bit of the Big Easy to L.A. with their filé (pronounced 'fee-lay') gumbo, jambalaya, oysters on the half shell, special seafood platters, and Mama Gloria's homemade bread pudding with whiskey sauce. · $20/AA

Harold & Belle's Creole Restaurant, 2920 W. Jefferson Blvd., 323/735-9023—Harold & Belle's has gained a national reputation as one of the best Creole restaurants outside of New Orleans. File gumbo loaded with shrimp, crab, sausage, chicken, and ham and beautifully presented in a crockpot is the number-one item on the menu. Live jazz on the weekends. Sunday brunch. · $30+/AA

Uncle Darrow's Cajun/Creole Eatery, 5301 Venice Blvd., 323/938-4293— Located down the street from Sony Studios, Uncle Darrow's sells winners like jambalaya as well as catfish and shrimp suppers (both fried to perfection in cornmeal), and turkey, chicken, and Creole link po-boys, homemade ice cream, and praline candy. Take-out only. · $10/AA

Boulevard Café
3710 W. Martin Luther King Jr. Blvd., 323/292-7900
Since 1984, Boulevard Café has served countless celebrities, politicians, athletes, and loyal locals. Its interior is modest and best suited for family-style dining. Paintings by local artists (many for sale) and photographs of the famous people who have dined here take up almost every inch of available wall space. Beef short ribs (no knife needed, thank you), chicken and dressing, fried chicken, red snapper, fried catfish, steaks, chitterlings, and gumbo are just a few of the down-home offerings. • **$15+/AA**

✳Coley's Kitchen Jamaican Restaurant
4335 Crenshaw Blvd., 323/290-4010
"A taste of Jamaica in the heart of L.A." is what Coley's Kitchen, the area's premier Caribbean restaurant, is all about. The decor, with its

Outside Uncle Darrow's eatery, where the Creole cuisine is served up fast and hot.

unique works of art, pastel-pink walls, and lace curtains, recalls the colorful Jamaican countryside, and Coley's Jamaican meat patties are considered the best in the city by many critics (the secret, they say, is in the crust!). Other house specialties include jerk chicken, curried goat, kingfish escoveitch, vegetarian delight, and brown stew fish. Traditional island beverages—sorrel, Irish moss, ginger beer, and soursop—are made fresh on the premises. • **$15+/AA**

Dulan's Restaurant
4859 Crenshaw Blvd., 323/296-3034
Located in the heart of L.A.'s African American community and just 15 minutes from downtown, Dulan's is housed in a large Spanish-style hacienda with a lovely outdoor patio perfect for alfresco dining. You can enjoy fried chicken, smothered pork chops, meatloaf, catfish, chicken and sausage jambalaya, short ribs, collard greens, and mashed potatoes. On Sundays Dulan's opens only for its famed gospel and jazz brunch. • **$20/AA**

Phillip's BBQ Carryout
4307 Leimert Blvd., 323/292-7613
When locals refer to Phillip's as "a hole in the wall," truer words never were spoken. Phillip's is all of a sliding plastic window at the end of a short hallway, surrounded by dirty white walls. Here you place and receive your order. Strange, yes, but don't let this scene scare you away from some of the best barbecue in L.A. • **$10/AA**

Simply Wholesome
4508 W. Slauson, 323/294-2144
Recognizing the need for "alternative" foods in the predominantly Black Crenshaw area of Los Angeles, Simply Wholesome serves triply as a restaurant, grocery store, and community center. The extensive natural foods menu will satisfy almost any craving. Sandwiches include tuna and avocado, turkey burgers, and lentil burgers. Entrées "on the healthy tip" range from spinach corn enchiladas to vegetarian lasagna. What's more, Simply Wholesome offers more than 25 thirst-quencher combinations from "Guava Explosion" and "Apple-Banana Fruit Slush" to "Peach Pizazz." • **$10/AA**

✳Sushi Nozawa
11288 Ventura Blvd., Studio City, 818/508-7071
At Sushi Nozawa, it is only about the fish. Forget the tacky decor and the strip mall location; neither has anything to do with the quality and creativity of the food coming from the kitchen. A word to the wise—sit at the sushi bar where menus are unnecessary. Everyone's meal is selected by chef Nozawa himself, so whatever Nozawa feels like slicing, you're eatin'! If a California roll is the limit of your Japanese dining adventure, eat somewhere else! For those who want to sample the best sushi and sashimi L.A. has to offer, this is it! • **$20+**

Nightclubs

✳Babe's and Ricky's Inn
4339 Leimert Blvd., 323/295-9112
Considered by many to be one of L.A.'s best clubs with the best decor, best live blues, and best crowd, period, Babe's and Ricky's has

Behind the Velvet Rope

Daddy's, 1610 Vine St., 323/463-7777—Who's ya daddy? If the answer is the hottest bar/lounge in L.A., you've come to the right parent.

Lola's, 945 N. Fairfax Blvd., 213/736-5652—With over 100 devilish martini concoctions and an equally sinful and eclectic international menu, Lola's turns to heat up most L.A. nights.

POP, 836 N. Highland—Without question, this is the place to be on a Friday night in L.A.

Voodoo Lounge, 4120 W. Olympic, 323/930-9600—This is L.A.'s premier dance club, with the pulsating floor extending to the great outdoors. The glass-enclosed VIP rooms have a slightly perverted elitist/peep show quality, which only adds to the club's decadent ambience.

a new location. It's a great addition to Leimert Park and a perfect venue from which to introduce music fans to one of the city's most eclectic neighborhoods. Sunday gospel performances are a featured plus. • **Music charge**

B.B. King's Blues Club
1000 Universal Center Dr., Universal City, 818/622-5464
B.B. King's Blues Club and Restaurant features a down-home southern menu with "opening acts" like southern-fried fingers, howlin' hot wings, and quick-fried dill pickles. "Main performances" include red beans and rice, barbecued ribs, delta-fried catfish, "The King" steak, and jambalaya kabobs. Of course, there's plenty of great live jazz and R&B music. The thrill is back! • **Music charge/AA-invested**

Comedy Act Theater
3339 W. 43rd St., 323/677-4101
The late Robin Harris got his start at the Comedy Act Theater, and you can bet he won't be the last famous comedian to come out of a

venue that offers newcomers a chance to introduce themselves. With up to eight different comedians appearing each night, cracking on the audience is par for the course. But that's OK because the Comedy Act serves plenty of munchies along with the good humor.
• **Cover charge/AA**

✴Conga Room
5364 Wilshire Blvd., 323/938-1696
Slick, sexy, and sassy is the only way to describe the scene at the Conga Room, L.A.'s hot new Latin music/salsa dance club You'll see a whole lotta shakin' goin' on here. Celebrity investor Jimmy Smits often puts in an appearance to add to the already electric ambiance produced by the colorful murals of giant conga drums, sensuous mood lighting, and infectious Latin beat. The attached Comedor restaurant serves a wonderful pre- and post-show Latin American menu. The grilled Chilean sea bass on a bed of banana leaves is upstaged only by the live 15-piece band. For those who don't cha cha or merengue, lessons are available. • **Cover charge/Dinner $30+**

✴5th Street Dick's Coffee Company
3347 W. 43rd Pl., 323/296-3970
At 11:30 on any pleasant night in L.A., a crowd spills out of 5th Street Dick's, piping hot cups of coffee and slices of carrot cake in hand, to wait for the second set of jazz to start. Other folks can be spotted playing chess or bid whist at the club's sidewalk tables. Upstairs, it's live, straight-ahead jazz played by local and nationally known acts—all part of the cool, laid-back culture of this re-emering neighborhood. A unique scene indeed. • **Cover charge/AA**

✴Jazz Bakery
3233 Helms Ave., Culver City, 310/271-9039
The Stanley Turrentine Quartet, Stanley Jordan, and Brian Bromberg are just a few of the jazz greats who show they really know how to cook at the Jazz Bakery. Located in the historic Helms Bakery building, this restaurant offers a beautiful, spacious setting for entertainment, enhanced by a rotating jazz art gallery, all dedicated to the preservation of the one true American art form, jazz. •
Music charge

Marla's Memory Lane
2323 W. Martin Luther King Jr. Blvd., 323/294-8430
Marla Gibbs, Florence on *The Jeffersons* and star of her own television series, *227*, takes special pride in providing quality entertainment to her Crenshaw neighborhood. Marla's Memory Lane serves up good food, live jazz, and lots of old-school R&B and world music to dance to. • **Cover charge most nights/AA**

✳Odessa
680 S. Coast Hwy., Laguna Beach, 949/376-8792
After the success of his first restaurant venture, Georgia's former basketball star-turned-restauranteur Norm Nixon opened, with a little help from his famous friends, Odessa, a swank jazz/supperclub in Laguna Beach. The menu is pan-Asian/California fine dining with entrées like seared ocean scallops in a light Chardonnay sauce accented with an asparagus/potato risotto. The jazz room hosts big-name local talent from up and down the California coast. Those who prefer to listen to their jazz down low retire to the VIP dining room and lounge. • **Music charge/Dinner $40+/AA-invested**

The Townhouse
6835 La Tijera Blvd., 310/649-0091
The legendary Townhouse is always packed with politicians, celebrities, neighborhood regulars, and loyal friends. It boasts an extensive wine list, two fireplaces, live entertainment nightly, dancing, Monday sports nights (the club has nine TVs, so you won't miss a thing), banquet facilities, and, if that's not enough, a full-service restaurant with an all-American menu. House specialties include porterhouse steak, smothered chops, fried catfish, blackened snapper, and Alaskan king crab legs. • **Cover charge/Dinner $20+/AA**

✳World Stage
4344 Degnan Blvd., 323/293-2451
The World Stage bills itself as a "performance gallery" dedicated to "seeking light through sound." It's a natural setting for workshops, concerts, jam sessions, readings, and rehearsals requiring a relaxed, intimate venue. The small arena seats only about 45 people, yet the music and vibes it delivers are so powerful, a larger stage might diminish the intensity of the message. • **Music charge/AA**

Festivals

Folks in L.A. love their jazz, and what better way to enjoy it than outdoors in nature. The Long Beach Jazz Festival is set in Rainbow Lagoon Park, a backdrop so scenic, Universal Studios couldn't design anything better. Local neighborhoods also take on a Hollywood atmosphere when celebrations turn residential blocks into festive tar-covered dance halls.

UCLA Jazz & Reggae Festival
UCLA Intramural Field, 310/825-9912
Sunday, it's all day cool jazz with performers from the Roy Hargrove Quintet to Roy Ayers. Monday officially kicks off the summer with a ragamuffin reggae party with Dennis Brown, and Freddie McGregor rockin' the crowd. Thousands of students and music fans from all over the city join in the fun at the UCLA Jazz & Reggae Festival. The international food and crafts marketplace is as large a draw as the performers. • **Memorial Day weekend/Admission charge**

Playboy Jazz Festival
Hollywood Bowl, 310/449-4070
The Playboy Jazz Festival is one of the most celebrated all-star jazz fests in the country. Past performers included the music of Al Jarreau, Wynton Marsalis, Ruth Brown & Friends, Pete Fountain & His New Orleans Jazz Band, Dee Dee Bridgewater, Sheila E & E-Train, Grover Washington Jr., Ray Charles, and Etta James and the Roots Band! And with Bill Cosby as the master of ceremonies, you know it's going to be a party. • **Second weekend in June/ Admission charge**

Long Beach Jazz Festival
Rainbow Lagoon Park, 562/436-7794
Stanley Clark, Roy Ayers, Lee Ritnouer, Chuck Mangione, Gil Scott Heron, Oscar Brown Jr., and Norman Brown are just a few of the jazz giants who have performed at the Long Beach Jazz Festival. Hosted at the base of the *Queen Mary* overlooking the Long Beach Marina, the picturesque surroundings are well suited to the festival's soothing sounds. • **Second weekend in August/ Admission charge**

Neighborhood Throw Down

Day of the Drum Festival/Simon Rodia Watts Towers Jazz Festival, Watts Towers Cultural Crescent Amphitheater, 323/485-1795—The simplest of sounds, the beat of a drum, rises to a crescendo at the Day of the Drum festival. Drum and dance performances include those from the countries Guinea, Polynesia, and Cameroon as well as from the American Latin Drum Ensemble. The Watts Jazz Festival celebrates America's only true art form with an assembly of the best local and national acts. Children's workshops, arts and crafts, and lots of food add to this lively weekend. · Last weekend in September/Free

Central Avenue Jazz Festival, Central Ave. between 42nd and 43rd Sts., 323/485-3351—Back in the day, Central Avenue was the heart of the Black community, a street where the jazz and blues sounds from now-legendary nightclubs filled the air nightly. Today, most of those spots are closed, but their musical memories live on and are celebrated at the Central Avenue Jazz Fest. The weekend starts off with a panel discussion with these renowned jazz greats, then you get the privilege to hear them play. Can't get any better than that. Yes, it does—it's all free! · First weekend in August/Free

Long Beach Blues Festival
Cal State University, Long Beach, 310/985-5566
Twenty-six blues acts in all, 30,000 die-hard blues fans, good food, unique arts and crafts, and good vibes make up the Long Beach Blues Festival. Bobby "Blue" Bland, Johnny Copeland, Gatemouth Brown, Marcia Ball, and Long John Hunter are just a few of this popular fest's past performers. • **Labor Day weekend/Admission charge**

Museums and Attractions

Biddy Mason Park and Monument
Broadway Spring Center, between Broadway,
Spring, and Third Aves.
She was born a slave, raised three children, fought to gain freedom

The Cabildo is Coming *by Viredo from the permanent collection of the California African American Museum*

for herself and her family, worked as a midwife and nurse, became a landowner, and founded Los Angeles's first African Methodist Episcopal church in her home. On November 16, 1989, the city proclaimed the first "Biddy Mason Day," and a plaque of recognition was erected at the Broadway Spring Center to commemorate the life of this amazing woman.

California African American Museum
600 State Dr., 213/744-7432
The California African American Museum, housed in a modern, industrial-style space, is devoted to the preservation and celebration of African American culture. With an emphasis on African American contributions to the development of California and the western

United States, the museum showcases exhibits, paintings, sculptures, and photographs from contemporary artists throughout the African Diaspora. Its Living History Theater schedules dramatic reenactments of historically significant events, literary readings, panel discussions, and video presentations. Permanent exhibits include displays such as "Ella Fitzgerald, Vocalist." • **Admission charge**

J. Paul Getty Museum
1200 Getty Center Dr., 310/440-7300
To appreciate the Getty Center, it is not necessary to be a scholar of fine arts and antiquities, just a lover of life. The Getty Center, located on 110 spectacular acres, is devoted to the preservation of cultural arts and humanities. The complex is truly an architectural wonder, each building equally distinctive and grand. The center's many walkways, courtyards, and balconies afford breathtaking panoramic views of Los Angeles. Permanent collections within the museum include Greek and Roman antiquities, European paintings, drawings, illuminated manuscripts, sculpture, and American and European photographs. Because of limited space, however, parking reservations must be made in advance, or entrance to the museum cannot be assured. • **Free**

La Brea Tar Pits
5801 Wilshire Blvd., 323/936-2230
If you arrive at the La Brea Tar Pits on the right warm afternoon, you may witness, with odd fascination, the churning of the soft asphalt entrapping insects, pigeons, and small animals just as it did more than 10,000 years ago. Morbid, yes, but the fact is that some 565 fossilized species, including saber-toothed tigers, wolves, and giant Columbian mammoths were retrieved from these celebrated pits and are currently on display at the on-site museum. The La Brea Tar Pits Museum's holdings include about 3 million items, the oldest a wood fragment dating back 40,000 years. Amazing! • **Admission charge**

Paramount Studios
5555 Melrose Ave., Hollywood, 323/956-1777
Touring the Paramount Studios lots is like stepping into one of the studio's most famous movies, *Sunset Boulevard*. So be ready for

your close-up. What's really cool about a visit here, in addition to hearing tales of the antics of past stars and directors on the Paramount lot, is the possibility of watching a movie being filmed. If television is more your thing, how about being part of a studio audience for Paramount's *Frasier*, *Moesha*, or *Dharma and Greg* shows? Tickets are available on a first-come, first-served basis. Oh, and make sure you look good when you hit the set—you never know which talent agent may be scouting for the next superstar! • **Admission charge**

Sony Picture Studios
10202 W. Washington Blvd., 310/244-4000
Sony Studios offers two-hour walking tours of its facility, including its massive wardrobe closets, backdrops, and stages, but no tours of live sets in production (you know how temperamental stars are—you wouldn't want to disturb their vibes, would you?). If you're a fan of *Jeopardy* or *Wheel of Fortune*, you can be part of these shows' studio audiences by calling the above number for tickets. • **Admission charge**

Watts Tower
1765 E. 107th St., 213/847-4646 (Watts Tower Center)
Did you know that Watts Towers, those funky, often-called-down-right-ugly futuristic works of art were designed and built by an Italian immigrant named Simon Rodia? It took this construction worker more than 30 years, countless pieces of found metal, tiles, and seashells, and plenty of vision, nerve, and determination to complete the towers. Adjacent to them is the Watts Towers Arts Center, a museum devoted to showcasing the work of young, talented local artists. The museum hosts several cultural lectures and studio workshops for kids throughout the year. Tours of the towers are available by appointment. • **Free**

Churches

Faithful Central Baptist Church
321 N. Eucalyptus St., Inglewood, 310/330-8000
A new, 4,000-seat sanctuary may not be large enough for this fast-

growing congregation. A new multicultural conference center also address the needs of the community.

First African Methodist Episcopal Church
2270 S. Harvard Blvd., 213/730-9180
Biddy Mason founded this historic church in her home in 1872. It was the first African American religious sanctuary in Los Angeles. Today, First African's notable programs include youth outreach and crisis prevention. First African is also known citywide for its dynamic gospel choir.

Second Baptist Church
2412 Griffith Ave., 213/748-0318
The original site of this church, founded in 1885 and the oldest African American Baptist church in L.A., was on Maple Street between Seventh and Eighth Avenues. The current building opened in 1926. Various outreach ministries make the church a vital part of the South Central community.

West Angeles Church of God
3045 Crenshaw Ave., 323/731-3012
West Angeles Church is one of the fastest growing churches in the country. With extensive ministry and outreach services, including television and radio broadcasts, West Angeles boasts a membership of more than 17,000. To address the growing congregation's needs, an ambitious $50 million expansion is underway. The sprawling new complex will include, among other edifices, the West Angeles Cathedral.

Recreation

Beaches

Manhattan Beach—A great family beach
Long Beach—The *Queen Mary* is permanently docked here.
Malibu—Surfers' heaven
Venice Beach—People watching and inline skating are the top activities.
Marina del Rey—Lovely harbor scene

Amusement Parks

Disneyland, 1313 Harbor Blvd., Anaheim, 714/781-4565
Knott's Berry Farm, 8039 Beach Blvd., Buena Park, 714/220-5200
Six Flags Magic Mountain, 26101 Magic Mountain Pkwy., Valencia, 805/255-4111
Universal Studios Hollywood, 100 Universal City Plaza, Universal City, 818/508-9600
Pacific Park, Santa Monica Pier, Santa Monica, 310/260-8744
Griffith Park, 4730 Crystal Springs Dr., 323/665-5188

Studio Tours

Studio Tour Tips
You'll be walking for at least two hours, so wear comfortable shoes. Tours are conducted Monday through Friday on a first-come, first-served basis. The admission charge is about $15 per person, cash only. Due to safety and insurance regulations, no children under 10 are allowed.

TV Audience Tips
Tickets are available five days before each scheduled show. A limited number of priority-seating tickets is available. Call 323/956-5575 for show schedules.

CBS Television City, 7800 Beverly Blvd., 323/852-2448
Universal Studios Hollywood, 100 Universal City Plaza, Universal City, 818/508-9600
NBC Studio Tour, 3000 W. Alameda Ave., Burbank, 818/840-3537
Warner Bros. Studios, 4000 Warner Blvd., Burbank, 818/954-1744

Memphis

Memphis. A city recognized worldwide as the home of the three Bs—barbecue, Beale Street, and the blues—Memphis is also home to an amazing group of African Americans who have shaped the city's, and the South's, rich history. One legendary native son was Robert R. Church Sr., the South's first African American millionaire, builder of the Church Park and Auditorium, and founder of Solvent Savings Bank. Civil and women's rights advocate and founding NAACP member Ida B. Wells, another Memphis native, challenged racial injustice in her newspaper *Free Speech and Headlight*. And let's not forget W. C. Handy, who wrote a little ditty on Beale Street called "Mister Crump's Blues," the first blues song ever published. Ever since, the list of musical greats emerging from this sultry southern town has grown and grown. Paragons of the "Memphis Sound" include Stax Records hit-makers Isaac Hayes, Otis Redding, Rufus Thomas, Al Green, and Wilson Pickett. Given this impressive list of august ancestors and living legends, it's no wonder so many folks are proud to claim Memphis as home.

Start your tour of Memphis downtown. The Main Street Trolley Line makes it easy to get around the area. All-day passes can be purchased from trolley operators for $2. First stop: the National Civil Rights Museum. Formerly the Lorraine Hotel, the site where Dr. Martin Luther King Jr. was assassinated, this museum houses an extraordinary collection documenting the struggles and victories of the Civil Rights movement. With recordings from that ill-fated day playing in the background, memories of that tragedy (if you're over 40) or a sense of great loss (if you're younger) will choke the air around you. But the museum is also a repository of hope and triumph, as represented by other exhibits and artifacts of a people *determined* to be free.

As you trolley-travel north on Riverside Drive, the mighty Mississippi lies to your left while the diverse residences and financial districts that make up downtown Memphis lie to your right. At the northernmost end of the line sits the Pyramid, an imposing multipurpose arena modeled after the massive tombs of pharaohs in northern Africa. The Pyramid is located next to Auction Square, once the site of an open-air slave market. Get off the trolley at North Parkway, walk a couple of blocks, and you're in "the Pinch" historic and entertainment district. Treat yourself to lunch at the Cozy Corner, where the barbecued Cornish hens and baked beans just don't *get* any better.

Last stop on the tour: Beale Street, home of the blues! Memphis's most famous street boasts block after block of history, music, and fun. It's where W. C. Handy birthed the blues and B.B. King perfected it. Once a center of African American commerce and culture, Beale Street preserves its musical legacy. At modernday honky tonks, you can listen to notables and local legends play the blues all night long. The Center for Southern Folklore, the Beale Street Blues Museum, the Orpheum Theater, First Baptist Beale Street Church, and a bronze statue of W. C. Handy himself are just a few sites to see as you boogie on down. Stop in B.B. King's Blues Club for a little barbecue and blues or two doors down to This Is It! for the hottest chicken wings and the coolest jazz this side of the Mississippi. Now, if only Beale Street really *could* talk!

Restaurants

OK, so we know Memphis is all about the barbecue. And with more than 200 restaurants around town, there is no way you can leave the city without sampling a tender pork butt, slow-smoked barbecue Cornish hens, or barbecue bologna and barbecue spaghetti—two "only in Memphis" delicacies. So if you O.D. on chopped pork, take an antacid and get over it! Where did you think you were going—Milwaukee?

Fine Dining

✳Aubergine
5007 Black Rd., 901/767-7840
Considered the finest dining experience in Memphis, Aubergine's creative French fare is constantly evolving; with each visit it just gets better and better. Past favorites include an intriguing spicy crab layered "napoleon," a tasty quail marinated in cloves and tarragon, and Aubergine's signature warm chocolate pyramid cake. Pure decadence.
• **$45+**

✳River Terrace
280 N. Mud Island Rd., 901/528-0001
There is nothing more romantic than watching the sun set with someone you love, especially while feeding them a morsel of your luscious black-bottom tart. OK, so you may not *want* to share this treat with them, but, hey, you still have the view! Asian- and Southwestern-influenced cuisine and a splendid view of the Mississippi make River Terrace a must-dine while in Memphis. • **$45+**

Casual Dining

A&R Bar-B-Que
1802 Elvis Presley Blvd., 901/774-7444
Rib tips, slabs of ribs, pork and beef shoulder, hot links, and hot wings make up the better part of A&R's menu. There are also several sandwiches to choose from, like smoked turkey breast, chopped pork, and chopped beef. Grandmother Pollard makes all the cakes and A&R's famous fried pies. Take-out only. • **$10+/AA**

✳Bar-B-Que Shop
1782 Madison, 901/272-1277
Consistency is the key at this bistro-like restaurant. Pork Boston butt, ribs, beef brisket, Texas toast, barbecue chicken, barbecue bologna, barbecue spaghetti (it's a Memphis thing!), and barbecue beans are specialties of this Memphis institution. The Bar-B-Que Shop's famous "Dancing Pigs" barbecue sauce (yes, the label really features dancing pigs!) is available for sale. • **$10+/AA**

Enough with the Barbecue Already!

✳McEwen's, 122 Monroe, 901/527-7085—McEwen's chic airy interior allows for plenty of room when the cooks raise the roof with fiery Louisiana Creole and West Indies dishes. Smoked catfish, a wonderful grilled pork chop paired with an andouille sausage dressing, and biscuits to die for lead the way. · $30+

Maxwell's, 948 S. Cooper, 901/725-1009—New American cuisine with a heavy dose of Asian influence describes the menu at Maxwell's, a restaurant known around town for a happenin' bar scene and appetizer pizzas with crusts made from blue corn or black sesame rice paper. · $20+

✳Cozy Corner Restaurant
745 North Pkwy., 901/527-9158
According to Chef Raymond Robinson Sr., "If it's cooked right, you don't need the sauce." But you may want just a little on the side for dipping, because at the Cozy Corner, it's that good! Barbecue ribs, chicken, Cornish hens (excellent!), pork shoulder, turkey, rib tips, and smoked sausage are what's on the menu. Sides include cole slaw, beans and bologna, and barbecue spaghetti. Don't let the exterior of this modest little take-out spot scare you away. • **$10+/AA**

Crumpy's Hot Wings
1381 Elvis Presley Blvd., 901/942-3427
1056 E. Brooks Rd., 901/345-1503
1724 S. White Station, 901/685-8356
2731 Rangeline Rd., 901/353-3232
2500 W. Goodman Rd., Hornlake, Mississippi, 601/342-1937
1584 Alcy Rd., 901/942-3427 (Crumpy's Restaurant)
Crumpy's take-out units serve mostly wings and "things," but you can also order burgers. The wings (as in the *whole* wing!) come in five degrees of heat: mild, regular hot, hot, x-hot, and suicide (!). The "things" are the sides that come with them: fries, carrot and celery sticks with blue cheese dressing, and a roll. Crumpy's Restaurant, on Alcy Road, serves up what owner Crump calls its "serious" hot plate

dinners: country-fried steak, meatloaf, fried chicken, and turkey and dressing—in huge portions for too little money. • **$10/AA**

✳Interstate Bar-B-Que Restaurant
2265 S. Third St., 901/775-2304

Jim Neely's Interstate Bar-B-Que is arguably the most famous and finest barbecue in Memphis. In 1989, *People* magazine rated it number two in a nationwide survey of the top 10 barbecue restaurants. Pork and beef ribs, chopped or sliced pork and beef, Texas beef links, smoked turkey breast, rib tips, and barbecue spaghetti are just a few of the hearty dishes ready to satisfy even the biggest appetite. • **$10/AA**

Leach Family Restaurant
694 Madison, 901/521-0867

On a typical weekday, Leach's cooks prepare at least 85 pounds of turkey necks, 80 pounds of fried chicken, and 60 pounds of ground meat for their famous meatloaf. They don't even open the doors without making sure there are enough greens and yams to go around! Other specialties include chicken and dressing, catfish, buffalo fish, ham hocks, and barbecued chicken, but don't leave without sampling Leach's delicious lemon cake or banana pudding. • **$10/AA**

✳Neely's Bar-B-Que
670 Jefferson, 901/521-9798
5700 Mount Moriah, 901/795-4177

Al Roker of the *Today Show* swears by Neely's barbecue, and we concur. At Neely's, barbecue comes in many forms: chopped or pulled pork, sliced beef, or turkey; ribs and rib tips; chicken; and sausage. The sauce, made daily, is thick, flavorful, and mild. There's also the bar-b-salad and the barbecue spaghetti dinner (a local favorite). The cole slaw is excellent, and a small order of fries at Neely's is not small at all! • **$10+/AA**

Nightclubs

Beale Street still sings the blues. With so many juke joints to choose from, the musical range is wide, from straight-ahead jazz to low-down, nasty blues.

Where the blues lives on—The Boogie Café on Beale Street

B.B. King's Blues Club and Restaurant
143 Beale St., 901/524-KING

When Riley B. King arrived in Memphis at the age of 22 with only his guitar and $2.50 to his name, his singing quickly earned him the nicknname Riley "Blues Boy" King. He later shortened that to "B.B." and...well, you know the rest! B.B. King's Blues Club and Restaurant features a down-home southern menu with "main performances" such as red beans and rice, delta fried catfish, "The King" steak, and jambalaya kabobs. Of course, there's plenty of great live jazz and R&B. The thrill is back! • **Cover charge/Dinner $10–$20/AA-invested**

Memphis Sounds Lounge
164 Union Ave., 901/527-4100

On Friday evenings, this club, located in the Days Inn Downtown, is packed with Memphis's who's who as well as tourists galore. Local celebs and visitors alike can be found lolling around, enjoying a good argument about politics, football, or the topic of the moment. The full-dinner restaurant serves American cuisine as well as standard bar fare. Live jazz on the weekends. • **Cover charge on weekends/Dinner $15/AA**

Rum Boogie Café
174–178 Beale St., 901/525-3891
Forget the Hard Rock Café! In addition to displaying an awesome collection of guitars autographed by the likes of Stevie Ray Vaughn and Robert Cray, the Rum Boogie proudly shows off other priceless Memphis music memorabilia, including (are you ready?) Isaac Hayes's cold-blooded cape! The original Stax Records sign looms over the bandstand, where local and national groups jam until all hours of the night. Cajun and southern fare menu, live blues nightly.
• **Cover charge on weekends/Dinner $15+**

✳This Is It!
167 Beale St., 901/527-8200
Some of the best live jazz in town literally spills out the front door of This Is It!—the most colorful club on Beale Street. The full kitchen serves up a classic American menu, famous for its chicken wings, the best and hottest on the strip. The wings' spicy heat ranges from mild to Watch Out! • **Cover charge on weekends/Dinner $10–$20/AA**

Willie Mitchell's Rhythm & Blues Club
326 Beale St., 901/523-7444
Beale Street truly comes alive weekends when Willie Mitchell's Rhythm & Blues Club throws open its doors and lets all that good live down-home R&B music come spilling out. Owned by and named after the famous musician and producer, Willie Mitchell's is *the* place to go in Memphis for great music, good home-style food, and dancing all night! • **Cover charge/Dinner $10–$15/AA**

Festivals

Barbecue and the blues—what else would Memphis celebrate with such passion?

Memphis in May International Festival

First Weekend:
Beale Street Music Festival, Tom Lee Park. No food, drinks, containers, cameras, or inline skates allowed.

Second Weekend:
International Weekend, various locations around the city and on the fairgrounds on the Mississippi. Call for a list of activities.

Third Weekend:
World Championship Barbecue Cooking Contest, Tom Lee Park.

Memorial Day Weekend:
Sunset Symphony, banks of the Mississippi. Bring your picnic basket, wine, blanket, and family to hear the melodic sounds of the Memphis Symphony Orchestra. The monthlong celebration climaxes with a fireworks display.

Africa in April Cultural Awareness Festival
Various venues, 901/947-2133

Each April Memphis brings the pageantry and mystery of African nations to its little corner of the world. Themes focus on the culture, rituals, history, and arts of that year's honored country. The African nations selected for that festival are unveiled during a five-day celebration featuring performance art, dance troupes, live music, and a colorful marketplace where vendors sell authentic African artifacts and fabrics. • **Mid-April/Free**

Memphis in May International Festival
901/525-4611

Memphis in May attracts more than 1 million visitors with concerts, ethnic foods, gallery exhibits, demonstrations, and a huge barbecue cooking contest, all dedicated to educating and enlightening the public about foreign cultures. The Beale Street Music Festival kicks off the first weekend in grand style. Some 75 fantastic performers from the worlds of jazz, rock 'n' roll, gospel, country, funk, and, of course, the blues get down on five stages for a party not to be believed! Past performers have included Eddie Floyd, Rufus Thomas, Koko Taylor, Dr. John, Wilson Pickett, Clarence Carter, and Bobby "Blue" Bland, to name a few. Add these performers to the talent that usually plays at the Beale Street clubs, and you could almost O.D. on the blues. But what a way to go!

The third weekend in May sees the World Championship Barbecue Cooking Contest, known to barbecue aficionados as "Hog Heaven." Some 225 teams fire up their smokers and hickory chips to compete with the "big hogs" for the modest distinction of "world champion." In addition to all the good eatin', the contest features such folksy awards as "Ms. Piggy," best hog caller, and other assorted praises to the pork. If you're not lucky enough to be a contest judge, just make sure you bring a mess of napkins, washcloths—oh, and an empty stomach! You don't want to miss out on anything. • **Month of May/Admission charge**

Memphis Music and Heritage Festival
Beale St., 901/525-3655
Local blues, jazz, honky tonk, and "just out to have a good time and jam" artists gather where it all started to remind the local folks that life without music is pretty tired. The Memphis Music and Heritage Fest was organized by the Center of Southern Folklore to showcase local musical talent, to celebrate local artists and craftspeople, and to eat a little barbecue along Beale Street. Can you think of a better way to usher in the fall season? • **Labor Day Weekend/Admission charge**

Memphis Arts Festival/Taste of Memphis
Memphis Botanic Garden, 901/761-1278
The Memphis Botanic Garden becomes even more beautiful when more than 150 artists gather among the flowers to show off their talent at the annual Arts in the Park. All media are represented, all pieces are judged, and everyone is invited to participate. Five stages strategically placed amidst the roses feature a variety of performances, from the Memphis Ballet to Nubian Theater to a tight groove on some down-and-dirty Memphis blues. The Taste of Memphis doesn't hold back, offering everything from slow-smoked barbecue to ethnic treats. • **Third Weekend in October/Admission charge**

Southern Heritage Classic
Liberty Bowl Stadium, 901/398-6655
Folks come from all over not one, but two states to root for their favorite teams, those from historical Black colleges Tennessee State University and Jackson State University. But with all that socializin' going on, who has time to watch the game? Halftime catches everyone's eye when the Battle of the Bands takes center stage to rock the stadium. In addition to the classic itself, golf tournaments, concerts, fashion shows, and profilin' make this the see-and-be-seen event of the year. • **Second Saturday in September/Admission charge**

Museums

Center for Southern Folklore
209 Beale St., 901/525-3655
The Center for Southern Folklore is a colorful, funky little museum dedicated to the preservation of the sounds that made Memphis famous. In addition to photographs and memorabilia, the center showcases live local blues, jazz, R&B, rockabilly, and gospel artists weekly in a smoke-free performance space. Enjoy a moonpie as you take a fascinating walking tour of Beale Street and are regaled with accounts of past and present musical quests, political upheavals, and historical facts about each landmark. • **Free (donations welcome)/Charge for mini-concerts**

Hunt-Phelan Home
533 Beale St., 901/344-3166
Nestled among the fragrant old magnolia trees, this restored antebellum home, built with slave labor in 1828 and filled with antiques dating back to the 1600s, is one of the oldest and most historically significant homes in Memphis. After the Civil War ended, a small schoolhouse was built on the sprawling grounds by members of the Freedman's Bureau. There, several hundred emancipated slaves were taught how to read and write. • **Admission charge**

Memphis Music Hall of Fame
97 S. Second, 901/525-4007
Everything you wanted to know about the Memphis sound, as revealed

If Beale Street Could Talk

As W. C. Handy's song says, "If Beale Street could talk…" Hmm, what would it say? Would it tell on itself and share tales of wild all-night brawls and balls? Would it reflect on the many injustices its residents have endured, of the corruption it has seen? Or would it just sing the blues? This famous strip is today filled with modern-day juke joints, junky souvenir stands, and plenty of rich African American history. Here are a few sites worth visiting while cruising Beale Street:

Center for Southern Folklore, 126–130 Beale St.—Dedicated to the preservation of southern folklore.

First Baptist Beale Street Church, 379 Beale St.—Built in 1881 by the Reverend Morris Henderson.

Handy Park, Third and Beale St.—Features a statue of W. C. Handy and live music most weekends.

Hunt-Phelan Home, 533 Beale St.—One of the oldest antebellum homes in Memphis.

Ida B. Wells Marker, Convention and Visitors Bureau on Beal St.—Honors Civil Rights movement crusader and editor of the Memphis *Free Speech*.

Old Daisy Theater, 329 Beale St.—Home of the Beale Street Blues Museum, which chronicles the evolution of the blues from slavery to the present day.

Orpheum Theater, Beale and S. Main Sts.

Pee Wee's Saloon, 317 Beale St.—Where W. C. Handy wrote "Mister Crump's Blues"—hence, the place where the blues was born.

Police Station, 159 Beale St.—This 24-hour museum recounts historic crimes committed in the Memphis area, including the assassination of Dr. Martin Luther King Jr.

W. C. Handy House Museum, 352 Beale St.—Features memorabilia from Handy's life.

Virtually untouched by time, the outside of the Civil Rights Museum remembers the Rev. Dr. Martin Luther King.

by photos, rare recordings, video and audio presentations, and countless personal memorabilia and instruments, is all right here! This museum houses the largest collection of W. C. Handy memorabilia in the world, the largest collection of Elvis Presley memorabilia outside Graceland, and an extensive collection of Stax and HI record labels memorabilia and tapes. • **Admission charge**

National Civil Rights Museum
450 Mulberry St., 901/521-9699

Considered by some the most important museum in the country, the National Civil Rights Museum tells us from whence we (African Americans) came and where we are going. From Michael Pavlovsky's massive welcoming statue, *Movement to Overcome*, to the background strains of Mahalia Jackson's "Precious Lord, Take My Hand," the

Check It Out

Art Museum of the University of Memphis, Communication and Fine Arts Building, 3750 Norriswood, 901/678-2224—The museum holds permanent collections of Egyptian antiquities and West African art. Temporary exhibitions are shown year-round in the main and adjacent galleries. · Free

Graceland, 3734 Elvis Presley Blvd., 800/238-2000—The only building Elvis will never leave, Graceland is a campy, outrageous journey through the life and times of a man who was larger than life. · Admission charge

Slavehaven/Burkle Estate Museum, 826 N. Second St., 901/527-3427—This small antebellum cottage was once a waystation on the Underground Railroad for thousands of runaway slaves. Secret cellars and trap doors reveal the hiding places and escape routes of the fugitives from bondage as they plotted their way north to freedom. · Admission charge

Sun Studios, 706 Union Ave., 901/521-0664—B. B. King, Charlie Pride, Rufus Thomas, Little Milton, Elvis Presley, Roy Orbison, and countless others recorded hits for Sun Records at this studio.

museum tells a long, moving story. Permanent interactive exhibits include a "ride" on the city bus with Rosa Parks, a walk up the steps of Central High School with the Little Rock Nine, and a sit-in at the Woolworth's lunch counter in Greensboro, North Carolina. Formerly the Lorraine Hotel, the museum is the site where Dr. Martin Luther King Jr. was assassinated, and pilgrims come from around the world to "say goodbye" to the great man. The powerful images, sounds, and feelings of that fateful day when Dr. King was murdered in Memphis are recaptured at the museum; many visitors are deeply affected by this exhibit. For showcasing civil rights memorabilia and presenting audiovisual displays of the monumental events that shaped America's history, the National Civil Rights Museum is a must-stop for people of all races. • **Admission charge**

Churches

Collins Chapel CME Church
678 Washington Ave., 901/525-2872
Listed on the National Register of Historic Places and built in 1841, the Collins Chapel CME Church was established before the founding of the CME denomination.

First Baptist Church
379 Beale St., 901/527-4832
Formally known as Beale Street Baptist Church, this was the first brick multi-story church in the country built by and for African Americans. It too is listed on the National Register of Historic Places.

Full Gospel Tabernacle
787 Hale Rd., 901/396-9192
With the Reverend Al Green (yes, *that* Al Green!) at the pulpit, you *know* the choir at this church has *got* to be good!

Mason Temple
930 Mason, 901/578-3800
Mason Temple is the international headquarters of the Church of God in Christ. It is also the site of Dr. Martin Luther King Jr.'s "I've Been to the Mountaintop" speech, delivered the day before his assassination.

Mississippi Boulevard Christian Church
70 N. Bellevue Blvd., 901/729-6222
This church houses arguably the largest African American congregation in Memphis.

Recreation

Memphis Queen Line Riverboats
45 S. Riverside Dr., 800/221-6197
Go rollin' down the river—the mighty Mississippi, that is—in an old-fashioned riverboat that features daily sightseeing and dinner cruises.

Golf and Tennis

Public courses in the greater Memphis area:
Pine Hill Golf Course, 1005 Alice, 901/775-9434
Bellvue Tennis Center, 1310 S. Bellvue, 901/774-7199
Riverside Tennis Center, 435 South Pkwy. W., 901/774-4340

Miami

Miami. For many this city is a smoldering cauldron of non-stop debauchery, where anything goes—and that's why everyone does. For others, Miami is as pure as all outdoors, where the visitor's only goal is to be at one with sun, sand, and sea. With miles and miles of sparkling beaches, saucy hot bodies showing off the results of laborious sit-ups and step classes, and the shimmering Atlantic just steps away, Miami offers plenty of reasons to cancel that trip to the Caribbean. For years, Miami was America's best-kept secret, known only as the city of a million golf courses. Folks believed all Miamians drove 25 miles an hour, and "*hot, hot, hot!*" was used only in reference to the weather.

Well, damn the media and their 24/7 television coverage! Today, Miami is *the* destination for celebrity spying and movie and fashion shoots. The city's newfound fame makes it the world's plumpest oyster, and *everyone* is clamoring to shuck their way into its pearly delights.

Although the irresistible lure of Miami Beach can be overpowering, start your tour of Miami with a trek through the neighborhoods—an ethnic pepper-pot mix that saves the city from sinking head first into total superficiality. First stop: Overtown, one of Miami's oldest Black communities. There's no better way to start the morning than at Overtown's premier down-home eatery, Jackson's Soul Food, where you can down a plate of steamed catfish, grits, scrambled eggs, and piping hot biscuits. After breakfast, head to the blocks between N.W. Second and Third Avenues and

N.W. Ninth and Tenth Streets, an area being restored to its original glory under the auspices of the recently established Historic Overtown Folklife Village. Note the side of the Lyric Theatre, which features one of the finest murals in the city, a tribute to great African Americans past and present.

A couple of blocks southwest of Overtown is Little Havana, home to Miami's large Cuban American community. The heart of this community is Calle Ocho, or S.W. Eighth Street, where the pungent fragrance of cigars, hand-rolled Havana-style, permeates the air, and the smoky bouquet clashes with the mouthwatering aroma of chicken and rice wafting from the many eateries lining the strip.

Southeast of Little Havana is the picturesque Coconut Grove. Developed by Bahamian laborers in the 1880s, Coconut Grove was the site of the first Black community on the south Florida mainland.

Head north on I-95 to another of Miami's flourishing African American neighborhoods, Liberty City. The community's pride shines bright through the signature chromatic murals that decorate many structures.

Little Haiti is the center of Miami's Haitian American community. Within the heart of the village are the sights, sounds, and smells of the area's renowned Caribbean Marketplace, a colorful, maddening bazaar where anything and everything is sold.

Next, take the John F. Kennedy Causeway to Miami Beach, which perhaps should be called Fantasy Island for it offers to fulfill the wildest, most decadent dreams imaginable. The Art Deco District in South Beach is what all the rest of the fuss is about. At night, Ocean Drive pulsates with reckless in-line skaters, curious tourists, dressed-to-impress drag queens, models, artists, exhibitionists, and college kids—all drawn like flies to the magical, candy-colored lights of the most famous adult playground in the world. With the fabulously restored hotels of South Beach serving as fantastic backdrops, the beautiful (and not so beautiful) people can be found hopping in and out of the Beach's several open-air bars, restaurants, and nightclubs all night long. The infectious beat of Latin music vibrates from every other club, commanding normally stiff hips to shake uncontrollably, release all inhibitions, and surrender every ounce of moral fiber to the crisp sea air. Ahhhhh, as Will Smith sings, "Welcome to Miami!"

Restaurants

In Miami, the Caribbean's influence is evident on nearly every menu. Cuban, Haitian, Bahamian, Trinidadian, and Jamaican fare are some of the savory cuisines available throughout southern Florida. Flaky empanadas stuffed with spicy shredded beef, pungent curried goat, traditional rice and peas, tasty boiled fish and a dense johnny cake, fiery jerk pork and tender oxtails are just a few enticing menu selections awaiting to tickle your taste buds in Miami.

Fine Dining

✳Ortanique on the Mile
278 Miracle Mile, Coral Gables, 305/446-7710
Christened after a citrusy fruit indigenous to the Jamaican plains (a cross between an orange and a tangerine), Ortanique is just as tart and tantalizing as its namesake. Its decor brings the richness of the islands to the Gables with a lush dining room bathed in soft tropical greens and yellows and lavishly accented with exotic flowers and, of course, its signature fruit.

Serving some of the very best New World Caribbean cuisine in the country, Ortanique introduces you to a plethora of seasonings and spices. A trio of ceviches offers a wonderful tangy sampling; seafood entrées include black grouper kissed with the signature ortanique liqueur sauce; and desserts continue the decadent decline with delicious banana fritters drunken with dark rum and sobered up with a scoop of cinnamon ice cream! Ouch! • **$40+/AA**

Casual Dining

✳Bahamian Connection Restaurant
4490 NW Second Ave., 305/576-6999
This small no-frills neighborhood spot transports you to the islands with sweet aromas from the kitchen and friendly banter among the regulars. Breakfast at the Bahamian Connection consists of boiled fish swimming in lemon, onion, and pepper. It may sound a bit plain, but nothing could be further from the truth. And served with what one devoted regular calls "the best johnny cake in Miami," breakfast doesn't get much better than this. At lunchtime, fried or

If You're Driving Up the Coast, Stop In...

✳Betty's Restaurant & Catering, 601 NW 22nd Rd., Fort Lauderdale, 954/583-9121—In the comfortable dining area, you'll find local politicians, national celebrities, sports figures, and devoted regulars chowing down on Betty's delicious southern-style breakfasts. Chopped steak with onions served with eggs and hot biscuits is a great way to start the day. · $10+/AA

✳Ellington's 2009, Harrison St., Hollywood, 954/920-9322—Named after the Duke himself, Ellington's pays tribute to the master nightly with terrific live jazz, sensuous ambience, and a sophisticated dinner menu. Sunday jazz brunch is a must. · $25+/AA

✳Riverwalk Eatery, 215 SW Second St., Fort Lauderdale, 954/760-4373—One of Lauderdale's favorite and brightest dining spots, Riverwalk serves a menu of savory American classics as exciting as the restaurant's decor. Must-tries include the zesty chili and warm, corny cornbread laced with delicious extras and any of several vegetarian delights. · $15+/AA

✳Tom's Place, 7251 N. Federal Hwy., Boca Raton, 561/997-0920—Boca's premier barbecue spot, this large, comfortable family restaurant has been around for years, serving up great food to Boca Raton's well-heeled patrons. Barbecued ribs, sliced beef, baby backs, and sides galore are among the items on Tom's extensive menu. · $10+/AA

Tom Jenkins Bar-B-Q, 1236 S. Federal Hwy., Fort Lauderdale, 954/522-5046—This charming Texas-style restaurant rustles up a pile of tangy chopped pork barbecue, smoky, tender ribs, chicken, collard greens, mac and cheese, and, of course, barbecue baked beans. · $10+/AA

steamed conch, steamed fish, and oxtails are among the favorites. · **$10/AA**

Casa Juancho Restaurant
2436 SW Eighth St., 305/642-2452
When it comes to fine dining *en Español*, Casa Juancho is where the well heeled go for the freshest seafood and tender beef, prepared on an

oak-burning grill. Start with the oak-roasted peppers stuffed with cod-fish mousse (sounds strange, tastes great!), then sample the shrimp, fish grilled in garlic sauce, or the oak-grilled prime sirloin topped with Spanish blue cheese. For the hopeless romantic in all of us, mariachis stroll from table to table to serenade the lovely señoritas. • **$35+**

✳Jackson's Soul Food
950 NW Third Ave., 305/377-6710
Miami's historic Overtown district has a lot to be proud of these days, and Jackson's Soul Food is one of them. This modest neighborhood spot serves a serious down-home breakfast with early morning preparations starting at 5:45. So big props go to the staff who are in the back cooking the smothered chicken wings, liver and onions, and pork chops with eggs, grits, and flaky homemade biscuits. • **$10/AA**

✳People's Bar-B-Que
360 NW Eighth St., 305/373-8080
Since 1961, People's Bar-B-Que has offered healthy portions of real-deal soul food at terrific prices. In addition to great barbecue chicken and ribs, People's buffet line serves up meat loaf, beef stew, fried fish, pork chops, and baked ham, as well as a large assortment of side dishes. On Sunday, it becomes a serious destination for banana pudding. • **$10+/AA**

Tap Tap
819 Fifth St., Miami Beach, 305/672-2898
Tap Tap is an authentic Haitian café disguised as an elaborate gallery showcasing the finest in Haitian and Caribbean art. Or is it the other way around? Every wall, doorway, ceiling, and crevice is covered with a kaleidoscope of brilliant color that exhibits the flamboyance of Haiti—inspired by the vibrantly painted Tap Tap buses that transport people across the Haitian countryside.

Start your culinary ride with lightly fried conch fritters in a mild watercress sauce, then ease into creamy pumpkin soup. Grilled chicken with carrots, cabbage, and watercress sauce; grilled snapper in a citrusy, lime sauce; shrimp in spicy Creole sauce; and stewed goat in tomato chayote sauce are just a few of the island delights at Tap Tap. • **$20+/AA**

Off the Beaten Path

Caribbean Delight Restaurant, 236 NE First Ave., 305/381-9254—Right downtown, this modest spot serves it up on the authentic Jamaican tip with plenty of jerk chicken, akee and salt-fish, and rice and peas. · $10+/AA

Ruby & Jean's Restaurant, 2190 NW 183rd St., 305/626-8100—This simple sit-down eatery serves lots of good soul food favorites. · $10+/AA

Sango Jamaican & Chinese Takeout Restaurant, 9485 SW 160th St., 305/252-0279—When you can't decide between the curried goat or the mushu pork, satisfy both cravings at Sango, the one-stop-shopping eatery. · $10/AA

Shaker's Conch House, 5330 NW 17th Ave., 305/693-6033—Shaker's does conch served every which way you can think of, along with other tasty island delights. · $10/AA

Versailles
3555 SW Eighth St., 305/444-0240
There is no way you can go to Miami and not revel in the Cuban experience. Versailles is about as authentic as you can get, serving great, classic Cuban fare, 24 hours a day at down-and-dirty prices. And don't let the fancy French name fool you. The kitchy decor and pseudo-resemblance to its namesake palace just add to the fun, bustling atmosphere. • **$15+**

Nightclubs

South Beach is one giant samba line where, on any given night, throngs of revelers swing in and out of open-air venues to a ceaseless salsa beat. But if your rumba is a little rusty, you can get your groove on any number of throw down dance clubs around the Miami Beach area.

*Bar Room
320 Lincoln Rd., Miami Beach, 305/604-0480

In the cycle of nightclubs, this place is enjoying its 15 minutes of fame. But, given how fickle club kids are, who knows how long Bar Room will be the darling of the beach. Until then, arrive early if you want to get in. House and techno music rock the international crowd. • **Cover charge**

*Champagne
1060 NE 79th St. Causeway, 305/754-6036

Located about 20 minutes from downtown Miami, Champagne is a much more mellow scene compared to the congested South Beach mob scene. This upscale lounge honors jazz royalty with colorful wall murals paying tribute to Sir Duke Ellington and Lady Billie Holiday. Champagne serves a classic continental menu with an emphasis on fresh seafood. Live music from the city's most talented traditional jazz bands is featured every weekend. • **Music charge/AA**

*Chaos
743 Washington Ave., Miami Beach, 305/674-7350

This club is out of control, very high energy, very NYC, very fat, very naughty. Music is all over the board, because at Chaos, it's all about the party. • **Cover charge/AA**

Groove Jet
323 23rd St., Miami Beach, 305/532-5150

Thursday is the night to run through Groove Jet, when Russell Simmons and his boyz rock the house. R&B, house, and hip-hop music are featured. • **Cover charge**

*Mango's Tropical Café
900 Ocean Dr., Miami Beach, 305/673-6743

This is the spot to break out that new red Spandex skirt and shake the results of four months of step class to the infectious sounds of salsa, merengue, and rumba. • **Cover charge**

*Marlin Bar Marlin Hotel
1200 Collins Ave., Miami Beach, 305/604-5000

Friday nights at the Marlin, all the folks get together to talk plenty of yang during happy hour, then party the night away. • **Cover charge**

✳Penrods on the Beach
1 Ocean Dr., Miami Beach, 305/538-1111
During the week, Penrods swings to a Latin beat, but on Saturdays, the people take over and the stars come out at night. • **Cover charge**

✳Timba
2898 Biscayne Blvd., 305/428-0500
Timba offers a cool, laid-back lounge atmosphere with jazz, R&B, hip-hop, and world music to please ears hungry for variety. • **Cover charge**

Festivals

Some kind of fun, funky festival is always going on any given day in one of Miami's colorful neighborhoods. The Martin Luther King Jr. Parade & Festival and the Miami/Goombay Festival attract the largest crowds, and not just from the Black community. Lets face it—we know how to party!

Martin Luther King Jr. Parade & Festival
Martin Luther King Jr. Blvd., 305/835-2464
More than 400,000 souls show up for this festival, one of the city's biggest community events. The parade route winds through 25 blocks of the Liberty City neighborhood, emptying into Martin Luther King Jr. Park at NW 62nd and 32nd Avenues. Rides, games, live music, stage performances, and lots of great food await the parade goers. • **MLK Holiday weekend/Free**

Sunstreet Festival
Calder Race Course, 305/751-8648
Just an old-fashioned carnival that grooves to a soulful beat, Sunstreet Festival is one of Miami's largest community events. African American pride swells as local musicians take the stage, some to praise God with the all-out Gospel Extravaganza, others to

Check Out These Performers While in Town

Black Door Dance Ensemble, 305/385-8960—Neoclassical ballet and modern dance performances. · AA

Body Nation Dance Theatre, 305/625-9310—Caribbean, reggae, folk, and modern dance performed in original and authentic costumes. · AA

Freddick Bratcher and Company, 305/448-2021—A modern dance troupe that showcases the ethnic diversity of southern Florida.

belt out familiar tunes on the R&B stage. In addition to games and rides for the kids, and dance and spoken word performances, the festival sponsors the Miss Sunstreet pageant and an oratorical contest for high school students eager to show off their verbal prowess to family and friends. • **Last weekend in February/Free**

Bob Marley Caribbean Festival
AT&T Amphitheater, Bayfront Park, 401 Biscayne Blvd.

Not just a party, this is a party with a purpose. The Bob Marley Festival not only honors the reggae giant's memory with a day of great music, but also encourages attendees to help out their community by donating nonperishables to Camillus House, a local charitable organization that distributes food and resources to the needy. • **Second Saturday in February/Admission charge**

Carnival Miami/Calle Ocho Festival
SW Eighth St., 305/644-8888

Considered the largest Latino festival in the country and one of the city's biggest annual events, Carnival Miami is a weeklong 23-block street party featuring music, food, dancing, and fun. Free concerts at Bayfront Park vibrate the downtown area with the rousing sounds of salsa and merengue. The last day of the fest, called Calle Ocho, more than a million people pack the street fair. Thirty blocks along Eight Street are closed off, while at least 30 stages resound all at once with live music. The result is a thunderous roar, yet somehow

Historic Overtown Folklife Village

Located between NW Second and Third Avenues and NW Ninth and Tenth Streets, Historic Overtown Folklife Village has spearheaded the rebirth of two historic blocks in one of Miami's oldest neighborhoods. Like so many communities across the country that fell prey to urban decay, Overtown desperately needed revitalization. The efforts of Dorothy Fields, founder of the Black Archives History and Research Foundation of South Florida, Inc., gave Overtown the new lease on life it deserved.

Established in 1896, "Colored Town" was where Blacks were allowed to live. And live they did, building successful businesses, hotels, churches, schools, and nightclubs. Luminaries like Ella Fitzgerald, Cab Calloway, and Nat King Cole performed in Overtown, and boxer Joe Louis and baseball legend Jackie Robinson vacationed here during the winter. Historic Overtown Folklife Village refuses to allow its history to be forgotten. Long-term goals include converting these blocks into a pedestrian mall dotted with restaurants, retail units, and office space. Call 305/638-6064 for current details. Newly renovated Overtown landmarks include:

Cola Nip Building—Owned and operated by African Americans at the turn of the century, this was the first manufacturing plant in Dade County's Black community.

D.A. Dorsey House—Built in 1915 by real estate magnate Dorsey, this site is now a children's museum that relates the Black experience in Dade County from a "multicultural perspective."

Greater Bethel AME Church—This church was built in 1896, the year the City of Miami was incorporated.

Lyric Theater—Built in 1913 by African American entrepreneur Geder Walker, this community theater is ready to relive its glory days.

Mt. Zion Baptist Church—This church was also built in 1896.

The historic Lyric Theater is one of the first buildings tenderly restored to its original beauty, by the Historic Overtown Folklife Village.

the syncopated sounds blend into one rhythm. Hundreds of vendors sell everything from chicken empanadas to short red-and-gold lamé dance skirts, perfect attire for evening parties at area clubs—*if* you have any energy left, that is! • **First week in March/Free**

Roots & Culture Festival
N. Miami Ave. between 54th and 62nd Sts., 305/751-4222
Imagine hundreds of thousands of bodies in motion, arms swaying in the air, some folks weeping with pleasure, all singing the anthem "One Love" in unison with reggae queen Rita Marley. Little Haiti's North Miami Avenue swarms with jubilant members of the

Caribbean community as they gather to celebrate the Roots & Culture Festival. Some 40 of the hottest Haitian, reggae, R&B, and Latin bands excite the masses until the late evening hours. Spoken word performers and colorful dance troupes also take the stages, vendors peddle unusual artifacts and jewelry, and rides and games entice the kids. And of course, there's Caribbean fare a-plenty for hungry revelers. • **May/Free**

Miami/Bahamas Goombay Festival
Downtown Coconut Grove, 305/372-9966
More than 600,000 folks from all over the state descend on Coconut Grove during the Miami/Bahamas Goombay Festival, America's largest Black heritage festival. You'll swear you're in Nassau when you hear the "rake 'n' scrape" bands, which groove to drums, whistles, cow bells, and combs, and inspire brilliantly costumed "junkanoo" dancers and high steppers to make their way down Grant Avenue to celebrate the Caribbean influence in the Americas. Some 300 vendors line the streets to proffer everything from delicious Bahamian eats to authentic Caribbean clothing and handcrafted items—such as that much-needed wide-brim hat you've been needing to protect you from Miami's noonday sun. • **First weekend in June/Free**

Miami Reggae Festival
AT&T Amphitheater, Bayfront Park, 401 Biscayne Blvd., 305/891-2944
Local bands and top-notch nationally known groups play this annual weekend festival to celebrate the music of the islands. • **First weekend in August/Music charge**

Caribbean Carnival
Opa-Locka Airport, 305/435-4845
The outrageous sights, sounds, dances, foods, and colors of the Caribbean explode the second weekend of every October when Mardi Gras comes early to Miami. Revelers in elaborate costumes— some of which weigh more than the wearer!—strut gracefully through the streets along with towering stilt walkers, marching steel drum bands, and the crowned king and queen of the festival. In the evenings, Soca Fest takes to the stage with over a half a dozen bands performing into the early morning light. On Sunday, the party really

gets started when more than 25 bands compete in the Grand Parade of Masquerade Bands. • **Second weekend in October/Admission charge for some events**

Museums

African Heritage Cultural Arts Center
6161 NW 22nd Ave., 305/638-6771

A spectacular multi-arts center located in the middle of the 'hood, the African Heritage Cultural Arts Center encompasses four complexes and includes a dance studio, visual arts complex, art gallery, black box theater, and scene shop. The Amazaldi Gallery showcases some of the nation's most influential artists, including William Falkner, Jacob Lawrence, and many local talents. • **Donations accepted**

Black Heritage Museum
Gulf Stream Elementary School
20900 SW 97th Ave., 305/232-3535

The material on display at the Black Heritage Museum is only a minuscule representation of the extensive collection of Black heritage

Gallery Hoppin'

Carlos Art Gallery, 3444 Main Hwy., Suite 9, Coconut Grove, 305/445-3020—A wonderful collection of original Haitian art. • AA

Dinizulu Gene Tinnie, 525 NW 29th St., 305/751-9791—Talented local artists collectively showcase a spectrum of artifacts from the African Diaspora. • AA

Gallery Antigua Inc., 5130 Biscayne Blvd., 305/759-5355—A collection of mixed media includes prints, sculptures, and posters. • AA

Haitian Art Factory, 835 NE 79th St., 305/758-6939—A colorful medley of Haitian paintings and artifacts. • AA

from around the world collected by the museum's president, renowned Civil Rights activist Priscilla Gwendolyn Stephens Kruize. Left homeless by Hurricane Andrew in 1992, the majority of the museum's collection remains in storage until a permanent address is secured. But through generous efforts from the government of Ghana, the museum opened a branch at the DuBois Center in Accra in 1999. Future overseas sites include Zimbabwe, South Africa, Brazil, and Suriname. The permanent exhibit features rare chairs from the African Diaspora, a touching collection of artifacts celebrating the Black mother and child, and several items honoring Dr. Martin Luther King Jr., including an autographed book given to Kruize. A visit to the museum would not be complete without meeting Priscilla Kruize herself, the museum's curator and a font of information. • **Donations accepted/AA**

Historical Museum of Southern Florida
101 W. Flagler St., 305/375-1492
Located in the Miami-Dade Cultural Center, the Historical Museum of Southern Florida features, among other exhibits, an important permanent retrospective of the history of African Americans in southern Florida and their significant contributions to Miami's development. • **Admission charge**

Churches

Ebenezer Methodist Church
2001 NW 35th St., 305/635-7413
In 1898, four pioneering families joined together to establish the Ebenezer Episcopal Church. A local mill donated the lumber used to build the first structure between 1906 and 1907 in the now-historic neighborhood of Overtown. Over the years, Ebenezer underwent many changes, but it was the economic hardships that befell the Overtown community in the 1970s that forced Ebenezer to relocate to its current home.

Greater Bethel AME Church
245 NW Eighth St., 305/371-9102
One of the oldest African American congregations in the city, the

Greater Bethel AME Church is part of the Historic Overtown Folklife Village restoration project. Founded in 1896, Greater Bethel is listed on the National Register of Historic Places.

Macedonia Missionary Baptist Church
3315 Douglas Rd., 305/445-6459
Macedonia Missionary Baptist Church originated in 1894 when 56 members left the Union Chapel, an integrated but separated church, to organize a new congregation where they could worship without fear of persecution within their own sanctuary.

Masjid Al-Ansar
5245 NW Seventh Ave., 305/757-8741
This orthodox Muslim mosque is the oldest and largest Masjid in southern Florida.

St. John's Institutional Missionary Baptist Church
1328 NW Third Ave., 305/372-3877
St. John's Institutional Missionary Baptist Church was established on June 17, 1906, under the name the Second Baptist Church, then changed to St. John's Baptist Church. In 1940, St. John's parishioners joyously marched from their former sanctuary into a brand new church built exclusively for them. Back then, St. John's was not only the first Black church in Miami to move into a new building, but the first to be built by an African American contractor, McKissack & McKissack. Today, this beautiful Overtown edifice is listed on the National Register of Historic Places.

Recreation

Beaches

When you're talkin' Miami, you're talkin' beaches. Whether it's showing off your lime green thong in the infamous South Beach area, or basking in the rays after a morning of Bal Harbour shopping, or strolling mile after magnificent mile on Miami Beach, in this town, life is a beach! If you want more exercise than turning the pages of that latest mystery you're reading, check out parks at Key Biscayne,

In Miami, life really is a beach!

where you can golf, tennis, bike, do water sports, and, of course, lie on the beach.

Golf

Golf is a way of life in Miami; there are countless courses to choose from. Contact the Greater Miami Convention & Visitors Bureau at 800/933-8448 for a list of the area's finest courses and golf resorts.

Black Enterprise Golf and Tennis Challenge
Doral Golf Resort and Spa, 800/209-7229

This is the crème de la crème of social events. Publisher Earl Graves and the *Black Enterprise* family assemble prominent African Americans in business, finance, politics, and marketing for a weekend of relaxation, networking, and lots of fun. Nightly corporate-sponsored receptions keep the entertainment, food, and bar flowing until late in the evening. During the day attendees enjoy tennis and golf tournaments (lessons for beginners are available). Between rounds, the ladies at the ultra-luxurious Doral spa pamper guests with soothing herbal wraps and relaxing deep-tissue massages.

Past years' highlights have included former Boston Celtic Cedric "Cornbread" Maxwell as a formidable bid wist opponent, golf legends Lee Elder and Charlie Sifford coaching folks on their golf swings, and former Atlanta mayor Maynard Jackson and his wife sharing a friendly laugh with friends old and new. • **Labor Day weekend**

New Orleans

New Orleans. The mere mention of the name conjures up mystery and excitement. Ask anyone who's ever been to the "Big Easy" and they'll likely exclaim, "It's my favorite city!" And what's not to love? Splendid St. Louis Cathedral in Jackson Square provides an elegant backdrop to the sidewalk fortune tellers, hotdog vendors, and street performers who proffer their wares. The grave of the high voodoo priestess, Marie Laveau, located at St. Louis No. 1 graveyard on Basin Street, attracts pilgrims daily. And the food! Sit down to a hot bowl of okra gumbo, a plate of red beans and rice, a side of "pok chops," French bread to sop up the juice, and a cold Dixie beer. This is as good as it gets! Evenings, jazz, zydeco, and low-down, dirty blues fill the always-humid air.

Located in the heart of the city is the world-famous French Quarter. The day doesn't start right without a breakfast of fried catfish, grits, and hot, homemade biscuits. Next, burn off those calories with a walk to the Historic French Market, where locals have shopped for 200 years. Just past the rainbow of fresh produce and rows of hot sauce and Creole seasoning, the real fun begins. You can spend hours sifting through table after table of deliciously junky souvenirs in search of the ultimate bargain. Serious shoppers comb Royal Street for exquisite antique jewelry and furniture.

Next, step outside the Vieux Carré to see how the locals live. Hop on the Canal Street streetcar for a ride through the Garden District and down St. Charles Avenue, past some of the most beautiful homes in the country. Take a cab ride through Tremé, America's oldest African American suburb. The neighborhood has lost its former luster, but you can hear about its illustrious past from area locals when you stop for lunch at Dooky Chase's; order a bowl of Ms. Leah Chase's famous Creole gumbo.

After a power nap, you'll be ready to hit the most infamous street in the Quarter: Bourbon Street. A stroll down this naughty pedestrian path exposes you to outrageous strip joints, gay dance clubs, funky jazz bars, and countless T-shirt joints and daiquiri shops. Even in the afternoon, Bourbon Street reeks of stale beer and yesterday's trash. But, hey, don't let that stop you! Bourbon Street is a must-stop for every visitor. Besides, Mike Anderson's Seafood restaurant is one of the best spots to gorge on oysters on the half shell, the best crawfish bisque, and stuffed crab. After dinner, head over to Snug Harbor Jazz Club and groove to the mellow sounds of New Orleans's master of jazz, Ellis Marsalis. Not ready to turn in? After the set, sneak off to Harrah's Casino for a little late-night blackjack. Around 1:30 a.m. is the perfect time to head to Café du Monde for a cup of steaming hot café au lait and a plate of warm beignets. Make sure your camera has film, so you'll have proof for your friends back home that you and your buddies indulged in a true French Quarter delicacy—the powdered sugar on everyone's face will testify! It's now 3 a.m. and a nightcap is in order. No surprise, there's no last call in New Orleans and a bar is always open. In fact, you can get your drink to go for the walk back to the hotel! Twenty near-perfect hours in New Orleans. Now I ask you, how can one city be so good at being so bad?

Restaurants

Food and New Orleans is a marriage that will never be broken. Meals are so memorable that every activity is planned around them. Where else can you feast on three pounds of boiled crawfish ("crayfish" is northern jargon!) and spicy potatoes served on yesterday's newspaper, shrimp étouffée, overstuffed fried oyster po-boys, a mile-high muffuletta sandwich, and fiery hot sausage hamburgers? Many imitate but few can duplicate the love and skill that go into preparing a good Creole meal. Bread pudding with raisins that have soaked in rum for over a year. Real dirty rice with fresh parsley and chicken gizzards. *These are a few of our favorite foods.* Get your fork ready and worry about that diet when you get home!

Fine Dining

✳Dooky Chase's
2301 Orleans Ave., 504/821-0600
Few New Orleans restaurants have gained the national recognition Dooky Chase's enjoys. The reason behind the success and longevity of this culinary institution? Quite simply, Leah Chase, proprietor and ever-gracious hostess, claims the "goal at Dooky Chase's is to provide our customers with a delicious meal and serve it elegantly, in the manner in which we deserve to be treated." Dooky Chase's offers a complete dinner menu, à la carte dining, and a lunch buffet Monday through Friday. Entrées include crawfish étouffée, shrimp *Clemençeau* (shrimp sautéed in garlic butter and mixed with vegetables), veal grillades, fried oysters, and stuffed lobster. And let's not forget Creole gumbo and Mamere's crab soup for starters! • **$20+/AA**

✳Olivier's Restaurant
204 Decatur St., 504/525-7734
You never know which musicians or celebrities may fall into Olivier's, located across from the House of Blues, for a bowl of gumbo and French bread. Blair Underwood and his wife were seen enjoying a plate of Olivier's famous oysters, served two ways: oysters Rockefeller and pecan-breaded oysters. Other house specialties include Creole Rabbit, Poulet au Fromage, Taster's Platter (fried seafood), Pork Medallions, and Beef Bourgignon. The Gumbo Sampler allows you to try three versions of Louisiana gumbo. Yummy! • **$20+/AA**

Dickie Brennen's Steakhouse
716 Iberville St., 504/522-CHOP
Leave it to the first family of New Orleans dining to elevate steak to new, decadent heights. Imagine an eight-ounce filet mignon, medium rare, drizzled with a rich béarnaise sauce, surrounded by plump fried oysters and creamy spinach. Or your favorite chop topped with a mountain of tender crabmeat sautéed in spiced butter. If that's not enough to send you into artery-clogged shock, the lus-

Jackets Are Suggested

The following are New Orleans dining establishments worth a splurge for special occasions:

✳**Bayona**, 430 Dauphine St., 504/525-4455—If you're tired of Creole cuisine (how could that be!), Bayona offers the best in nouvelle cuisine. The velvet shrimp are amazing! · $35+

✳**Commander's Palace**, 1403 Washington Ave., 504/899-8221—This exquisite mansion-turned-restaurant is the ultimate in Creole fine dining. · $40+

✳**Galatoire's**, 209 Bourbon St., 504/525-2021—Traditional Creole cuisine in an elegant, although slightly intimidating, setting. · $40+

cious bananas Foster bread pudding topped with homemade ice cream and warm rum-raisin crème will definitely do you in! But what a way to go! • **$45+**

Casual Dining

Bennachin
133 N. Carrollton, 504/486-1313
The name means "one pot," which is how the many African dishes, such as jambalaya, are prepared at this neighborhood restaurant. Bennachin's customers are treated to a tantalizing blend of African cuisines, served in a casual down-home setting decorated with African artifacts and paintings. Favorites include *kembel-ioppa* (sautéed lamb strips and bell pepper with ginger), *bomok-chobi* (baked stuffed trout), and *bennachin* (beef jambalaya served with sautéed spinach). The prices are right, too. Daily lunch specials typically run under $5, and the portions are generous. • **$15/AA**

Eddie's Restaurant
2119 Law St., 504/945-2207
The Baquets, one of New Orleans' oldest restaurant families, have

Local Flava

Dunbar's Fine Foods, 4927 Freret St., 504/899-0734—Traditional New Orleans dishes like gumbo, red beans and rice, fried chicken, and cornbread are on the menu at this well-known neighborhood spot. · $10/AA

✳**Loretta's New Orleans Authentic Pralines**, 1100 N. Peters, Stall 17, French Market, French Quarter, 504/529-6170—You'll find the best pralines in the city here, along with praline sauces, assorted fudges, and other good stuff. · AA

Montrel's Creole Café, 4116 Marigny, 504/288-6374—Montrel's provides an enjoyable dining experience with friendly service and good traditional Creole dishes. · $15+/AA

Rita's Olde French Quarter Restaurant, 945 Rue Chartres St., 504/525-7543—Rita's serves Creole and Cajun meals "with a soulful flair." · $15+/AA

served delicious food in their community for more than 50 years. Eddie's po-boy sandwiches—oyster, catfish, shrimp, or hot sausage, all "dressed," of course—make lunchtime a heavenly meal. For dinner, start with filé (pronounced "fee-lay") gumbo or oyster-stuffed bread. Red beans and rice, breaded veal, stuffed shrimp in seafood sauce, and trout *Baquet* (broiled trout with lump crabmeat) are some of the favorites served daily. • **$15+/AA**

✳**Felix's Restaurant & Oyster Bar**
739 Iberville St., 504/522-4440
It's all about oysters at this popular Bourbon Street seafood joint. The perfect dining orgy for the pearl-baring lover starts with a bowl of creamy oyster stew. If you sit in the side room, you can watch the talented shuckers open oyster after oyster, and serve them up raw with a side of hot sauce and horseradish for your slurping pleasure. Fried oyster po-boys are the real specialty of the house and Felix's serves them as they should, overstuffed with butter, pickles, and a cold beer on the side. • **$15+**

✳Mike Anderson's Seafood
215 Bourbon St., 504/524-6334

Whether it's fried, broiled, baked, or raw, Mike Anderson's got your seafood! Highly recommended: crawfish bisque. Bisque is a thick brown spicy stock that's packed with crawfish tails and stuffed crawfish bodies. Because crawfish bisque is so labor-intensive, few places serve this New Orleans delicacy. Thank you, Mike Anderson, for recognizing and preserving one of life's little pleasures! • **$25+**

Palmer's Jamaican Restaurant
135 N. Carrollton Ave., 504/482-3658

Palmer's Jamaican Restaurant is considered one of the best in a city flooded with great eateries. This neighborhood spot, about 10 minutes from the Quarters, is not fancy but the food is fabulous. Palmer's must-tries include the chicken roti, the shrimp *Joanne* (sautéed shrimp on a slice of eggplant), *mélange de Rebecca* (shrimp and chicken sautéed with vegetables in a Chardonnay cream sauce), and Jamaican chicken. Top off your meal with a cup of Blue Mountain coffee. A lunch buffet is served daily. • **$10+/AA**

✳The Praline Connection
542 Frenchmen St., 504/943-3934
901-07 S. Peters St., 504/523-3973 (Gospel & Blues Hall)

Proprietor Curtis Moore describes the menu at the Praline Connection as "down-home cooking that no one wants to prepare anymore." The restaurant's Sunday gospel brunch is the best way to sample it all. Live inspirational music and an extensive buffet will satisfy both hungers. Pass on the breakfast bar and head straight for the buffet's terrific filé gumbo, red beans and rice, fried chicken, stuffed bell peppers with crabmeat, BBQ ribs, and fried catfish. Don't forget dessert: super-sweet bread pudding with praline sauce and, of course, fresh pralines (pronounced "praw-leens," not "pray"). • **$20 +/AA**

✳Two Sisters Restaurant
223 N. Derbigny St., 504/524-0056

Two Sisters Restaurant sits on the outskirts of the French Quarter near Tremé, and it's well worth crossing North Claiborne to get there. That's because Two Sisters is the *real deal* Creole/soul food restaurant in New Orleans! The outside of the restaurant looks like it never recovered from the last hurricane, but inside it smells like heaven. City officials to national celebrities swear by this small homey spot. Specials change daily, but you can be sure the following will be there to greet you: stewed shrimp with okra, stewed turkey wings, jambalaya, fried chicken, fried fish, and chitterlings. • **$10/AA**

✳Uglesich Restaurant & Bar
1238 Baronne, 504/523-8571
Don't let the exterior fool you. Uglesich looks like a dump, and one healthy gust of wind would probably flatten the joint. But the consistently good food has kept folks coming back for years. Specials include raw oysters, po-boy sandwiches, and fried seafood. • **$15+**

✳Zachary's Creole Cuisine
8400 Oak St., 504/865-1559
This bright, charming restaurant, located in the now-trendy uptown Carrollton neighborhood, sits next to old, double-shotgun cottages, just like the one from which Zachary's was fashioned. Lunchtime at this very popular restaurant finds local politicians and executives talking shop over an ample plate of red beans and hot sausage. Noteworthy entrées include stuffed trout with shrimp and crab dressing, 7th Ward Chop, jambalaya pasta, and Kelly's seafood platter. • **$20+ AA**

Nightclubs

Funky Butt at Congo Square
714 N. Rampart St., 504/558-0872
There's always a party going on at the Funky Butt! Live music nightly, good food, and friendly folks. What more do you want? • **Cover charge**

✳House of Blues
225 Decatur Ave., 504/529-2583
"Hey, pocko way!" House of Blues throws midnight dance parties that rock until 4 a.m., hosts local and nationally known live bands nightly, serves a delicious Creole and American menu, and offers plenty of two-stepping on the outside backyard patio. • **Cover charge**

Jazz History

The roots of jazz are firmly planted in New Orleans's soil. Old Congo Square (now Louis Armstrong Park), located on the edge of the French Quarter, is considered the birthplace of modern jazz. Back in 1817, the square was the only place in New Orleans where enslaved Africans were allowed to converse in their native tongues and play their native music. Over time, this music evolved to incorporate other harmonies and syncopations, including Black spirituals, the blues, and work songs. White musicians often gathered at the square to take note of this new musical style and adapt it as their own. Legend has it that the first band to call its music "jazz" was a white band that introduced Dixieland jazz to the North. (That's OK. We know where jazz *really* came from and, more importantly, who keeps it alive today!)

Jazz first came to the world's attention through the legendary sounds of Jelly Roll Morton, Buddy Bolden, and Louis Armstrong, all New Orleans natives. Fast forward to the fabulous fifties, when Crescent City produced the "godfather" of New Orleans funk, Professor Longhair, and his Mardi Gras "second line" dance songs. The Professor's modernday apostle, Dr. John, as well as Fats Domino, R&B queens Irma Thomas and Ruth Brown, and songwriter Allen Toussaint began to commercialize the New Orleans sound. In the late sixties, the funky percussion of the Neville Brothers, led by the angelic voice of Aaron Neville, rocketed New Orleans to the top of the soul and pop charts. In the mid-eighties, young jazz trumpeters Wynton Marsalis and Terence Blanchard brought us back full circle to the tradition now known as "straight-ahead jazz." Today, this musical jambalaya is served up hot and steamin' at nightclubs throughout the city and showcased by music festivals held throughout the year.

*Mid City Lanes
4133 S. Carrollton Ave., 504/482-3133

OK, where else can you bowl a strike and then jam to the soulful sounds of Marva Wright while waiting for your next turn? Only at the Mid City Lanes, where live blues, zydeco, jazz, and R&B are featured Tuesday through Saturday evenings. • **Cover charge**

JaksonSquare, in the French Quarter, is a great place to catch wonderful street performers.

New Showcase Lounge
1915 N. Broad, 504/945-5612

Not all of the good music is found in the French Quarters. The New Showcase is located in the heart of the community and hosts some of New Orleans's premier groups, like bass player Walter Payton and his Snapbean Band, vocalist Betty Shirley, and the James Rivers Movement. You haven't lived till you've seen Rivers throw down on the electric bagpipes! • **Cover charge some nights/AA**

✷Preservation Jazz Hall
726 St. Peters St., 504/523-8939
For the serious jazz enthusiast, a jam session at Preservation Jazz Hall is not to be missed! Famous for showcasing everyone from Pete Fountain to the Olympia Brass Band, Preservation Hall is considered one of the original jazz venues in the French Quarter. • **Cover charge**

Prime Example
1909 N. Broad, 504/947-0763
This dance club rocks on the weekends when a DJ comes in to spin everything from hip-hop, R&B, and oldies to soft rap. The interior is much slicker than that of its neighbors, and the crowd is a little younger and hipper. Live music is featured on select nights; call for a calendar of events. • **Cover charge/AA**

✷Snug Harbor Jazz Bistro
626 Frenchman St., 504/949-0696
Each night New Orleans's best local talent jams at Snug Harbor. Legendary Ellis Marsalis appears weekly, as does Charmaine Neville, swayin' and singing her show-stopper, "Baby, Meet Me With Your Black Drawz On!" Located on the edge of the French Quarter, Snug Harbor always guarantees a terrific time. • **Cover charge**

✷Sweet Lorraine's
1931 St. Claude Ave., 504/945-9654
The outside of this local hangout is scary. Tacky silver tinsel hangs from its dilapidated wooden frame, and the neighborhood, on the far edge of the French Quarter, sits far from the bright lights of Bourbon Street. But once inside Sweet Lorraine's, you'll feel like Dorothy falling into Munchkin Land. The high-tech decor is rivaled only by the state-of-the-art band stage, host each weekend to the city's best musicians. For real local flavor, check this place out. If you're lucky, maybe Michael Ward will be performing. His electric jazz violin is awesome. • **No cover charge/AA**

✷Storyville District
125 Bourbon St., 504/410-1000
Featuring live jazz nightly, this new hot spot also serves a mean jazz brunch. Happy hour is the best time to enjoy the music and some of

the coldest raw oysters in the city! Any native will tell you: It's the only way to eat them! • **Cover charge**

Tipitina's
501 Napoleon Ave., 504/897-3943
Tipitina's French Quarter
233 N. Peters, 504/895-8477
Tipitina's on Napoleon Avenue is not for everyone. It's loud, wild, and totally out of control. The clientele leans toward the young college crowd. But, hey, don't let that stop you if you want to hear great live bands and party until they throw you out! Packed nightly to capacity, Tipitina's was one of the earliest places to host the Neville Brothers on a regular basis. Tipitina's in the French Quarter is more civilized, but get there early if you want a seat. But with the music that's being thrown down there, who could sit? • **Cover charge**

Festivals

New Orleans doesn't need a reason to throw a party or plan a parade. According to locals, the fact that the good Lord allowed you to wake up that morning is reason enough to celebrate! Whether it's a neighborhood social club celebrating the weekend or the two weeks of insanity known as Mardi Gras, New Orleans is *always* ready to throw down.

Mardi Gras
Citywide festivities, 504/556-5005
"Laissez les bon temps rouler!" means "Let's get this party started *right*!" Or somethin' like that. No matter the exact translation, imagine more than a million of your nearest and dearest friends parading in the streets, fighting over flying plastic beads and painted coconuts, and prancing around in ridiculous costumes they would never be caught dead in back home! Outrageous, rowdy, and *way* too much fun, Mardi Gras never fails to excite, shock, and intrigue—and it has always been that way!

Christian European countries celebrated Mardi Gras to enjoy a last hurrah before the start of Lent. Back in the early 1700s, French settlers began observing the event in Louisiana with masked balls and

Not to Be Missed

While in town, try to get invited to a Mardi Gras ball so you can see New Orleans high society step out in all its finery. African American balls include the Zulu Ball, the Bunch Ball, the Original Illinois Club Ball, and the Black Pirates Masquerade Ball.

Friday: Bunch Ball, Zulu Ball

Saturday: Endymion Parade

Sunday: Bacchus Parade

Tuesday (Mardi Gras): Zulu Parade, Rex Parade

raunchy street parades. Well, nothing has changed, and Mardi Gras today is considered the biggest free party in America. The festivities get started after January 6 (King's Day) and continue until Fat Tuesday. Mardi Gras Day parades start at 8:30 a.m., when the African American Zulu krewe begins to sashay down Jackson and Claiborne Avenues. Their elaborate truck floats comprise just one of some 15 different parades that will make their way downtown, where the city's mayor toasts each krewe's king and queen.

High school marching bands from all over the state join in the parades, as do musical groups such as the Olympia Brass Band and the Second Line Walking Club. The Mardi Gras Indians don spectacular feathered costumes—expensive handmade extravaganzas that sometimes weigh as much as the wearer. All day long city streets are lined with enthusiastic revelers, most of whom are hoarse by the end of the day from screaming, "Throw me something, Mister!" • **March 7, 2000; February 27, 2001; February 14, 2002**

French Quarter Festival
French Quarter, 504/522-5730
How could you not love a festival that boasts the world's largest jazz brunch? Started back in 1982 to bring locals back to the Quarter after street construction and repairs prior to the World's Fair kept them away, the annual French Quarter Festival now attracts more than 250,000 music and food lovers from all over the world.

The Second Line

The second line is a street dance/walk in which handkerchief wavin' and hip shakin' accompany a funky brass band beat—all to honor the newly deceased. It started back in the day when jazz musicians played their tribute to departed fellow musicians by parading through the city streets to the graveyard. First in the procession came the band, then the coffin, and then the family and friends of the deceased—the "second line." Musicians played a respectful, solemn song until the procession reached the grave site, but once the coffin was buried, they broke into a high-spirited tune that instantly transformed mourners into rejoicers celebrating their dearly beloved's release into heaven. This dancing and carrying-on continued all the way back to the *repás* (reception) and then well into the night.

Today, the second line, considered New Orleans's official dance, is performed—brass band, colorful costumes, feathers and all—at weddings, birthdays, political inaugurations, and of course, music festivals. Remember: New Orleans doesn't need an excuse to party. Any day will do!

A gala fundraising party on Thursday night kicks off the weekend events. More than 100 hours of live music performances take place throughout the Quarter, featuring everything from Cajun, gospel, and Dixieland jazz to classical and international sounds, satisfying every musical taste. More than 60 food booths line Jackson Square and Woldenberg Riverfront Park offering a taste of every food imaginable, from local favorites to international delicacies. A prelude to the city's Jazz & Heritage Festival, this event offers the most exciting backdrop of any music festival in the country: the world-famous Vieux Carré. • **Second weekend in April**

New Orleans Jazz & Heritage Festival
New Orleans Fair Grounds, 504/522-4786
Without question, the New Orleans Jazz & Heritage Festival is the greatest music and food event in the United States! No fewer than 70 bands on 12 stages offer jazz, gospel, Cajun, zydeco, R&B,

A colorful scaffolding covered with cardboard second-liners welcomes the crowds to the New Orleans Jazz & Heritage Festival.

blues, rock, folk, and funk performances over a seven-day period. Wear your running shoes to dash from stage to stage—you won't want to miss Sister Shirley Caesar raising the roof of the Gospel Tent with her spiritually charged rendition of "Amazing Grace." At the Congo Square stage, wave your white handkerchief to salute the Wild Magnolia Mardi Gras Indians as they dance in full costume to the hip-shakin' classic "Do What You Want To." CBS anchor and Jazz Fest devotee Ed Bradley never misses a chance to jump on stage and shake his tambourine with New Orleans's own Neville Brothers, the festival's most well attended and hotly anticipated closing act.

The fest also features hundreds of artists and craftspeople from all over the United States, cultural and cooking demonstrations,

Suggestions for a Great Jazz Fest

1) Take the bus to the fairgrounds; you'll have fewer headaches and it's a lot cheaper.

2) Get there early and go straight to the food vendors before the lines get ridiculous.

3) Don't leave without sampling the following: pheasant, quail, and andouille gumbo; oysters Rockefeller bisque (alone worth the trip!); Ghana's *jama-jama* (sautéed spinach); softshell crab po-boys; creamy crawfish sacks (like nothing you've ever tasted!); and a frosty ice cream-flavored snow ball.

4) Don't forget sunscreen, a hat to protect yourself from sun or rain, and comfortable shoes that can get muddy or wet.

dancing with the second-line strutters, a Children's Pavilion with games and storytellers—and eating and more eating! Tasting the 120-plus specialty foods peddled by some 50 vendors is as big a draw as the music! From seasoned connoisseurs to the pickiest palates, no one walks away from Jazz Fest hungry or unsatisfied! • **Last weekend in April, first weekend in May/Admission charge**

Reggae Riddums International Arts Festival
Marconi Meadows, City Park, 504/367-1313
Some 15 local, national, and international acts bring the best in Caribbean, reggae, and calypso music to the lush grounds of City Park for this unique and exciting event. The Reggae Riddums International Arts Festival was established to promote world peace and unity and celebrate positive, uplifting music.

In the past, reggae fans have enjoyed groups such as Inner Circle, Steel Pulse, Mighty Sparrow, and Burning Spear. While jammin' to world beat music, indulge in the best West Indian and local New Orleans dishes, from jerk chicken and filé gumbo to Haitian rum cakes and refreshing island drinks. • **Second weekend in June/AA**

***Essence* Music Festival**
Louisiana Superdome/Ernest N. Morial Convention Center,
800/ESSENCE
The *Essence* Music Festival gathers together impressive musical talents, distinguished speakers, and original arts and crafts for the purpose of uplifting the spirit and stirring the soul. Empowerment seminars featuring nationally renowned speakers, celebrities, and authors are held daily at the Morial Center. Book signings, Black art exhibitions, and unique gifts and cultural items are a few of the many added extras worth checking out.

Evening concerts showcase the best in today's contemporary performers. The main stage rocks with today's hottest rap as well as all-time R&B favorites. Past performers have included superstars Maxwell, Usher, Patti LaBelle, Luther Vandross, and Frankie Beverly and Maze. The smaller satellite "superlounges" provide more intimate settings for everything from old-school funk bands to laid-back jazz artists. Celebrities hang out in up-in-the-sky suites, but people-watching opportunities abound. Evidently, wardrobe planning starts months in advance, with the men trying their best to outshine the women! That's right, you'll see several dozen men strutting their stuff in head to toe brights, from chartreuse bowler hats to the tip of their lime green snake skins. Where are the fashion police when you need them? • **July Fourth weekend/Admission charge/AA**

Bayou Classic Extravaganza and Football Game
Louisiana Superdome, 504/587-3663
Folks from all over the country converge on the Crescent City for what many consider the biggest, baddest party of the year. The annual Bayou Classic is all about which team will get to claim bragging rights: Grambling University or Southern University. The halftime "Battle of the Bands" between the two schools' high-steppin', world-famous marching ensembles stirs up more enthusiasm than the football game itself! If you are fortunate enough to be invited to watch the game from one of the many corporate suites, you'll see that this is where the heavy-duty partying and networking takes place. Many folks don't get to see too much of the game, since it interferes with all the mayhem and suite hopping going on! Only in N'awlins! • **Thanksgiving weekend/AA**

Museums

❋Amistad Research Center
Tulane University-Tilton Hall, 6823 St. Charles Ave., 504/865-5535
Amistad Research Center houses the largest collection of African American historical documents in the United States. Included are millions of clippings and manuscripts, the Aaron Douglas Collection celebrating 19th- and 20th-century artists, and the William Bertrand and Victor DuBois collection of African art. • **Free**

❋Louisiana State Museums
The Cabildo, 701 Chartres St., Jackson Square
The Presbytere, 751 Chartres St., Jackson Square, 800/568-6968
Bookends to the St. Louis Cathedral, the Cabildo and the Presbytere museums offer a look into the state's colorful past. Photography, documents, and paintings comprise the bulk of the exhibit with emphasis on the contributions of African Americans in shaping New Orleans and the state of Louisiana. • **Admission charge**

❋Musée Conti Wax Museum
917 Conti St., 504/525-2605
Just like the movie only better! This museum contains life-size wax figures depicting some of Louisiana's most famous and infamous residents, including several African Americans who made their marks on history. • **Admission charge**

New Orleans Historic Voodoo Museum
724 Dumaine St., 504/523-7685
It's everything the name suggests and then some. Through documents, artifacts, and photographs, mysteries unfold in this collection devoted to our secret obsession with voodoo. The museum even features a working altar and plenty of history on Marie LaVeau, the most famous voodoo priestess of them all. Walking voodoo tours of the French Quarters are available. • **Admission charge**

New Orleans African American Museum of Art,
Culture, and History
1418 Gov. Nicholls Street, 504/527-0989
After years of hard times and sheer neglect, Faubourg (French for

"suburb") Tremé, the oldest African American neighborhood in the United States, is enjoying a much-deserved renaissance. At the eye of this resurgence is the New Orleans African American Museum of Art, Culture, and History. Located in the restored Meilleur-Goldwaite House, the museum is dedicated to sharing the rich and brilliant history of New Orleans and Tremé. Within the confines of the main house are the Villere House and the Villere Street Gallery, showcasing exciting contemporary art from local and national artists. • **Admission charge**

Old U.S. Mint
400 Esplanade Ave., 800/568-6968
Formally the old Federal and Confederate Mint, the U.S. Mint is now the home of permanent jazz and Mardi Gras exhibits that include an extensive collection of carnival costumes, photographs, and musical paraphernalia chronicling the history of jazz and Mardi Gras in Louisiana. • **Admission charge**

River Road African American Museum & Gallery
Tezcuco Plantation, Burnside, 504/644-7955
It's a hike, but worth the trip. River Road African American Museum was founded to tell the story of the hundreds of slaves who were purchased and brought to Burnside, Louisiana. Photographs, artifacts, historical documents, and other rare memorabilia preserve the heritage and contributions of these African Americans. • **Mon–Fri by appointment only/AA**

Churches

First African Baptist Church of New Orleans
2216 Third St., 504/366-9712
The First African Baptist Church is the oldest African American Congregation of record in the state, founded in 1817.

St. Augustine Church
1210 Governor Nicholls St., 504/525-5934
St. Augustine is the second-oldest African American Catholic church in America. Located in the historic neighborhood of Tremé,

St. Augustine orginally was built as "a place of Catholic Worship
for Free People of Color and African Slaves."

St. Louis Cathedral
721 Chartres St., 504/525-9585
The oldest continually active cathedral in the United States, St.
Louis Cathedral is the corner stone of Jackson Square in the center
of the French Quarter.

Recreation

Audubon Park Golf Club, 6500 Magazine St., 504/865-8260
Audubon Park Tennis Courts, 6320 Tchoupitoulas St.
City Park Golf Course (Bayou Oaks), 1 Palm Dr., 504/583-9386
City Park Tennis Center, 1 Palm Dr., 504/483-9383
Pontchartrain Park Golf Course, 6514 Congress Dr., 504/288-0928

High Rollers

Bally's Casino Lakeshore Resort, 800/57BALLY, This large riverboat gambling casino rarely leaves shore these days, so you can board anytime the gambling bug bites—or make that quick exit when the dice stop rolling your way. The resort is owned by African American businessman Norbert Simmons. • AA

Harrah's Casino, 512 S. Peters St., 800/HARRAHS, With their second try, Harrah's got it right with a great location smack in the center of town, across from the Riverwalk. In addition to featuring every game known to man, Harrah's keeps patrons entertained with nightly stage performances and live jazz bands.

New YorkCity

New York City. Most folks either love it or hate it. But what's to hate? Sure, New York is big. It's also dirty, sometimes unfriendly, always noisy, and expensive as all get-out—parking can cost you as much as $12 for a half hour! What's to love, you ask? Picnicking with your main squeeze while groovin' to the mellow sounds of a free summer concert in Central Park. Searching for buried treasures like vintage Chanel handbags and bakelite bracelets at the Sixth Avenue flea market. Picking up the latest vibrant Senegalese prints from the African fabric market on the corner of 125th and Adam Clayton Powell Jr. Boulevard in Harlem. Now, how could anyone not love all that!

New York is "on" 24 hours a day, in perpetual motion and constantly changing. Prosperous executives, who once clamored for an East Side address, have turned to renovating abandoned brownstones, making Harlem, USA, once again one of the chic-est neighborhoods in which to live. Forty-second Street, all cleaned up and lookin' fine with trendy new restaurants and grandly rejuvenated theaters, is ready for an encore. Make no mistake: Crusty corners still abound throughout the city. Hell's Kitchen still looks like it, cheesy Alphabet City (Avenues A through D) appeals only to club kids, and Ninth Avenue between 42nd and 45th needs to dial 9-1-1-Fashion Emergency. Yet even with these unsightly blemishes, the brilliant lights of the Big Apple outshine its dim corners any day of the week!

New York City is a walking town, so put on your most comfortable shoes and prepare to cover some ground! Follow the Duke's advice and take the A train uptown to Harlem. Get off on 125th Street (or "One-Two-Fifth Street," as the young set say), where your first landmark is the Cotton Club, the legendary night spot where Cab Calloway and Bill "Bojangles" Robinson once strutted their stuff and subsequently put Harlem on the map.

Across 125th Street, the ever-present sidewalk merchants continue to ply a fascinating assortment of wares on the streets of Harlem. Reggae cassettes, pungent incense, new and used books, fake Ray-Ban sunglasses for $5, and wanna-be designer handbags are just a few of the many items you can find for sale on Harlem sidewalks. Prices, of course, are negotiable.

Still going strong after 70 years, the Apollo Theater is a Harlem icon, its proud landmark marquee brightly highlighting the week's headline act. A block away, the intimate Studio Museum in Harlem exhibits contemporary art by local as well as nationally and internationally known Black artists. The outdoor African market on the corner of Adam Clayton Powell Jr. Boulevard is a great place to bargain for stoic-faced wood statues, brightly colored fabrics, the latest world music cassettes, and unique ethnic jewelry.

If it's lunchtime, head a couple of blocks north to Well's Restaurant, at 133rd Street and Adam Clayton Powell Jr. Boulevard. Here, a meal of chicken and waffles with a side of collard greens is worth the wait. Across from Well's is Striver's Row, a historic residential section known for its stately brownstones and famous former residents like Eubie Blake and W. C. Handy. The area is also home to Mother AME Zion Church, New York City's first Black church, and the Abyssinian Baptist Church, where the late Congressman Powell served as pastor.

Hop back on the A train headed downtown to catch a quick nap at your hotel before having cocktails at the penthouse bar at the Peninsula Hotel, where the Cosmopolitans are good, but the view of Fifth Avenue is spectacular! Celebrity star gazing and nouvelle soul cuisine are served at Soul Café. The night is young, so what's it going to be—old school or jazz? Hey, it's New York, why not both? For terrific local talent, check out Smalls' or the Blue Note in the village for big-name acts. At the end of the second set, head to NYC's number-one dance club, Nell's, where the party is still going strong after 15 years.

Three a.m. and still not ready to call it a night? Well, plenty of after-hours clubs downtown don't close until noon the next day, but they require correct responses to a few discreet inquiries, you know.

You've already spent a very full day in New York City and have yet to hit Times Square, Central Park, South Street Seaport, Fifth Avenue, Soho, Tribeca, the Upper West Side, Greenwich Village, Chinatown, and a Broadway play! Better get a good night's sleep, after all!

Restaurants

There is no possible way to list the countless varieties of foods available in New York City. Fried chicken and fluffy waffles from Well's in Harlem; heavenly pastrami and chopped chicken liver piled a mile high at Kaplan's deli in Midtown; dim sum smorgasbord on Sunday afternoon anywhere in Chinatown; spicy sausages and creamy cannoli in Little Italy eateries; roast pork, peas, and rice from La Caridad; hot slices of New York-style pizza on just about any corner—these are just a minuscule sampling of some of the Big Apple's delicious ethnic cuisine. Again, what's not to love?

Fine Dining

✳Bambou
243 E. 14th St., 212/358-0012
Bambou is one of the most handsome Caribbean fusion restaurants in the country. Celebrities like Stevie Wonder regularly pop in to enjoy its tropical charm. Start with an absolutely luscious bowl of *aubergines saveur coconut* (eggplant soup) or a crab cake with avocado butter; then dive into the rich bouillabaisse Caraibe with scallops, mussels, clams, and lobster in a light coconut broth or the dazzling dorade royale stuffed with sweet potato purée and crowned with ginger sauce. Top the evening off with warm chocolate soufflé cake and a cup of Blue Mountain coffee. • **$35+/AA**

✳B. Smith's Restaurant
320 W. 46th St., 212/315-1100
In the mid-1980s, it took a visionary like Barbara Smith to change the old caked-on makeup of Eighth Avenue with her new, hip eatery,

"You Want a Table for *Tonight*?"

Balthazar, 80 Spring St., 212/965-1414—The first name in intimidating restaurants, Balthazar is the see-and-be-seen French bistro of the decade and is usually as chock-full with celebrities as its excellent bouillabaisse is with fish. · $40+

Carmine's, 200 W. 44th St. 212/362-2200—If you think you can pop in here for dinner just before the curtain goes up, let's hope your tickets are for tomorrow night! Carmine's offers southern Italian food served family-style—that is, if your family includes the entire block! · $25+

Le Cirque 2000, 455 Madison Ave., 212/794-9292—Considered the ultimate New York dining experience, Le Cirque 2000 features a gorgeous Beaux Arts dining room, snooty clientele, a one-month waiting list, and a French menu to die for. · $65+

B. Smith's Restaurant. So it is no surprise that after years in her inaugural location, Smith transfers her sense of style to new digs on the staunch, historical 46th Street, a block better known to New Yorkers as Restaurant Row.

Intriguing choices from Smith's "international eclectic" menu include Tutu Man's chicken with a charred banana chutney; "pan-tanned" smothered pork chops in "ancestral" gravy (I guess that means like Mama use to make!); and, our favorite entry (drum roll please), "So Slow Roast Dry Rub Buttah Ribs, Bookers Bourbon Black Strap Lacquer, Moppin Sauce and Monkey Bread!" Live music five nights a week. • **$35+/AA**

✳Jezebel's
630 Ninth Ave., 212/582-1045
With its sophisticated down-home cuisine and seductive dining room, Jezebel's is considered one of Manhattan's premier restaurants. The baskets of sweet potato muffins, hot biscuits, honey-glazed fried chicken, cornmeal-coated catfish, smothered pork chops, and jumbo shrimp scampi are just a few of the classic menu items. But $9.50 for

bread pudding with bourbon sauce? That's outrageous! For that price, they had better bring the whole pan!• **$35+/AA**

✳Michael Jordan's Steakhouse
Grand Central Station, 23 Vanderbilt Ave., 212/655-2300
Masculine, polished, and trés sexy describes both the man and his restaurant. Michael Jordan's Steakhouse, located inside the equally opulent and newly restored Grand Central Station, exudes New York sophistication. Its slick contemporary lounge is perfect for cocktails and conversation before jumping on the next train home. The handsome dining room, with its high-back leather chairs and mahogany accents, attracts more of the high-powered executives crowd then the see-and-be-seen Michael groupees. The traditional steak house menu offers all the usual suspects, except they're served with a little more flair than the competition—just like the owner. • **$45+/AA-invested**

✳Sugar Bar
254 W. 72nd St., 212/579-0222
The celebrity friends of proprietors and recording artists Nick Ashford and Valerie Simpson, like best buddy poet Maya Angelou, pop into this restaurant whenever they're in town. Yet Sugar Bar's unpretentious character keeps this hot spot a friendly neighborhood haunt rather than another uppity, over-priced eatery. The restaurant, filled with African artifacts handpicked by Ashford himself, offers an international menu featuring barbecued salmon with sweet corn risotto, pepper-crusted tuna with mango curry, and cinnamon-rubbed loin of pork with candied squash. • **$35+/AA**

Casual Dining

✳Daphne's Caribbean Express
233 E. 14th St., 212/228-8971
Daphne's Caribbean Express serves up fresh, delicious, and quick island fare to time-strapped executives and those looking for a good, cheap meal. Curried chicken, oxtail, stew beef, jerk chicken, codfish and callaloo, and stuffed roti are the favorites at Daphne's. On Thursdays and Fridays, Chef Daphne adds a little soul food to the menu, along with vegetarian and daily specials. • **$10/AA**

Cheap and Cheerful in the Big City

✳**Carnegie Deli**, 854 Seventh Ave., 212/757-2245—This place serves deli sandwiches piled so high with meat, you'll have enough for tomorrow's lunch. · $15+

Gray's Papaya, 2090 Broadway, 212/799-0243—This restaurant is king of the cheap eats. Hot dogs and orange drink—how much more "New Yorkish" can you get? · $5+

✳**La Caridad**, 2199 Broadway, 212/874-2780—Can't decide between rice and peas or Singapore mi fung? At La Caridad, you can order both! This is one of New York's most popular ethnic eateries. · $15+

Ollie's, 200B W. 44th St., 212/921-5988—Good classic Chinese dishes, especially dumplings, are the specialties here. Ollie's is always packed. · $10+

✳**Dayo**
103 Greenwich Ave., 212/924-3161
Dayo is known as "that funky Greenwich Village restaurant with quirky animated coconut head figures shaking to the reggae beat." It serves great New World cuisine, a combination of Caribbean and southern favorites including jerk chicken burritos, walnut-crusted catfish, a dish called "vegetarian island" (assorted vegetables), coconut shrimp, and Dixie-fried chicken served with candied yams and a mountain of greens. The all-you-can-eat brunch is famous with the after-church crowd! • **$20+/AA**

✳**Island Spice**
402 W. 44th St., 212/765-1737
✳**Negril**
362 W. 23rd St., 212/807-6411
If you can't make it to Jamaica this year, don't worry, mon! Island Spice and Negril bring the islands to New York! Island Spice is located in the heart of the theater district, while Negril caters to the

funkier downtown crowd that's ready to "lime" the night away! Tropical drinks and codfish fritters with avocado salsa get you going. Then, you can't go wrong with the jerk chicken, ginger lime chicken, shrimp Negril, oxtails and beans, or the whole red snapper. • **$20+/AA**

✳Justin's
31 W. 21st St., 212/352-1734
Hip-hop entrepreneur extraordinaire Sean "Puffy" Combs's restaurant was destined to be a hit from day one. And with friends like Mariah Carey dropping in for dinner on any given night, you can believe the star gazers are four-deep at the bar and every table is booked every night. Not only that, the chef can *burn*! The South Carolina catfish over velvety grits is on the money, as are the beef oxtails, roasted lobster, and macaroni and cheese and sweet yams sprinkled with raisins. All are served with plenty of sass, ambience, and high prices to match! Dress to impress. • **$35+/AA**

Soul Food to Go

Monck's Corner, 644 Ninth Ave., 212/397-1117—Honey chicken, Carolina shrimp Creole, baked ham, fried whiting, and oxtail stew are among the delicious hot meals brought to you by the folks who gave you Jezebel's. · $10/AA

Soul Fixin's, 371 W. 34th St., 212/736-1345—With a client list that includes filmmaker Spike Lee and singer Tony Braxton, this place is cheap and cheerful with great service, attitude, and, of course, serious down-home food like barbecued chicken, fried whiting, meat loaf, and sweet potato pie. · $10/AA

T.J.'s Southern Gourmet, 92 Chambers St., 212/406-3442—Pork chops, fried chicken, meatloaf, and fried fish sandwiches are all priced under $4 at T.J.'s, and served in nothing flat! Sides of serious potato salad, fresh collard greens, yams, and sweet cornbread are big hits with the Wall Street crowd. · $10/AA

The Best of Harlem

Amy Ruth's, 113 W. 116th St., 212/280-8779—The newest reason to head uptown is Amy Ruth's sweeter-than-sweet peach cobbler, chicken livers and scrambled-egg breakfast, and homemade honey. This cute diner is popular with locals, tourists, and the after-church crowd. · $10+/AA

Emily's Restaurant, 1325 Fifth Ave., 212/996-1212—Emily's contemporary dining room is a hot spot for cooling down after work. Patrons enjoy a simple dinner of down-home delights such as Jamaican jerk chicken and Emily's famous barbecued baby back ribs. Live jazz Thursday evenings. Brunch is served Saturdays and Sundays. · $20/AA

Londel's, 2620 Frederick Douglass Blvd., 212/234-6114—Londel's is a lovely neighborhood spot specializing in "New York-style" cooking, or a mix of Cajun, southern, and international cuisines. Live music most weekends. · $20/AA

Miss Mamie Spoonbread Two, 366 W. 110th St., 212/280-8779—Proprietor and author Norma Jean Darden's newest entry into the restaurant scene takes its recipes from her best-selling book, Spoonbread & Strawberry Wine. The ambience is as warm and comforting as the menu, and in NYC we can all use a little lovin'. · $10+/AA

Strictly Roots, 2058 Adam Clayton Powell Jr. Blvd., 212/864-8699—The slogan at Strictly Roots is "We serve nothing that crawls, walks, swims, or flies." That leaves vegetarian fare and all-natural beverages, fresh and quick. · $10/AA

Well's Restaurant, 2247 Adam Clayton Powell Jr. Blvd., 212/234-0930—This is where it all began more than 60 years ago! Fried chicken, thick golden waffles, and lots of gooey syrup, for a taste that is by now renowned. If you've never tried chicken and waffles, do yourself a favor and get over here, fast! Live music on the weekends. · $10/AA

✳Little Jezebel's Plantation
529 Columbus Ave., 212/579-4952
Little Jezebel's Plantation transports the long, lazy days of summer spent sitting on grandma's porch down South to Manhattan's Upper West Side. Charleston she-crab soup, hot and spicy shrimp, swamp fox southern-fried chicken, and baked beef short ribs are just a few of the scrumptious offerings at Little Jezebel's. There's also brunch and tea and desserts like southern pecan rum cake. • **$20/AA**

Pink Tea Cup
42 Grove St., 212/807-6755
What other soul food restaurant can claim to be a resident of Greenwich Village for the past 40 years? At the Pink Tea Cup, the most famous soul food restaurant in Manhattan, notables such as Spike Lee stop in often for a hearty breakfast. Large portions of the following await you: smothered pork chops, barbecued beef, and frogs' legs sautéed in wine sauce. Fried chicken with apple fritters is a breakfast favorite. • **$15+/AA**

✳Shark Bar
307 Amsterdam Ave., 212/874-8500
Every celebrity from Luther Vandross to Diane Sawyer has eaten at the Shark Bar at least once. But since its more lustrous days, the service has suffered, the food has dulled, and waiting 30 minutes for a reserved table no longer charms. Even so, the Shark Bar remains one of the hottest upscale soul food restaurants in the country, with the PYT set keeping the bar beautiful and the dining room packed. Sweet potato muffins, corny cornbread, grilled oyster appetizers, pan-blackened catfish, shrimp étouffée, honey-dipped fried chicken, and seafood gumbo grace the now-famous southern menu. Oh, and try not to stare at the rap star sitting at the table next to yours lickin' his fingers. After all, he's only human! The Sunday brunch is legendary. • **$30/AA-invested**

✳Soul Café
444 W. 42nd St., 212/244-7685
"The Rebirth of Cool Dining" describes Soul Café, Malik Yoba and Michael Vann's wildly successful new soul food restaurant. With investors Roberta Flack and Natalie Cole on board, Soul Café is

Harlem Nights

Lenox Lounge, 288 Malcolm X Blvd. (formerly Lenox Ave.) 212/427-0253—A fabulous facelift has transformed the famed Lenox Lounge from cheesy bar to oh boy! Its new, sexy jazz room is attracting NYC's beautiful people from around the island and heating up the nights, just like old times. · Cover charge/mature crowd/AA

Perk's Fine Cuisine, 553 Manhattan Ave., 212/666-8500—Big-name and local entertainers nightly heat up the downstairs stage at Perk's while the kitchen serves up a mean continental menu. · Cover charge/ Dinner $20/AA

✳**St. Nick's Pub**, 773 St. Nicholas Ave., 212/283-9728—This local favorite is as old as black thread, but that just adds to its charm! St. Nick's Pub is still the place for great live local jazz, five nights a week, and cheap drinks. · No cover charge/AA

✳**Showman's Lounge**, 2321 Eighth Ave., 212/864-8941—Established in 1940, the Showman's Lounge is the oldest nightclub in Harlem and still going strong! It's often filled with German or Japanese tourists enjoying great music from local jazz artists and mingling with the neighborhood regulars while dining on good down-home-style food. · No cover charge/Two-drink minimum/Dinner $20/AA

Manhattan's sexiest celebrity-packed scene. Patti LaBelle, Magic Johnson, Jasmine Guy, Veronica Webb, Maze, Boyz II Men, Montell Jordan, and Dru Hill have all dined on its Creole fried catfish and seafood gumbo. Add Wynton Marsalis and Stevie Wonder to the list of luminaries who've popped in for dinner and ended up delighting the dining room with a song or two. Now that's a dessert worthy of seconds! Soul Café hosts live music on weekends and a lively bar scene, making it a veritable "meet market." • **$30/AA**

Sylvia's Restaurant
328 Malcolm X Blvd., 212/996-0660
Arguably the most famous soul food restaurant in the United States, Sylvia's has fed notables from boxer Muhammad Ali, soul stylist

Aretha Franklin, and religious leader/politician Jesse Jackson to singer Barbra Streisand, to name a few. In 1979, Gael Greene, food critic for *New York* magazine, dubbed proprietor Sylvia Woods "the Queen of Soul Food." This started a stampede by downtown customers who normally wouldn't be caught dead north of 96th Street to dine at Sylvia's in "big, bad Harlem." The rest, as they say, is history.

Breakfast is always packed with business people starting the day with southern-fried chicken and eggs or pork chops and grits. Daily lunch and dinner specials include stewed chicken and dumplings, turkey wings with down-home dressing, and pork chitterlings. A jazz brunch is featured on Saturdays and a gospel brunch on Sundays. • **$15+/AA**

Nightclubs

If you can't find good music in New York City, you're not looking in the right places! Greenwich Village is all about jazz with legendary clubs like the Blue Note and Sweet Basil's throwing down with the biggest names in the business nightly. Across 110th Street, places

Vintage Village Jazz

✳The Blue Note, 131 W. Third St., 212/475-8592—Arguably the most influential jazz club in the city, possibly the country, and definitely the most expensive of them all. Big-name talent featured nightly. Dinner menu served. · Cover charge

✳Smalls', 183 W. 10th St., 212/929-7565—Smalls' is small, but it's also cheap and cheerful. Great local groups and national acts. · Cover charge/AA

Sweet Basil, 88 Seventh Ave., 212/242-1785—Famous for its jazz brunch, Sweet Basil hosts big-name and local talent, and the food is good. · Cover charge

✳Village Vanguard, 178 Seventh Ave., 212/255-4037—You've gotta step down to get into one of New York's oldest night clubs. Big-name talent nightly. · Cover charge

Off the Hook

These clubs are the 54, Area, and Garage of the new millennium. All are guaranteed to yield at least one pseudo-celebrity sighting, a splitting headache from the loud music, a wait of at least an hour before entry, and a $20 cover charge for the privilege.

NV, 289 Spring St., 212/929-NVNV—Hip-hop, funk, '70s disco. The "it" club of the moment.

Life, 158 Bleecker St., 212/420-1999—Wall-to-wall club kids, beautiful people, and wannabes.

Club New York, 252 W. 43rd St., 212/997-9510—Serious Latin dance night, made famous by Puff Daddy and Ms. Jennifer.

Webster Hall, 125 E. 11th St., 212/353-1600—Gay, straight, bridge 'n' tunnel, upper eastside—everyone parties here.

like the Lenox Lounge, Showman's Lounge, and St. Nick's Pub showcase musical forefathers who continue to play the blues and tell all the old stories to new generations of jazz lovers.

Birdland
315 W. 44th St., 212/581-3080

The old Birdland nightclub Uptown was a great neighborhood spot with terrific music, food, and people. The new Birdland's proprietors also guarantee a pleasurable dining and musical experience. The club features live music nightly, and good thing: The acoustics are fabulous and the sound system, crystal clear. With nationally known acts like the Count Basie Orchestra on the bill, you won't want to miss a note. Southern-style dinner menu available. • **Cover charge/Two-drink minimum/Dinner $20**

Cotton Club
656 W. 125th St., Harlem, 212/663-7980

The Cotton Club first gained notoriety in the late 1920s when it opened as a segregated night spot hosting whites only. Back then, the club attracted a gangster and celebrity clientele that included the infamous and famous alike: Dutch Shultz, Bing Crosby, and Cole Porter, to name a few. The Cotton Club also launched the careers of legendary African American entertainers Cab Calloway, Duke Ellington, Lena Horne, and Bill "Bojangles" Robinson. It thrived at its Harlem location until the mid-1930s, when the owners attempted to relocate it to Midtown Manhattan. That venture failed in 1940, and the club stayed shut for the next 38 years. The Cotton Club returned to Harlem in the late 1970s to offer a live gospel brunch and dinner show and a delicious southern-style buffet. • **Cover charge/Gospel brunch $25+/AA**

Festivals

New York in the summertime is one big festival! With a nonstop schedule of parades and outdoor concerts, no avenue is exempt from being transformed into a street fair. Central Park Summerstage offers free live performances from diverse groups like the Robert Cray Band, Hugh Masekela, the Sugar Hill Gang (the original rappers), and funkmaster Bernie Worrell.

In fact, New York hosts more free events than any other American city, from that granddaddy of festivals, the Ninth Avenue Food and Street Fair, to the outrageous Greenwich Village Halloween Parade. Check out **www.ny.com** for a complete list of events. Here's a short list of some of the best the city offers:

Ninth Avenue Food Festival, Ninth Ave. between 42nd and 55th Sts. Memorial Day weekend.

National Puerto Rican Day Parade, Fifth Ave. between 42nd and 86th Sts. Second Sunday in June.

Amsterdam Avenue Summer Festival, Amsterdam Ave. between 86th and 96th Sts. Third Sunday in June.

Gay Pride Day, Fifth Ave. between 52nd and Christopher Sts. Last Sunday in June.

African American Day Parade, Adam Clayton Powell Jr. Blvd., Harlem. Mid-August.

West Indian American Day Carnival, Eastern Pkwy. between Utica Ave. and Grand Army Plaza, Brooklyn. Labor Day.

Feast of San Gennaro, Mulberry St. between Canal and Houston Sts. Second and third week in September.

NYCVB

Harlem shows off its elegant façade along Striver's Row.

Broadway Fall Festival, Broadway between 86th and 96th Sts. Sponsored in part by the NAACP. Last Sunday in October.
Village Halloween Parade, Sixth Avenue from 22nd St. through Greenwich Village. Halloween night. (Finding a good spot from which to watch the parade is tough, but it's the best of them all and worth the effort!)

Take the A Train (or the 2 or 3) to Harlem

Astor Row, W. 130th St. between Malcolm X Blvd. and Fifth Ave.— These palatial homes were built in the 1880s by prominent New Yorker John J. Astor.

Morris Jumel Mansion/Museum, 1765 Jumel Terrace at 160th St., 212/923-8008—Best known as the temporary headquarters of General George Washington during the Battle of Harlem Heights. The oldest single-family home in Harlem, the Jumel Museum houses historical artifacts from the Revolutionary War.

Raven Chanticleer African American Wax Museum of Harlem, 316 W. 115th St., 212/678-7818—This museum features wax figures of notable African Americans like Dr. Martin Luther King Jr.

St. Nicholas Historic District, W. 137th to 139th Sts. between Adam Clayton Powell Jr. and Frederick Douglass Blvds.—Also known as Striver's Row, these blocks were home to Eubie Blake and W. C. Handy.

Harlem Week
Various venues, www.discoverharlem.com

What once was a few days' celebration to promote this historic community, Harlem "Week" has since expanded to a month of outdoor concerts, block parties, educational forums, empowerment workshops, sports tournaments, and food festivals. Technology seminars, health fairs, and investment workshops provide additional food for thought and self-improvement. Most anticipated are the weekend concerts; past performers have included Tito Puente, Bob Marley, the Chi-Lites, Jon Lucien, and The Persuaders, to name a few. The Jazz Mobile parked at Grant's Tomb at 122nd Street and Riverside Drive draws thousands of music lovers from all five boroughs. During the festival month, Harlem also throws open its doors for tours of its museums and historic brownstones. • **All of August/Free**

Museums and Attractions

Brooklyn Heights Promenade
End of Montague St., Brooklyn
Stroll along this famous promenade for the city's most spectacular view of downtown Manhattan and the Brooklyn Bridge.

Chrysler Building
405 Lexington Ave. at 42nd St., 212/682-3070
This building offers the best example of art deco architecture in the city.

Empire State Building
350 Fifth Ave. at 34th St.
This has *got* to be the most romantic edifice in the world, just ask King Kong, Cary Grant, and Meg Ryan! The 102-story art deco landmark is still worth the climb. Allow 15 to 45 minutes to board the elevator. • **Admission charge**

Greenwich Village
South of 14th St. and north of Houston between
First St. and the West Side Hwy.
People watching in Washington Square Park, shopping for vintage clothing at St. Mark's Place, trolling East Sixth Street for great Indian food, and cheering on the brothers playing hard-core hoops at Sixth Avenue and Fourth Street are just some of the reasons why Greenwich Village is *the* place for hanging out in New York City.

Metropolitan Museum of Art
1000 Fifth Ave., 212/535-7710
Just walking up the grand marble stairway to the Met is a thrill. African, Egyptian, and Islamic art, and a revolving fashion exhibit are just a small sampling of what its galleries have to offer. • **Admission charge**

Museum of Modern Art (MOMA)
11 W. 53rd St., 212/708-9480
Once inside MOMA, you're privy to the largest collection of drawings in the country, more than 6,000 pieces, along with paintings,

Pay off All the Credit Cards Before You Hit ...

Canal St. between Third and Eight Aves.—This is the best place to get knock-off Chanel and Prada handbags and fake Rolex watches for a mere $20.

Century 21, 22 Coutland, 212/227-9092—Floors of designer clothes, shoes, men's ties, and accessories. The locals swear by this place!

Eighth St., Greenwich Village—Home to funky boutiques geared toward the hip-hop and body-piercing crowd.

Fifth Ave. between 50th and 60th Sts.—Home to some of the most exclusive stores in the world.

Flat Iron District, Broadway and Seventh Ave. between 16th and 23rd Sts.—Chic boutiques mix it up with high-end designers in this trendy district.

Garment District, Broadway and Seventh Ave. between 34th and 42nd Sts.—Sample sales abound at the end of each market season (November, December, May, June). Pick up everything from designer coats to high-end costume jewelry.

Madison Ave. between 57th and 72nd Sts.—This is the real-deal high-rent district! Be prepared for price-ticket shock.

Soho between McDougald and Broadway—Ultra-exclusive Japanese designers, loft apartments renting for $2,000 a month, sidewalk cafés, and "If you must ask for the price list, why bother?" art galleries describe Soho to a tee!

prints, photographs, design objects, and a lush sculpture garden. MOMA hosts free jazz concerts all summer long. • **Admission charge**

Rockefeller Center
Fifth and Sixth Aves. between 49th and 50th Sts.
Say "Hi!" to the gang on the *Today Show*, enjoy outdoor dining in the summer, and watch the skaters avoid collisions on the ice rink

NYCVB

The Apollo Theater still holds center court on 125th Street in Harlem USA.

during the winter months. Witness the lighting of the huge Christmas tree every first Tuesday in December.

Schomburg Center for Research on Black Culture
515 Malcolm X Blvd., 212/491-2200

Considered one of the largest collections celebrating the history and culture of the African Diaspora, the Schomburg Center was established in 1926 when the personal collection of Arturo Alfonso Schomburg, a Puerto Rican savant was accepted by the Division of Negro Literature, History, and Prints of the New York Public Library's 135th Street branch. With more than 5 million artifacts, photographs, audio- and videotapes, manuscripts, films, periodicals, and prints, the Schomburg is one of the nation's chief promoters and preservers of the legacy of the Americas' African descendants.

Solomon R. Guggenheim Museum
1071 Fifth Ave., 212/423-3500

Thank you, Frank Lloyd Wright, for designing the graceful curves of the Guggenheim Museum, which arguably draws as many "oohs" and "ahhs" as the museum's exquisite collection of 19th- and 20th-century art. • **Admission charge**

Statue of Liberty
Hudson River, 212/269-5777

Even if you're not much of a patriot, a trip to Lady Liberty will give you goosebumps and have you singing "God Bless America" in no time! Her size and stature overwhelm, and the 15-minute boat ride to Liberty Island on a clear day offers a great view of the Manhattan harbor. • **Admission charge**

Studio Museum in Harlem
144 W. 125th St., 212/864-4500

This intimate museum, nestled in the heart of Harlem, is known for its permanent collection of traditional African art, 19th- and 20th-century African American art, and 20th-century Caribbean and African art. Throughout the seasons, the Studio Museum highlights the talents of renowned as well as local Black artists and offers family art workshops, art demonstrations, and music concerts. • **Admission charge**

World Trade Center
1 World Trade Center
Having drinks at the World Trade Center's 107th-floor bar, Window on the World, is the best way to see it all!

Churches

Abyssinian Baptist Church
132 W. 138th St., 212/862-7474
The Abyssinian Baptist Church is considered the largest Black Protestant congregation in the United States. Not only is it recognized nationwide for its outstanding choir, but Congressman Adam Clayton Powell Jr. and Rev. Adam Clayton Powell Sr. both pastored here. The church's basement houses a small museum that pays tribute to the Powells.

Cathedral Church of St. John the Divine
1047 Amsterdam Ave., 212/316-7540
The largest Gothic cathedral in the world, St. John the Divine is a magnificent work of art.

Convent Avenue Baptist Church
420 W. 145th St., 212/234-6767
This popular church is best known for the beautiful limestone structure that houses it, along with the unique and colorful hats worn by its fashionable parishioners.

Masjid Malcolm Shabazz
151 W. 128th St., 212/663-8990
Not only is this mosque erected on the site of the first church established in Harlem back in 1896, it is currently the only place of worship registered as a city, state, and national landmark.

Mother AME Zion Church
140-146 W. 137th St., 212/234-1545
Mother AME Zion, the first Black church in New York City, was attended over the years by such prominent African Americans as Frederick Douglass, Sojourner Truth, and Paul Robeson. It also

served, as did many other Black churches, as a station along the route of the Underground Railroad.

St. Phillips Church
204 134th St., 212/862-4940
Former members of St. Phillips Church, founded by slaves as well as freemen, include African American luminaries Langston Hughes, W. E. B. Du Bois, and Supreme Court Justice Thurgood Marshall. The church's current façade was designed by Black architect Vertner Tandy.

Recreation

Central Park
59th to 110th Sts. between Central Park W. and Fifth Ave., 212/360-3444
What to do, where to start? How about in-line skating to disco music with the Central Park pros? Or what could be better than a lazy day picnicking on the Great Lawn, stretched out with the Central Park South skyline over you? To indulge your romantic side, stroll with your significant other around the gorgeous Bethesda Fountain or have lunch at the Boathouse Café. There are many things to do in Central Park; this short list will get you started:
Belvedere Castle, mid-park at 79th St.
Bicycle, Boat, and Gondola Rentals, boathouse at E. 72nd St.
Carousel, W. 65th St.
Central Park Zoo, 64th St. and Fifth Ave. (America's oldest public zoo)
Conservatory Gardens, E. 105th St. and Fifth Ave.
Ice Skating and Inline Skating, E. 72nd St.
Tennis Courts, E. 96th St. entrance
Skating Wollman Rink, 63rd St. entrance

Colonel Young Park
**W. 143rd to 145th Sts. between
Malcolm X Blvd. and Harlem River Dr.**
Named after one of America's first Black army officers, Col. Charles Young, this park hosted games for the old Negro Professional Football and Baseball League.

Holcombe Rucker Memorial Playground
W.156th to 158th Sts. between
Frederick Douglass Blvd. and Harlem River Dr.

Julius ("Dr. J") Erving and Tiny Archibald have played on these basketball courts dedicated to humanitarian Holcombe Rucker, organizer of basketball tournaments to benefit Harlem youth.

Jackie Robinson Park
W.145th to 155th Sts. between
Edgecombe and Bardhurst Aves.

A Harlem favorite, this park boasts an Olympic-sized swimming pool, a softball field, basketball and volleyball courts, and a nature center.

Marcus Garvey Park
120th to 124th Sts. between
Mount Morris Park W. and Madison Ave.

This park contains the Mount Morris Watchtower. It also features an Olympic-sized swimming pool and a recreation center.

Riverbank State Park
145th St. and Riverside Dr. between 137th and 145th Sts.

This park offers one-stop shopping for athletes. It boasts a regulation-size football field, a 400-meter track, softball fields, an Olympic-sized pool, tennis courts, roller- and ice-skating areas, indoor recreational facilities, and picnic grounds as well as basketball, handball, and paddleball courts.

Philadelphia

Philadelphia. Despite the increasingly divisive lines of racial tension that have challenged its claim as the "City of Brotherly Love," Philadelphia remains a beautiful municipality of historical significance. A drive up 76 West along the famous Schuykill River is worth getting stuck in traffic just to admire the cute little gingerbread houses on Boat House Row, whose owners leave their Christmas lights up all year 'round, no doubt for commuters' enjoyment. An exit onto Lincoln Drive puts you in the heart of Mt. Airy and Germantown, two of Philly's prominent African American neighborhoods, where many of the elegant homes are constructed from Pennsylvania fieldstone. In the summertime, Fairmount Park comes alive. Free outdoor concerts at the Dell East Theater feature headliners from old-school funk to contemporary smooth jazz.

Philadelphia's charm spreads from the cobblestone streets of Old City, downtown, northwest to the rejuvenated neighborhood of Manayunk. With so much ground to cover, you should start downtown at the Afro-American Historical and Cultural Center, where you'll find a comprehensive, revolving collection of contemporary art, dedicated to the triumphs of African America's spirit and culture. Refresh your memory of fifth-grade American history class with a walk through Independence National Historical Park. First stop: the Liberty Bell, encased in glass, probably to prevent a third crack from penetrating its fragile dome. At the helm of the mall is Independence Hall, most noted as the site of the signing of the Declaration of

Commissioned by the Philadelphia Mural Arts Program, artist Meg Saligman's mural "Common Threads", located at Broad and Spring Garden Streets, is one of over 1,900 wall paintings beautifying the city.

Independence. Cross the street and you're in historic Washington Square. Formally named Congo Square, this is where the city's enslaved Africans were sold and traded during colonial times. Up Sixth Street at the corner of Lombard you'll find the stately Mother Bethel AME Church, the world's first, established in 1787.

It wouldn't be a trip to Philly without a walk down world-famous South Street. It's great fun to check out the "sights" coming and going from the tattoo parlors, bohemian boutiques, and body-piercing shops. Before you leave South Street, pop into Jim's Steaks for an authentic Philly cheesesteak sandwich loaded with onions and sweet peppers. A word to the wise, however: Order your sandwich with real provolone cheese, not cheese wiz—unless, of course, you actually *like* cheese wiz! No matter how the sandwich is prepared, split it with a friend because more good eating is in store! If you zig-zag back across town to the Reading Terminal Market, you'll find some 80 vendors packed into their stalls like smoked oysters, offering samples of every food known to man. In this chaotic maze of edible delights, Delilah's small, colorful bistro commands attention. Serving healthy-sized portions of fried catfish, smothered chicken, and macaroni and cheese, Delilah's is a hit with hungry executives.

Located smack dab in the middle of Broad and 15th Street is Philadelphia's City Hall, an amazing example of French Renaissance Revival architecture run amuck. It doesn't matter that the building sticks out like a perpetually sore thumb, it's a must-see attraction for anyone who appreciates vision on a grand scale! Retrace Rocky Balboa's triumphant jog up the steps of the Philadelphia Museum of Art. On your way back down the Ben Franklin Parkway, give a salute to the All Wars Memorial to Colored Soldiers and Sailors at 20th Street, a tribute to African American war heroes.

It's time to catch that second wind: Warmdaddy's, Philadelphia's premier African American-owned supper club, seats for dinner no earlier than 8 o'clock; nightly performances of live blues by local and national talent have the place jumpin' by 9. Philadelphia is known for its dance clubs, so when in Center City, as downtown is also called, head to the eclectic dance floor at Brave New World, where the party people swing to a new world beat. If it's 2 a.m., still early for some towns, it's time for Philly to roll up the sidewalks. Not bad for a town founded by down-and-out Quakers! Not bad at all!

Restaurants

Fagetaboutit! How can you not love a city that worships creme-filled vanilla Tastykakes; that lives for warm, salty, knotted pretzels slathered with yellow mustard; and that considers cheesesteak sandwiches smothered in onions and sweet peppers fine dining? Until recently, Philadelphia was famous foodwise only for its working-class indulgences. Over the past 10 years, however, Philly has gained recognition as one of the best restaurant cities in the nation. In addition to fine dining, Philadelphia's ethnic neighborhoods—Chinatown, South Philly Italian Market, and its African American communities—add to the flavors that make this city especially savory.

Fine Dining

✳Buddakan
325 Chestnut St., 215/574-9440
Interested in meeting new friends while dining on Szechuan-crusted tuna with wasabi sour cream and Japanese gnocchi? At Buddakan, Philadelphia's premier pan-Asian dining experience, a day-glow Buddah statue presides at the center of the 20-seat illuminated communal table. This double-level, ultra-chic eatery serves unique East-meets-West dishes like wok-smoked salmon. At night it turns into the see-and-be-seen spot for hip Philadelphia bar crawlers. • **$30+**

✳Girasole Ristorante
1305 Locust St., 215/985-4659
If the cheery sunflowers don't put a smile on your face, the tender grilled and marinated octopus is guaranteed to. Girasole (Italian for "sunflower") is a lovely authentic Italian restaurant with wonderful pasta dishes like farfalle pasta with smoked salmon and papardelle with mushrooms and sundried tomatoes. You just gotta enjoy! • **$35+**

✳ Mélange Café
1601 Chapel Ave., Cherry Hill, New Jersey, 856/663-7339
Located just outside the city in this Jersey suburb, Melange Café features New American cuisine with Louisiana and Italian influences

Mélange Café

Chef Joe Brown tantalizes the taste buds nightly at his restaurant, Mélange Café.

in a subtle, fine-dining atmosphere. Start with the excellent pan-smoked tomato crab bisque, then choose between the chicken maque choux with scallops, pasta pescatore, roast rack of lamb, or the bayou filet mignon with sea scallops and shrimp in brandy cream. With a menu like this, Mélange has no problem enticing customers to leave Philadelphia for a night. • **$30+/AA**

Honey, What's Our Credit Card Limit?

✳**Kansas City Prime**, 417 Main St., Manayunk, 215/482-3700—Here you'll find melt-in-your-mouth chops, larger-than-life lobsters, and ultra-tender Japanese kobe steak—considered the most expensive meat in the world. But look at it this way: You'll have 28 days to pay the bill! · $50+

✳**Le Bec Fin**, 1523 Walnut St., 215/567-1000—Considered not only the best French restaurant in Philadelphia, but also one of the best and most expensive in the United States. Is it worth it? Unfortunately, yes! Go for lunch to soften the blow to your wallet. · $100+

✳**Striped Bass**, 1500 Walnut St., 215/732-4444—You won't find seafoam blue walls or fishnets and plastic starfish as part of the decor in this ultra-sophisticated seafood restaurant. · $50+

✳**Zanzibar Blue**
200 S. Broad, 215/732-5200
Zanzibar Blue offers something none of the other restaurants on Philadelphia's exclusive Walnut Street restaurant row do: an international menu and world-class live jazz performed nightly. Start your evening with your choice of roasted tomato lobster bisque, Dungeness crab empanadas, coconut chicken tempura, or andouille sausage bruschetta. Take your time deciding between Asian barbecued yellowfin tuna, tangerine Szechuan duck, Moroccan oven-roasted chicken, or sirloin steak au poivre. After you've ordered, sit back, relax, and enjoy the music, the sophisticated crowd, and the handsome surroundings that are Zanzibar Blue. Also open for Sunday brunch. • **$35+/AA**

Casual Dinning

Astral Plane
1708 Lombard St., 215/546-6230
If Astral Plane ever decides to have a garage sale, it will have no trouble getting rid of all the stuff scattered throughout the restaurant.

Vintage posters from the glory days of the Copacabana, autographed celebrity 8x10s, and scads of little knick-knacks give Astral Plane enough ambience for three restaurants. The menu is just as eclectic, featuring creamy pastas, delicious seafood, and tempting chicken dishes. Tarot card readings by the restaurant's table-hopping psychic are great fun for dessert. • **$25+**

Delilah's
Reading Terminal Market, 12th and Arch St., 215/574-0929
30th St. Amtrak Station, 30th and Market, 215/243-2440
Terminal B, Philadelphia International Airport
Terminal E, Philadelphia International Airport
What smells so good? At Delilah's Reading Terminal location, the aromas of southern-fried chicken, chopped chicken barbecue, Virginia country ham, smothered turkey "chops," and Cajun fried catfish, served with sides like collard greens and macaroni and cheese, lead the hungry straight to her counter to find out! Delilah's cozy dining-room environment, located smack dab in the middle of the station's bustling food emporium, is a godsend for busy commuters, ravenous travelers, and other patrons. • **$10/AA**

Dwight's Southern Bar-B-Q
4345 Lancaster Ave., 215/879-2497
It's all about the barbecue at Dwight's—long ribs and short, chopped beef, pork, and chicken—with sides of broccoli and cabbage, macaroni and cheese, and corn on the cob to round out the menu. Service is take-out only, but you probably won't make it to your car without sneaking a bite from your order! • **$10+/AA**

✳Jamaican Jerk Hut
1436 South St., 215/545-8644
One of South Street's busiest restaurants, the Jamaican Jerk Hut does a mostly take-out business in the winter months since its tiny dining area seats only about 20. In the spring, however, this island-style eatery brings tropical ambience to the Philly coast when the veranda opens for dining under the stars. Local favorites include curried conch and fried plantains, spicy Jamaican sweet-and-sour chicken over jasmine rice, succulent jerk pork with rice and peas, and curried shrimp roti with sweet mango chutney relish. BYOB. • **$20+/AA**

Neighborhod Haunts

Champagne, 21 E. Chelten Ave., 215/849-7366—Located in the heart of Germantown, Champagne is an upscale supper club specializing in seafood dining and night-time entertainment including karaoke, live R&B bands, and dancing to oldies, R&B, and reggae. Of course, there's an impressive champagne menu and lots of late-night fare for midnight cravings. · $20+/AA

✳**Diane & Tom's Café**, 26 W. Maplewood Mall, 215/842-1996—"Where home-cooking is only a mouthful away!" claims the slogan at Diane & Tom's. Yeah, but do you know anyone who can prepare shrimp Alfredo over fettuccine or chicken stir-fry like this at home? For such a small, unassuming spot, this café offers a rather sophisticated menu specializing in pastas, vegetarian dishes, stir-fries, and gourmet salads. Open for breakfast. · $10+/AA

Moody's on the Pike, 6834 Limekiln Pike, 215/924-7077—This popular Philadelphia spot attracts a mature clientele with food and a good time. Moody's traditional American cuisine includes lobster tails, fried shrimp, porterhouse steaks, stuffed flounder, crab cakes, and skillet-fried chicken, as well as that famous sweet potato pie. · $25+/AA

Magnolia Café
1602 Locust St., 215/546-4180
Creole cuisine usually doesn't translate well outside of New Orleans, but Magnolia Café somehow got the recipes down right, remembered to add just enough cayenne pepper, and even hauled in a Dixieland band to keep the joint jumpin' all night long! You can't miss this restaurant—it's the one with the large tree out front festooned with Mardi Gras beads. The menu is typical New Orleans, yet some items are more authentic than others. The gumbo is inconsistent, but the Cajun margaritas, blackened fish, oyster po-boy sandwiches, chicken mamou pasta, and sweet potato pecan pie are on the money. • **$25+**

✳**Warmdaddy's**
4–6 S. Front St., 215/627-2500
Warmdaddy's decor may be rich and modern, but once the band sets the stage on fire with that real down-home blues, you'll swear you're in a backroads juke joint! And what goes better with the blues than some down-home cookin'? Warmdaddy's colorful menu features Crazy Clara's fish fingers, real ol'-fashioned southern-style chitter-lings, down-home smothered chicken and waffles, Big Moose's fried chicken and baby back ribs combo, backwoods-fried cornmeal cat-fish, and vegetable jambalaya. Whatever you do, save room for the ever-so-seriously-delicious bread pudding with bourbon sauce. • **Music charge/$25+/AA**

Nightclubs

Philadelphia is notorious for its former warehouses-turned-interna-tional-dance-clubs. The majority of these stand shoulder-to-shoul-der on Columbia Boulevard, along the Delaware River waterfront. The party usually doesn't get started until after 11 p.m., and parking is tight on the strip, so cabbing it is the way to go. Besides, who wants to walk, after parking several blocks away, in four-inch heels? The club sound too "techno" and a little too "bump, bump, bump" for you? Philly also has great jazz and blues clubs, and the suburbs boast dozens of neighborhood joints where R&B and old-school tunes never go out of style.

✳**Brasil's Restaurant and Night Spot**
112 Chestnut St., 215/413-1700
When was the last time someone enticed you to samba? Or wined and dined you on a Rodízio feast of sausage, chicken, pork loin, or sirloin tips over rice, beans, and fried bananas? Brasil's offers a truly international experience: the only authentic Brazilian cuisine in the area and the best in Brazilian jazz and Latin samba music. Its Saturday night jams are the bomb!

✳**Warmdaddy's**
4–6 S. Front St., 215/627-2500
This is the only place in Philly where you can hear down-and-dirty

Shake Your Groove Thang!

Brave New World, Seventh and Arch St., 215/413-4000—World music, reggae, urban contemporary, and R&B. · Admission charge/AA

Club Egypt, 520 N. Columbus Blvd., 215/922-6500—Techno, Top 40, dance hits, and urban contemporary. · Admission charge

Katmandu Pier 25, 417 N. Columbus Blvd., 215/629-1101—Top 40, dance hits, and urban contemporary. Outdoor dancing during summer. · Admission charge

Pegasus, 3801 Chestnut St., 215/386-0260—Urban contemporary, R&B, old school, and hip-hop. · Admission charge/AA

blues favorites like "Girlfriend, Your Husband Been Cheatin' on Us!" while meetin' and greetin' big time on the side at the long bar with the smoking section up front. Warmdaddy's has it all, and it's all wrapped up in a chic, upscale setting. • **Music charge/AA**

✳Zanzibar Blue
200 S. Broad, 215/732-5200
Zanzibar Blue features world-class jazz seven nights a week in a gorgeous, supper club atmosphere. National and local talents, continental cuisine, and a popular bar area make it one of the city's favorite late-night haunts. • **Music charge/AA**

Festivals

Philadelphia enjoys a number of music and ethnic festivals throughout the spring and summer months. In addition to the events mentioned below, there are weekly neighborhood multicultural events ready to welcome newcomers to their little corners of the city.

Penn Relays, Franklin Field
University of Pennsylvania, 215/898-6145
This tradition-rich track-and-field event is one of the most explosive

shows of solidarity, sportsmanship, and survival-of-the-fittest competition in the country. Bill Cosby, the Penn Relay's number-one fan, never misses a chance to cheer on the hundreds of young men and women who come from every corner of the country to compete in numerous running, jumping, and throwing events. Competitors with names like Carl Lewis, Michael Johnson, and Renaldo Skeets Nehemiah have gone on to fame and the Olympics. Others go home filled with pride, knowing they did their best, and that's grand.
• **Last weekend in April/Admission charge**

Odunde African Street Festival
African Market Place, 23rd and South Sts., 215/732-8508
The Odunde African Street Festival is a colorful ceremonial welcome to the new year for African and African American people. The processional to the Schuykill River for the offering of fruits and flowers to Oshun, the Goddess of the River, is the highlight of the day's joyous activities. • **Second Saturday in June/Free**

All That Corporate-Sponsored Jazz

Corestates Jam on the River, Penn's Landing, 215/636-1666—Each year Philadelphia welcomes the music and culinary delights of the "Big Easy" (that's New Orleans, y'all!) to Penn's Landing on the waterfront. For three days, the joint jumps with terrific music including blues and R&B, gospel, jazz and jazz fusion, zydeco, and reggae. · Memorial Day weekend/Admission charge

Mellon Jazz Festival, various venues, 610/667-3559—The Mellon Jazz Festival showcases the best in local and national talent throughout the city with 10 exciting days of terrific jazz. Past performers have included Branford Marsalis, Roy Hargrove, Jon Lucien, the Rippingtons, and Lou Rawls. · Mid-July/Music charge for some venues

Peco Energy Jazz Festival, various venues, 215/636-1666—The Peco Jazz Fest starts the year off right with live music staged at nightclubs and venues citywide. · Second week in February/Music charge

Neighborhood Block Parties

African American Extravaganza, Penn's Landing, 215/457-4725—Arts, music, food and performance festival. · August

African American Heritage Festival, Fairmount Park, 215/684-1008—Black Family Reunion celebrates family and friends. · July

Caribbean Festival Penn's Landing, 215/879-9352—Celebrating the culture, foods, and sounds of the Caribbean. · August

Cecil B. Moore Avenue Jazz-Blues Festival, 15th St. and Cecil B. Moore Ave., 215/763-8996—Local talent rocks the neighborhood.

Junkanoo Festival, Point Breeze Civic Association, Dickinson to Morris Sts., 215/336-9790—Parades, music, food, and fun.

Sunoco "Welcome America" Celebration
Various venues, 800/770-5883
Philadelphia throws its doors wide open for the biggest party of the year. More than 2.5 million people descend on the city for the 10-day festival. The weekend before the Fourth usually kicks off with the Great Gospel Gathering, featuring the area's most powerful and angelic voices, and strong enough in spirit to raise the roof of the convention center. Outdoor jazz concerts, dance performances, and art exhibits fill up the week. You can even get free admission into Philly's world-famous museums. And if that's not enough, the Mummers, Philly's answer to Mardi Gras revelers (sans floats), sashay through the city streets showing off their outrageous costumes and good humor. To top it all off, on the Big Day, everyone and their mamas gather around the base of the Philadelphia Museum of Art and along the Ben Franklin Parkway to listen to the Philadelphia Pops Orchestra. Special Pops guests like Dionne Warwick and Smokey Robinson close the show, along with 40 sensational minutes of ear-splitting, eye-dazzling fireworks, carefully choreographed to the nation's favorite contemporary and patriotic songs. God bless America—for real! • **Ten days prior to the Fourth of July/Most events free**

Artistic Expression

Held the second weekend in November, the Philadelphia Art Expo (New Apollo of Temple, Temple University, 1776 N. Broad St., 215/629-3939; free) is the largest and certainly one of the most impressive gatherings of work by African and African American artists. The vast floor of the Apollo arena is transformed into an intricate maze of colorful sculptures, oil paintings, and prints available for admiration or purchase, and artists are in attendance to discuss and sign their works. Many attendees are amazed at the quality and quantity of the art presented.

The Philadelphia Art Expo is the brainchild of Mercer Redcross of October Gallery. Its purpose is to create a broader awareness of the talents of African American artists. In 1985, the first Expo drew a meager 200 curiosity seekers. Today, 200 is the number of artists in attendance from 45 states and six countries around the world. In addition to the exhibits, seminars are conducted daily and live performances by local talent round out the offerings. Past years' attendance has been estimated at 40,000 over the three-day period, so the word must be out!

Pan-Hellenic Council Greek Picnic
Belmont Plateau, Fairmount Park, 215/851-0822
We're talkin' more folks than you have probably ever seen in one place at one time: More than 200,000 African American fraternity and sorority members, their friends, and families descend on Belmont Plateau to party hardy and raise money for charity. And just in case you have any energy left after the picnic, local nightclubs plan scores of late-night parties to top off the festivities. • **Last weekend in July/Free/Charge for evening events**

Museums

Charles L. Blockson Afro-American Collection
Temple University, Broad St. and Montgomery Ave.,
215/204-6632
Ever since he was a young student, Charles Blockson understood the

Up and Down the Parkway

Academy of Natural Sciences, 1900 Ben Franklin Pkwy., 215/299-1000— This is the oldest science research institute in the Western Hemisphere. Its permanent exhibit, "Butterflies," takes a look at the insects' role as preservationists of the rainforest. · Admission charge

All Wars Memorial To Colored Soldiers and Sailors, 20th St. and Ben Franklin Pkwy.—This impressive 18-foot monument paying tribute to three centuries of African American war heroes is located across from the Franklin Institute Science Museum.

Franklin Institute Science Museum, 20th and Ben Franklin Pkwy., 215/448-1200—Four floors of some 500 interactive science exhibits and demonstrations and an IMAX movie theater are among the sights here. · Admission charge

✳**Please Touch Museum**, 210 N. 21st St., 215/963-0667—This innovative museum offers hands-on and interactive exhibits for the cultural enrichment of children. · Admission charge

Rodin Museum, 22nd and Ben Franklin Pkwy., 215/763-8100—More than 120 sculptures and drawings including Rodin's most revered and famous sculpture, The Thinker. Donations accepted.

importance of his ancestral legacy; he preserved it through documentation. Over a span of 50 years, Blockson's collection has grown to more than 80,000 pieces, including books, manuscripts, prints, drawings, sheet music, and artifacts. An accomplished author and historian, Blockson spearheaded a state historical project that resulted in the production of 65 markers noting contributions made by African Americans. Placed throughout the city, the markers are identified in Blockson's *Philadelphia Guide: African American State Historical Markers*.

Philadelphia Doll Museum
2253 N. Broad St., 215/787-0220
This tiny showroom is filled with more than 300 Black dolls from the United States, the Caribbean, and Africa, from two-feet-high Black baby dolls in ivory christening gowns to soft handmade West

Gallery Hoppin'

Dizyners Gallery, 65 N. Second St., 215/627-8955—Custom jewelry designs as well as painting and sculptures by local African American artists. · AA

Lucien Crump Gallery, 6380 Germantown Ave., 215/843-8788—Local as well as renowned artists are on display in this modern neighborhood gallery. · AA

October Gallery, 68 N. Second St., 215/629-3939—Organizers of the Philadelphia Art Expo, the October Gallery features original artwork by world-renowned African American artists. · AA

Sande Weber Gallery, 2018 Locust St., 215/732-8850—Sande Weber is credited with introducing the talent of many local Black artists to the city's art community.

African dolls decked out in colorful dress. Executive director and serious collector Barbara Whiteman moved her doll collection from her home to its current location when lugging the figures around the country became too much for her. Her collection, in her own words, is "a summary of African American history, of how society has seen us and how we've seen ourselves." Each May, Whiteman hosts the International Black Doll Convention, the largest Black doll convention in the country. • **Admission charge**

Philadelphia Museum of Art
26th and Ben Franklin Pkwy., 215/763-8100
It's easy to get lost in this awesome structure, designed by Julian Francis Abele, the first African American to graduate from the University of Pennsylvania School of Architecture. Recognized as the third-largest museum in the United States, the Philadelphia Museum of Art houses 200-plus galleries filled with more than 400,000 works of art. Permanent collections include pieces from around the world, with emphasis on European paintings and Asian and African art. • **Admission charge**

Churches

African Episcopal Church of St. Thomas
6361 Lancaster Ave., 215/473-3065
Founded in 1792 for persons of African descent seeking religious expression and freedom from the segregated church, the Episcopal church was united under the leadership of Absalom Jones. In 1804, Jones was ordained the first African American priest in the nation. Rev. Jones's legacy of humanitarianism continues today through the church's many service programs.

First African Baptist Church
16th and Christian St., 215/735-1050
First African is one of the oldest Black Baptist churches in the country. Its members organized the first insurance company to serve the African American community.

Mother Bethel AME Church
419 Richard Allen Ave., 215/925-0616
In 1787, Richard Allen established the world's first AME church with a group of free Africans who called themselves the Free African Society and who left the segregated St. George Methodist Episcopal Church congregation in search of religious freedom. The group's first sanctuary was a blacksmith shop located on the same spot where Mother Bethel church stands today. Their church was the first property owned by African people in the United States, and Richard Allen went on to become the first bishop of the AME church. Today, Mother Bethel is one of the principal tourist attractions in downtown Philadelphia. Its beautiful stained-glass windows feature both religious and Masonic themes. Downstairs, the Richard Allen Museum houses 19th-century artifacts including the original church pews, the pulpit from which Allen preached, his tomb, and those of his wife and Bishop Morris Brown.

St. Peter Cleaver's Roman Catholic Church
1200 Lombard St., 215/735-0799
Named after Peter Cleaver, a 19th-century advocate for the emancipation of slaves, this church was dedicated for African American Catholics in 1892.

Tindley Temple United Methodist Church
762 S. Broad St., 215/735-0442
Former slave Charles Albert Tindley came to Philadelphia to study
for the ministry and aid those trying to escape from the South. The
Reverend Tindley's humanitarian example is still followed today
through his church's free meal and clothing programs.

Recreation

Atlantic City, New Jersey
888/ACVISIT
Only one hour from downtown Philadelphia, Atlantic City is
nowhere near the opulent playground that is Las Vegas. It does,
however, have its share of campy hotels and casinos, splashy
celebrity stage productions, endless shopping, all-you-can-eat buf-
fets, and, of course, that famous boardwalk and beach. Once you've
paid up all your casino markers, check out the African American
History Museum, 609/348-8906, on Kentucky Avenue, to learn
about Black life in AC during the early part of the 20th century.

Freeway Golf and Country Club
1858 Sicklerville Rd., Sicklerville, New Jersey, 609/227-1115
Located about 20 miles from downtown Philadelphia, Freeway is
the only African American-owned 18-hole golf course in the area.

Joe Frazier's Gym
2917 N. Broad St., 215/221-1115
Owned and operated by "Smokin' Joe" himself, Philadelphia's favorite son keeps busy these days encouraging young fighters and
mentoring kids.

St. Louis

St. Louis. It's where Scott Joplin introduced the world to ragtime. Where W. C. Handy composed the blues of the same name. Where three American favorites—iced tea, ice cream cones, and ice-cold beer—made their debuts. Throughout all these developments, the mighty Mississippi has kept a-rollin' by.

A visit to St. Louis would not be complete without a walk around Laclede Landing, once owned and occupied by African Americans. Now a riverfront entertainment district, Laclede's Landing was home to many wealthy free Blacks before the Civil War. The most celebrated of these settlers was Jacques Clamorgan, a wealthy West Indian fur trader-entrepreneur, whose family is credited with establishing and cultivating the 19th-century colored aristocracy in St. Louis. Cobblestoned Clamorgan Alley is named in his honor.

Adjacent to the Landing, surrounded by the beautifully manicured St. Louis Riverfront, is one of the country's most recognizable monuments (possibly because it evokes that set of golden arches hamburger-hungry Americans have come to know and love): the Gateway Arch. At its base sits the Old Cathedral (Basilica of Saint Louis King), the city's oldest church, ringing in at a good-lookin' 165-plus years old!

Two blocks west on Market Street is the Old Courthouse, site of one of the earliest and most significant fights for civil rights: the infamous Dred Scott trial. Scenes from this courtroom drama are reenacted daily, lest we forget. If you head west on Delmar, you'll reach the restored antebellum home of Scott Joplin, the father of ragtime.

While in Town, Swing By…

Martin Luther King Jr. Statue, Fountain Park, Euclid and Fountain—
Listed on the National Register of Historic Places, this impressive
11-foot bronze statue captures the passion and conviction of the
orator. The base of the statue is inscribed: "His Dream–Our Dream."

St. Louis Walk of Fame, 6504 Delmar Blvd., 314/727-STAR,
www.stlouiswalkoffame.org—Why bother going all the way to
Hollywood when the St. Louis Walk of Fame puts you toe to toe
with the brass stars of the stars! Maya Angelou, Josephine Baker,
Chuck Berry, Tina Turner, and Red Foxx are among the privileged
to be immortalized on the walk. Bronze plaques tell the stories of
these honorary St. Louis citizens.

Continue traveling northwest on Delmar to Grand Avenue,
make a right, then a left on St. Louis Avenue, and you're in the heart
of a historic Black neighborhood called The Ville. This district is
home to Sumner High School, the first high school west of the
Mississippi dedicated to the education of African American students.
Famous graduates include our girl Tina Turner, Chuck Berry, the
late tennis great Arthur Ashe, and Missouri Congressman William
L. Clay. The Reverend Dr. Martin Luther King Jr. is remembered
with a majestic statue in Fountain Park, located east of Kingshighway Boulevard between Delmar and Page. Many historical
events significant to African Americans occurred in the Ville. While
in the 'hood, stop by Robert's Cafeteria, where you'll have a hard
time deciding between the barbecued "porksteak" and the fried catfish platter.

After lunch, head south on Kingshighway Boulevard to Forest
Park, one of the largest urban parks in the United States. After a
stroll around the park, check out the Central West End, where
lovely early-20th-century homes rub sidings with clever, funky
clothing stores, open-air eateries, and wonderfully junky antique
galleries. If it's drama you crave, call ahead for tickets to the latest
production by the St. Louis Black Repertory Company at the Grand
Center, located in the arts and entertainment district. Enjoy some

local flavor at Gene Lynn's, where for years Mr. Lynn himself has taken the mic to croon love songs to all the lovely ladies. If Gene's groove is a little too mellow for you, let riverboat gambling entice you and the dice to roll on down the mighty Mississippi.

Restaurants

Quick, what famous foods are associated with St. Louis? Almost a century ago, iced tea, hot dogs, and ice cream cones were introduced at the Louisiana Purchase Exposition fair. Today, St. Louis is best known for robust brews, tangy barbecue, and crispy snoots. Snoots? Yes, and they do mean the "Rooter," but the flavor and texture is more like fried cracklin', and *that* taste and image we can handle!

Fine Dining

✴Fio's La Fourchette
7515 Forsyth, 314/863-6866

How can you not love a fine French restaurant that offers a complimentary second helping if the first serving fails to satisfy your hunger! But before you make room in your stomach for an all-you-can-eat-feast, know this: Fio's La Fourchette is no overpriced buffet palace. In fact, it's known for its rich five-course prix fixe menu. Pass on that second helping of veal medallions, and save room for the amazing Grand Marnier soufflé served with a lush custard sauce. • **$50+**

Casual Dining

✴Babalu's
8 1/2 S. Euclid Ave., 314/367-7833

This cheap and cheerful spot will make you long for a sandy beach, gentle breeze, and tall frosty rum punch. Well, at least you can get the drink at Babalu's, St. Louis's answer to an island getaway. Jamaican jerk pork skewers with mango salsa for dipping, chile-rubbed grilled salmon in a buttery citrus ginger sauce, and chicken rubbed, roasted, and carefully wrapped in a banana leaf are among the island favorites Babalu's serves on the mainland. • **$20**

✳Crown Cafeteria
2618 Martin Luther King Jr. Dr., 314/535-0590
The oldest African American-owned restaurant in St. Louis (circa 1947), Crown serves home-style cooking "like mama prepared down South." The handsomely decorated dining area fills up with the after-church crowd, who come to dine on tender roast pork, duck, chitterlings, turkey wings, pigs' feet, sweet potatoes, and chicken and dumplings. • **$10/AA**

Del Monico's Diner
4909 Delmar, 314/361-0973
Del Monico's is known throughout St. Louis as *the* spot for simple, down-home cookin'. For breakfast, Del Monico's serves everything from fried green tomatoes to salmon croquettes, but lunch is their main meal of the day. Entrées include baked chicken, ham hocks, smothered pork chops, prime rib, roast beef, and lots of sides of fresh greens, squash, and mashed potatoes. • **$10+/AA**

✳Duff's Restaurant
392 N. Euclid Ave., 314/361-0522
Alfresco dining doesn't get any better than at Duff's. When the weather is fine, folks wait up to 30 minutes for a sidewalk seat, well worth it to watch the world drift by and indulge in Duff's innovative New American menu. Must-tries include the Moroccan roasted vegetable, lamb sausage, and chickpea stew over couscous and the to-die-for chocolate brownie topped with whipped cream and drizzled with hot fudge. • **$25+**

Mama Campisi's Restaurant
2132 Edwards St., 314/771-1797
It's safe to say Mama Campisi's is one of the city's most popular tourist attractions. Blame its fame on the toasted ravioli, an "only in St. Louis" dish that features eggplant, mushrooms, and cauliflower stuffed into a lightly fried pasta. Mama's extensive classic Italian menu is great eating when nothing but red sauce will do. • **$25+**

✳Reynolds' Barbecue
6409 Natural Bridge, Pine Lawn, 314/385-3100
Ok, this place is about 20 minutes from downtown and not much

to look at, but the tangy rich homemade sauce, excellent rib tips, and crispy, crunchy snoots lure folks from all over the city. Reynolds' North Carolina-style hickory-smoked ribs, beef brisket, chopped pork (serious business!), barbecue chicken wings, tangy baked beans, and fresh lemonade are local favorites. After all, what else do you need with barbecue this good but a pile of napkins and some room?! • **$10+/AA**

✳Richard's Ribs
10727 Big Bend, Kirkwood, 314/966-1015
Another spot out in the boonies but worth the ride, Richard's Ribs is located about 20 minutes from downtown. This place may be small, but the food coming out of the kitchen packs a *big* taste. Try the divine pulled brisket, baby back ribs, pork steak, barbecue chicken, and wings. It would be a crime to leave without ordering the heavenly homemade peach cobbler or a slice of sweet potato pie—perfect for that ride back to town!• **$10+/AA**

✳Robert's Cafeteria
1444 N. Kingshighway, 314/367-4600
✳Robert's Grill
1408 N. Kingshighway, Suite 114
There is something about cafeteria dining we all love: the seduction of what appears to be an endless smorgasbord of different varieties of food, all ready for the picking. But how do you decide between smothered pork chops laced with fat transparent onions, or crispy chicken, fried in a cast-iron skillet just like your grandma's, when they both look so-o-o good? Cafeteria owners recognize this weakness for "the more we see, the more we want," and they play us diners like bassoons! Robert's is no exception, offering lots of great soul food for not much money. Figure on starving yourself before you go, and don't be ashamed if you pile up your tray. That's the way it was planned! • **$10+/AA**

Nightclubs

Laclede's Landing, the Central West End, and Soulard are pockets of the city where nightclubs and lounges celebrate their bluesy roots

Pure Drama

Liberty Playhouse of St. Louis, Midtown Arts Center, 3007 Washington Ave., 314/963-4653—This celebrated African American theater company presents three original performances a season.

St. Louis Black Repertory Company, Grandel Square Theatre, 3716 Grandel Sq., 314/534-3807—Offering the finest in stage and dance productions, "The Black Rep" presents poignant renditions of African American culture.

with live nightly music. To hang out with the local crew, check out some of the neighborhood African American-owned bars and lounges along West Florissant.

Backstage Bistro
3536 Washington Ave., 314/534-3663
From Terrance Blanchard to the Ahmad Jamal trio, some of the biggest names in jazz appear at the Bistro, St. Louis's premier jazz club. The Bistro features a decent American-continental menu, but it's nothing compared to the tasty tunes served up nightly. • **Music charge**

BB's Jazz, Blues & Soups
700 S. Broadway, 314/436-5222
Down on the Landing, BB's is the place for nothin' but the blues, a little sassy jazz, and some good comfort food.

Brione Nites
11836 W. Florissant, 314/830-2250
This is St. Louis's party club, where the folks get down to the sounds of Motown, old school, and R&B. • **Admission charge/AA**

Broadway Oyster Bar
736 S. Broadway, 314/621-8811
Broadway Oyster Bar takes the best of the Big Easy, such as Creole food, and mixes it with St. Louis blues to create one of the city's favorite nightclubs. National and local acts appear nightly; however,

the best main attraction is the raw oysters, especially those topped with sour cream, horseradish, and caviar! • **Music charge most nights**

Club VIVA!
408 N. Euclid, 314/361-0322
Living up to its high-energy name, Club VIVA! enlivens with Latin, Brazilian and African sounds, as well as reggae, soca, jazz, and the blues. After-work happy hour, live music most nights, and an international crowd guarantee big fun for those who like to mix and mingle. • **Cover charge**

✳Gene Lynn's Cocktail Lounge & Restaurant
348 N. Sarah, 314/652-6242
This is the kind of club you would want to own if you could: intimate, up-close-and-personal, and fun! And with all the clubs in and around St. Louis, Gene Lynn's gets props for being relaxed, festive, and unpretentious. It's just large enough to hold the right number of folks (a 35-plus crowd), most of whom know each other and happily welcome visitors to the fold. And then there's Gene Lynn, who personally greets every patron who enters his club. If you are a lucky lady, he may even sing to you! • **AA**

Ms. Whit's Candlelight Palace Lounge
9814 W. Florissant,
314/867-9066
That's Ms. Whit to you—or anyone else, chile! Don't even *think* about calling her anything but! One of St. Louis's favorite cool-out spots, Ms. Whit's is a rustic, comfortable, unpretentious neighborhood hangout, where the dart tournaments are fierce and the music is pure R&B! Ms. Whit herself DJs Thursday through Sunday evening. • **AA**

Spruill's Restaurant & Lounge
2625 Stoddard, 314/533-8050
A lot of great local music comes out of this upscale neighborhood lounge and restaurant. Spruill's is considered one of St. Louis's favorite jazz nightclubs, with live jazz every weekend and great American soul food fare nightly. • **Dinner $20+/AA**

Festivals

Black Dance-USA: A Celebration in Movement
Center of Contemporary Arts, University City, 314/367-3440
The weeklong Black Dance-USA festival gathers together some of
the country's leading choreographers and dancers to educate, entertain, and enlighten. St. Louis's top performers participate in workshops, seminars, and lectures; other workshops offered explore
topics such as African percussion for musicians and dancers, and
African song. In-school programs and dance recitals feature regional
and national dance troupes, attracting a diverse audience, all for the
love and furtherance of dance. Traditional West African, African
American jazz, tap, African, Caribbean, and hip-hop are among the
energetic dance forms explored. • **Memorial Day weekend/**
Admission charge

Juneteenth Heritage and Jazz Festival
Various venues, 314/367-0100, www.juneteenthjazz.org
The largest Juneteenth celebration in the country, this festival offers 10 days of visual arts, theater, dance, and great music, all to recognize the final emancipation of enslaved Texans on June 19, 1865.
Jazz and performance stage venues throughout St. Louis showcase
the city's brightest stars as well as the country's biggest names.
Stanley Jordan, Lonnie Liston Smith, Bobby Lyle, T. S. Monk, and
Nicolas Payton all have graced the festival stage. Not just for the
purpose of pure pleasure (but, hey, pure pleasure ain't bad!), the festival aims to educate younger generations on the joys of jazz
through seminars, lectures, and jam sessions with favorite performers. Of course, the festival's main purpose is to commemorate
Juneteenth and pledge never to forget the significance of that glorious day. • **Third week in June/Music charge**

Black Family Week
Various venues, 314/367-3440, www.betterfamilylife.com
The largest family-oriented event in the state of Missouri, Black
Family Week is filled with daily activities intended to unify and
strengthen the Black family, and prove to all those naysayers that it
is a whole, solid unit. Black Family Night at the Ballpark, Gospel
Festival, Black Family Week Parade, and "Hot Fun in the Summer

Freddy Cole performs at Spruill's, one of the Juneteenth Heritage and Jazz Festival venues.

Time" Summer Festival are among the many events produced to inform and entertain family and friends.

Better Family Life (BFL) is one of the most active sponsors of African American cultural events in St. Louis. Throughout the year, BFL hosts a number of special events, including a three-day Kwanzaa celebration. Check out their Web site, above, for a calendar of events. • **Mid-August**

Big Muddy Blues and Roots Festival
Laclede's Landing, 314/241-5875
Some 50,000 music lovers hit the cobblestone streets of historic Laclede's Landing for three days of some of the best blues, roots, and gospel in the country. First-class talent, showcasing national, regional, and local musicians, lights up five stages along the banks of the Mississippi. And it wouldn't be a blues festival without plenty of good down-home food to go with that good down-home music. • **Labor Day weekend**

Museums and Attractions

Black World History Wax Museum
2505 St. Louis Ave., 314/241-7057

Life-size wax figures of some of St. Louis's most influential residents, a remarkable replica of a section of a Middle Passage slave ship, and an authentic slave cabin from Jonesburg, Missouri, are three of the intriguing exhibits featured at the Black World History Wax Museum. The figures of Dred and Harriett Scott, George Washington Carver, John Barry Meacham, and Dr. Martin Luther King Jr. not only captivate viewers with their likenesses, but remind us of the achievements that earned these leaders their places in American history. Special traveling exhibits, along with a permanent collection of artifacts, memorabilia, and photographs, make this unique museum a must-stop while in St. Louie. • **Admission charge**

Forest Park

This gorgeous park smack in the middle of town is home to several museums as well as the St. Louis Zoo and every outdoor recreation attraction imaginable. Forest Park encompasses an 18-hole golf course, tennis courts, bike rentals and paths for safe riding, an ice-skating rink, a roller-skating rink, paddleboat and gondola rides in the Post Dispatch Lake, and the Turtle Playground, a section of the park that will charm even the oldest kids.

Riverboat Gambling

Casino Queen, 200 S. Front St., East St. Louis, 618/874-5000

Harrah's Casino at Riverport Casino Center, 777 Casino Center Dr., 314/770-8100

Players Island Casino at Riverport Casino Center, 777 Casino Center Dr., 314/209-3900

President Casino on the Admiral, St. Louis Levee below the Gateway Arch, 314/622-3000

While in the Ville, Check Out ...

The Ville is bordered by Dr. Martin Luther King Jr. Drive, Taylor Avenue, St. Louis Avenue, and Sarah Street. Once the center of the African American community, the Ville has preserved many of its historical landmarks. Contact the Greater Ville Historic Development Corporation, 314/534-8015, to arrange a tour.

Anne Malone Children's Home and Family Service Center, 2612 Annie Malone Dr.—The center was founded in 1888 as the St. Louis Colored Orphans' Home. The name was changed in 1992 when philanthropist Anne Turnbo Pope Malone donated $10,000 toward the completion of the center's current facility.

Homer G. Phillips Memorial Hospital, 2601 Whittier St.—Once the finest state-of-the-art medical facilities devoted to the training, of Black medical professionals and health care for African Americans. No longer a hospital, the building is listed on the National Register of Historic Places.

Sumner High School, 4248 W. Cottage Ave.—Arthur Ashe, Kenneth Billups, Tina Turner, Bobby McFerrin, Dick Gregory, and Robert Guillaume are just a few of the famous alumni of Sumner High. Opened in 1875, Sumner was the first high school west of the Mississippi devoted to the education of African

Missouri Historical Society Library and Collections Center
225 S. Skinker Blvd., Forest Park, 314/746-4599
Permanent exhibits explore the growth of St. Louis, the American West, and African American influences on the nation's early development. Exhibits examine African American contributions to contemporary music, sports, community outreach services, and civil rights efforts. • **Admission charge**

Old Courthouse
11 N. Fourth St., 314/655-1600
The site of the Dred Scott case, the Old Courthouse is one of

The Ville neighborhood Monument honors the ancestors of the historic African American community.

America's most significant historical landmarks. Dred Scott and his wife were denied freedom in 1857 when the Supreme Court ruled that slaves were not citizens. The repercussions of this case propelled the nation closer to civil war. Scott eventually received his

Gallery Hoppin'

Portfolio Gallery & Education Center 3514 Delmar Blvd., 314/533-3323—Lectures, workshops, and art classes are offered at the Portfolio Gallery. Headed by sculptor Robert Powell, the gallery showcases the talents of local and national artists. · AA

Hobnail Art Gallery, 4155 Lee Ave., 314/652-2677—Artist Vernon Smith proudly gives a personal tour of his gallery, which showcases more than 75 original works reflecting on the positive aspects of African American culture. · AA

Lithos Gallery, 6301B Delmar Blvd., 314/862-0674—Lithos Gallery features original paintings and sculpture from local and national African American talents, and live jazz on Friday evening. · AA

freedom from his owner shortly after the court's decision, but the victory was bittersweet: He died less than a year after his emancipation. In 1861, the steps of the Old Courthouse were the location of the last slave auction in St. Louis, but it wasn't much of an auction: The antislavery crowd refused to bid, and the protest signified that the world was a-changing.

St. Louis Art Museum
1 Fine Arts Dr., Forest Park, 314/721-0072
The museum features a small but impressive collection of paintings and artifacts by some of the country's most prolific African American artists, including Jacob Lawrence and Romare Bearden. It also boasts a permanent assemblage of African, Asian, Spanish, and Native American artifacts. • **Free admission**

Scott Joplin House
2658 Delmar Blvd., 314/533-1003
Although Joplin resided at this address only between 1901 and 1903, he composed some of his most significant arrangements here, including "Lost Opera," "A Guest of Honor," and his most famous

Tee Time

Forest Park Golf Course, 5591 Grand Dr., 314/367-1337
Pevely Farms, 400 Lewis Rd., 314/938-7000
Quail Creek Golf Club, 6022 Wells Rd., 314/487-1988

ditty, "The Entertainer," more commonly known as the theme from *The Sting.* Joplin received the most acclaim while living in St. Louis. His home was deemed a national landmark to commemorate his contributions to the St. Louis music scene, as well as to honor accomplishments by other St. Louis African Americans. • **Admission charge**

Vaughn Cultural Center
525 N. Grand Blvd., 314/535-9227
Under the direction of the local chapter of the Urban League, the Vaughn Cultural Center's mission is to increase the community's awareness of African American history and the arts. Gallery presentations of local artists and special cultural activities take place regularly. Call for a schedule of events.

Churches

Antioch Baptist Church
4213 W. North Market St., 314/535-1110
Antioch Baptist, established in 1884, is one of the oldest churches still standing in the Ville.

Central Baptist Church
2843 Washington Ave., 314/533-0747
The fourth-oldest African American church in St. Louis, Central Baptist is historically known as the site of the Missouri Equal Rights League, the state's first Black political activist organization established soon after the end of the Civil War.

First Baptist Church
3100 Bell Ave., 314/533-8003
Formally the First African Baptist Church, the city's first Black Protestant congregation was founded by the Reverend John Berry Meachum. One of St. Louis's most influential African Americans, a former slave and entrepreneur, Meachum purchased slaves, educated them, then freed them. Because his floating "Freedom School" sat anchored off shore, on one of his barges on the Mississippi River, Meachum managed to defy Missouri laws prohibiting the education of slaves. Hundreds of children were taught during the 1840s and 1850s.

Washington Metropolitan AME Zion Church
613 N. Garrison Ave., 314/533-0316
The oldest African Methodist Episcopal Zion church in St. Louis, the stunning edifice of Washington AME was designated a landmark in 1974.

Washington Tabernacle Baptist Church
3200 Washington Blvd. 314/533-8763
Historically known for hosting one of the largest Civil Rights rallies, spearheaded in 1963 by the Reverend Dr. Martin Luther King Jr., the Washington Tabernacle Baptist Church is also credited with the leadership development of a generation of local African Americans. This beautiful 1879 Gothic Revival church is a designated national landmark.

Washington, D.C.

Washington, D.C. The nation's capital. The District of Columbia. Dee Cee. Chocolate City. By whatever name, Washington, D.C., has come a long way from the boorish 1980s, a decade characterized by stuffy Republicans and starched-collar Capitol Hill staffers running to work in navy blue polyester suits and tennis shoes. Thank goodness the 1990s brought us Democrats behaving badly, the return and departure of Mayor-for-Life Marion S. Barry, the resurgence of the historic U Street corridor, and the emergence of first-class restaurants and cool, cozy clubs. What has not changed—and we pray it never will—is the ever-renewing beauty of this city on the banks of the Potomac.

As the seasons change, the landscape and pageantry that make D.C. one of the nation's most picturesque locales continue to allure. Each April, millions flock to Washington to stroll along the Tidal Basin beneath the almost-surreal pale pink buds of the world-famous cherry blossom trees. The landing in front of the Thomas Jefferson Memorial overlooking the basin provides unobstructed star gazing, making it one of the most romantic spots in the city on a warm summer's night. (It also offers a sneak-peek of the White House's backyard!) The proper way to welcome fall in D.C. is to take a long, winding drive through Rock Creek Park. At the southern end of the park, trees show off their new fashion colors while leaves make their ceremonial journeys to the ground, fluttering against a stunning backdrop of the enormous stone arches supporting Connecticut Avenue above. During the winter, legions of lobbyists, cell phones permanently attached to their ears, scarcely notice the majestic Corinthian columns that grace the numerous government buildings in and out of which they dart every day. Yet the nation's capital is the consummate tourist attraction, all year 'round.

The downtown Capitol Hill area alone deserves several days to explore the majestic monuments, museums, and galleries. Start your day with a huge plate of blueberry pancakes and crisp bacon at the Market Lunch at Eastern Market. On Saturday, this outdoor emporium hops with vendors selling everything from handmade jewelry, original arts and crafts, and fresh flowers to homemade cakes and sweet potato pies. From there it's a short walk to the grand steps of the U.S. Capitol. From the top of the steps, enjoy the spectacular bird's-eye view of the National Mall, which stretches 23 blocks beyond the Washington Monument to the Lincoln Memorial and is bordered by numerous Smithsonian museums. When you think of the historical events that have taken place on the Mall, from Marion Anderson's stirring rendition of "America, the Beautiful" to Dr. Martin Luther King Jr.'s "I Have a Dream" speech to the Million Man March, you'll feel you're walking on sacred ground.

No visit to D.C. would be complete without a drive through the city's diverse neighborhoods. The historic districts of Shaw and LeDroit Park, centers of Black business and culture during segregation and home to notables such as Duke Ellington, had long been neglected before recent renewal efforts revitalized them. The Gold Coast, an area north of Mount Pleasant and east of Rock Creek Park on 16th Street, is home to many of the city's African American nouveau riche.

Cross the district's other historic waterway, the Anacostia, to take a tour of the Frederick Douglass Home and to explore the revolving exhibits at the Smithsonian's Anacostia Museum of African American History.

Back in the northwestern section of town, Adams-Morgan is a bubbling caldron of African American, African, European, Caribbean, and Hispanic immigrant cultures, replete with great ethnic restaurants and bars. It's bordered on the south by the U Street corridor, during segregation referred to as Washington's "Black Broadway." This neighborhood has undergone an amazing transformation to become one of the city's hottest strips. Stop at the Islander Caribbean Restaurant for its signature dish of Calypso chicken, rice, and peas.

Then stroll down the street for an after-dinner cognac and the best in Brazilian jazz at U-topia, one of the city's most eclectic neighborhood bars. The late, late-night crew should make a beeline to Club 2K9, where dancing continues until the wee hours.

Restaurants

With its large international population, it's no surprise Washington, D.C., boasts the most diverse selection of ethnic restaurants in the country. D.C.'s Adams-Morgan community is a veritable melting pot of Ethiopian, West African, Caribbean, Italian, and modern American restaurants and bars. These foods too common for you? If it's Salvadoran, Malaysian, Persian, Turkish, or great soul food you seek, look no further—you've come to the right town! Enjoy!

Fine Dining

✳B. Smith's
50 Massachusetts Ave. N.E., 202/289-6188
Located in the Grand Hall of Washington, D.C.'s beautifully refurbished Union Station, B. Smith's restaurant brings charm, sophistication, and "southern fare with New York flair" to an appreciative audience. Savory entrées includ the infamous "swamp thing"—étouffée with sautéed lobster and scallops—and wonderful grilled lamb chops with lamb au jus. Live jazz is featured on Wednesday, Thursday, and Saturday evenings. • **$30+/AA**

✳BET on Jazz Restaurant
730 11th St. NW, 202/393-0975
The decor at this newest, high-profile BET (Black Entertainment Television) eatery is strictly Harlem Renaissance, with gorgeous art deco appointments and strategically placed banquettes filled to overflowing with young D.C. sophisticates. The menu is classified as "New World Caribbean," with kudos going to the piquant jerk chicken on penne pasta, the thick veal chop brown stewed in a Cabernet sauce, and the grilled grouper filet precariously balanced on a light, sweet plantain mash. Live jazz most nights; Wednesday happy hour is hot. • **$35+/AA**

D.C.'s Best

✳**Bombay Club**, 815 Connecticut Ave. NW, 202/659-3727—The best Indian cuisine in D.C. An excellent Tandoori salmon, extra-spicy crab Marsalla, and luscious butter chicken in an exquisite fine-dining setting. · $35+

✳**Cesco Trattoria**, 4871 Cordell Ave., Bethesda, Maryland, 301/654-8333—Superb Tuscan Italian cuisine with a fall-off-the-bone veal osso buco and a glorious roast pork chop. · $35+

✳**Kinkead's**, 2000 Pennsylvania Ave. NW, 202/296-7700—Arguably the best seafood restaurant—correction, best restaurant, period—in the district. · $40+

✳**DC Coast**
1401 K St. NW, 202/216-5988
DC Coast's interior is absolutely delicious, with cathedral ceilings, rich woods, and funky high-back overstuffed chairs in the lounge/bar area. And the food is amazing! Seafood rules here, from chilled raw oysters massaged with a splash of vodka and pickled ginger to rich lobster bisque, from mushroom-crusted halibut atop a large portabello mushroom and fluffy truffle-whipped potatoes to (in season) jumbo crab cakes balanced on top of a cornmeal-fried softshell crab. • **$35+**

✳**Georgia Brown's Restaurant**
950 15th St. NW, 202/393-4499
Bronze ribbons spin a graceful web across the ceiling while blond waves of maplewood surround diners at Georgia Brown's, D.C.'s most popular spot for nouvelle southern cuisine. Located just two blocks from the White House, this is one restaurant where the clientele crosses all racial, professional, and political lines. The extensive low country menu offers wonderful pan-seared sea bass with sautéed crayfish, barbecued Cornish game hen with red bliss mashed potatoes, and Carolina shrimp and grits (spicy hot and lovin' it!).

The Sunday jazz brunch at Georgia Brown's has become a Washington tradition. • **$30+/AA-invested**

✳The Savoy
1220 19th St. NW, 202/293-6848

With sassy and sophisticated decor and live jazz nightly, the Savoy lives up to its illustrious name, attracting a well-heeled clientele and serving up delish nouvelle southern cuisine. Located just a couple of stair steps beneath 19th Street, DC's illustrious restaurant row, the Savoy boasts beautifully appointed cherrywood accents and a spacious L-shaped lounge area that's cigar friendly and perfect for meeting and greeting.

The menu brims with good stuff. Appetizers include a wonderful seafood gumbo served over, get this, sweet polenta not rice and low country chicken livers sautéed in a spiced garlic relish. Entrées include Gullah shrimp and gravy over creamy yellow grits and pork chops delicately stuffed with well-seasoned kale. Save room for the sinful crème brûlée! • **$35+/AA**

✳Zanzibar on the Waterfront
700 Water St. SW, 202/554-9102

This one-stop entertainment center offers dancing nightly, along with live jazz on Tuesday and Thursday, free salsa lessons on Wednesday, and a serious oldies and world music dance club atmosphere on the weekend. A first-class menu of dishes reflecting the African, Caribbean, and Latin America diasporas permeates the vibrant dinning room with the pungent aromas of countless spices. Could it be the appetizer of mini-lamb kabobs brushed with garlic, cinnamon, and peppers and served on a sweet potato pancake? Or the Caribbean lobster in a light mushroom sauce with green banana dumplings? Dinner and dancing—what a novel idea! • **$35+/AA**

Casual Dining

✳Ben's Chili Bowl
1213 U St. NW, 202/667-0909

Virginia Ali and her husband, Ben, opened Ben's Chili Bowl in 1958. Back then, U Street was for Blacks the most fashionable place to be in segregated D.C. Today, Ben's famous chili dogs are enjoyed by

Good to Go

Full Kee, 509 H St. NW, 202/371-2233—Huge bowls of excellent Hong Kong noodle soup stuffed with fat shrimp dumplings and a tender roast duck are just two reasons why the lines are out the door at this modest Chinatown eatery. · $10+

Horace & Dickie's Seafood Carry Out, 809 12th St. NE, 202/397-6040—Everyone in D.C. knows that if you want a real fish sandwich and you've got only four dollars, head to Horace & Dickie's! The entire menu consists of fried fish, fried shrimp, crab cakes, chicken, fries, potato salad, slaw, and collard greens. That's it! Then again, what else do you need? · $5+/AA

Webb's Southern Fish & Ribs, 1351 U St. NW, 202/462-FISH—Great home cooking served in a styrofoam container! Chitterlings, baked red snapper, smothered pork chops, barbecued ribs, and big sides of greens, macaroni and cheese, and sweet potato pie. · $10/AA

such notables as Denzel Washington and Bill Cosby, who swears by Ben's half-smokes. All-beef chili dogs, chili con carne with cheese and onions, chili cheese fries, and turkey and veggie burgers round out Ben's menu. Nowadays, breakfast at Ben's is served only between 6 and 11 a.m., but the restaurant is open until 4 a.m. on weekends. • **$10/AA**

BET SoundStage
9640 Lottsford Ct., Largo, Maryland, 301/883-9500
The BET (Black Entertainment Television) SoundStage Restaurant offers a visually stimulating dining environment made possible via state-of-the-art video programming, an impressive collection of original works by African American artists, and a handsome, well-configured seating area. Its extensive menu features American and Caribbean cuisines, and it's known for its Sunday brunch. This is a great place to bring the gang to celebrate a birthday, promotion, or the end of another work week. • **$20+/AA**

Carolina Kitchen
8517 Colesville Rd., Silver Spring, Maryland, 301/585-4400
Carolina Kitchen specializes in home-style cooking served cafeteria style. Must-tries include perfectly seasoned jerk chicken, Creole chicken, thick slices of Mom's meatloaf, barbecued beef ribs, and smothered pork chops. There are 15 side dishes to choose from, but Carolina Kitchen saves the best for last: thick, moist sweet potato cake. All that's missing is a big scoop of vanilla ice cream on the side. What do you say, Lance, can you help a sister out? • $10/AA

Florida Avenue Grill
1100 Florida Ave. NW, 202/265-1586
Located just a few blocks from Howard University, the Florida Avenue Grill is arguably the most famous soul food restaurant in D.C. Open since 1944, the food at the grill is uncomplicated and just plain good! Breakfast is served daily until 1 p.m. Dinner favorites include chitterlings, meatloaf, beef liver and onions, ham hocks, and short ribs. And don't leave without sampling the banana pudding! • $10/AA

Heart & Soul Café
801 Pennsylvania Ave. S.E. 202/546-8801
Heart & Soul Café's extensive menu offers "soul food with a Creole flair." Blackened catfish, grilled salmon with orange pecan sauce, grilled shrimp in citrus vinaigrette, stuffed tenderloin pork chops, country-fried chicken, and collard greens and cabbage please diners' palates here. The café is busiest during its famed Sunday brunch. • $20+/AA

*The Islander Caribbean Restaurant and Lounge
1201 U St. NW, 202/234-4971
No doubt the success of the Islander is due as much to proprietor Addie Green, who absolutely swears by her customers, as it is to the food. "God sends the right people here to eat," she claims. "Therefore, my customers become more than just customers. They are now part of the family!" Addie's children hold various key positions at the restaurant, so the Green family serve their "other family" the best in Caribbean cuisine. Whole red snapper, king fish, curried shrimp, calypso chicken (Addie's grandmother's recipe!),

Making new friends at Zanzibar on the Waterfront

oxtail stew, and goat roti are just a few of the Islander's menu delights. • **$15+/AA**

Midtowne Café
4306 Georgia Ave., 202/291-8745
It's as if a Caribbean junkanoo carnival blew onto Georgia Avenue, breathing life into its dreary existence. Midtowne Café's interior is an explosion of funky candy colors mixed with live musical performances, popular disc jockeys, cool cocktails, and great food. An eclectic fusion of international flavors and cuisines makes for an exciting mix-matched menu. Check out the salmon brushed with an Asian barbecue sauce served over a bed of jalapeno cheese grits or the sizzling fried catfish served with Thai cucumber salad and a Japanese black-bean dipping soy sauce. De-lish! • **$30+ AA**

U-topia Bar and Grill
1418 U St. NW, 202/483-7669

Known for its funky, contemporary interior, friendly, multi-ethnic clientele, and live Brazilian jazz, U-topia is the kind of restaurant that represents the essence of Washington D.C. Menu standouts include the plump petit crab cakes served over sautéed spinach with a tomato basil butter sauce, the lush seafood bisque peaked with just the right amount of brandy cream, mucho garlicy shrimp over angel hair pasta, and mahimahi served over Spanish ratatouille. Live Brazilian jazz Thursday through Sunday nights. • **$25+/AA**

*Zed's
1201 28th St. NW, 202/333-4710

Voted one of Washington's 100 best restaurants by *Washingtonian* magazine, Zed's brings "indescribably delicious" cuisine to a city that has as many Ethiopian eateries as Addis Ababa. Try the *awazel fitfit* (pieces of *injera*— Ethiopian flatbread—soaked in red pepper sauce with beef), *infillay* (strips of chicken sautéed with onions and seasoned butter), or the shrimp *tibbs* (shrimp sautéed with onion, fresh garlic, and tomato). All dishes come with injera, which serves as your "fork." Meals are served communal-style on a large tray, so bring the whole gang along! • **$20+/AA**

Nightclubs

Clubs come and go, and D.C. has certainly seen its share of change over the years. For a region that purchases a large portion of the country's inventory of jazz CDs, its support of nightly live jazz venues is lukewarm at best. This has been an area of contention and extreme disappointment to local club owners. Yet, despite the inconsistent patronage, D.C. offers a lot of great music for you to enjoy.

Bukom Café
2442 18th St. NW, 202/265-4600

Whether it's reggae, highlife, or soukous, the music at Bukom pays homage to West Africa. So does the menu: devil chicken wings, ecowas okra soup, African curried chicken, oxtail stew, cassava leaves

I Love the Nightlife

Club 2K9, 2009 Eighth St. NW, 202/667-7750—Make no mistake, with its spacious dance floor, funky retro lighting, and steel-cage go-go platforms, Club 2K9 is all about the party—and only for those who left their inhibitions and modesty at home. Music ranges from hip-hop to old school and so does the clientele. Get there early for the soul-food buffet. · Admission charge/AA

Republic Gardens, 1355 U St. NW, 202/232-2710—Strictly for the young and the beautiful, Republic Gardens features urban contemporary music, live bands weekends, and an impressive light Caribbean fusion menu. · Cover charge/AA

Takoma Station Tavern, 6914 Fourth St. NW, Takoma Park, 202/829-1999—Takoma Station brings progressive and straight-ahead jazz, blues, reggae, and funk artists to its extensive lineup of stars. Full continental dinner menu. · Cover charge/Dinner $20/AA

Twins, 5516 Colorado Ave. NW, 202/882-2523—Twins packs in the crowds, who come to hear great straight-ahead or contemporary jazz. Nationally known artists such as the Roy Ayers Quartet, Jimmy McGriff, and vocalist Shirley Horn have performed here. · Cover charge/Dinner $10/AA

and beef, and *egusi* (goat cooked in a broth of melon seeds, egusi, and spinach). Only problem is, it's hard to enjoy the food while dancing! Live entertainment is featured Tuesday through Sunday nights. • **$20/AA**

DC Live
932 F St. NW, 202/347-7200
"Iron Mike" Tyson, local DJ guru Donnie Simpson, and basketballer Alan Iverson hang out here, so ...you get the picture. Three floors of high energy, with a music menu that ranges from progressive jazz, hip-hop, and old school to world beat, characterize DC Live. From "look at all that hair" to skirts that barely cover the derrière, stylin' elevates

people watching here to an art form. With so many fashion do's (and even more don'ts) at every turn of the head, the sights alone are worth the price of admission! • **Cover charge/AA**

✳MCCXXIII
1223 Connecticut Ave. NW, 202/822-1800
MCCXXIII dispels all of the rumors that D.C. doesn't have it going on! MCCXXIII is a high-styled, sexy, champagne-and-caviar, meet-and-greet, late-night party lounge/club. Leopard-print bar stools, chamois settees, and an oh-so-intimate dance floor glamorize the first level, while upstairs, a metal-grated catwalk serves as a bridge from the reservations-preferred bar to the private, flirt-till-it-hurts lounge zone. The narrow, contemporary bar menu is alluring, but it takes a back seat to the decadent and more appetizing cocktails. • **Cover charge some nights/AA-invested**

New Vegas Lounge
1415 P St. NW, 202/483-3971
This offbeat dark small joint packs the house on weekends with live R&B, courtesy of the Out of Town Blues Band. Led by Dr. Blues on vocals, these boys have the walls sweatin' by the end of the night with their Chicago- and New Orleans-style blues. There's no dance floor at the New Vegas Lounge, but that doesn't stop the crowd from gyratin'—in the aisles, at their tables, with the band, wherever! It's all about having a good time! • **Cover charge/AA**

Festivals

From the official start of the festival season in April with D.C.'s salute to the cherry blossom to its culmination with the much-anticipated Taste of D.C. on Columbus Day weekend, Washington's calendar bursts with special-event weekends.

Cherry Blossom Festival
Tidal Basin SW, 202/547-1500
Mother nature does not always comply with the annual Cherry Blossom Festival. Some years, the trees bloom too early; other times, April showers knock the delicate petals from their branches

before the parade begins. Yet, more years than not, the 6,000-plus Japanese trees famous for their pale pink blooms perform as scheduled for Washingtonians and visitors from around the world during two weeks that honor a most exquisite gift of national friendship. The best way to enjoy the show is to take the subway, bring a picnic basket, and amble along the Tidal Basin under the trees. Let the petals kiss your cheeks to say "hello" as they drift down to earth. • **First two weeks in April/Free**

National Capital Barbecue Battle
Pennsylvania Ave. between Ninth and 13th Sts. NW,
703/319-4040
The south lawn of the Washington Monument never smelled so good! During this highlight of a D.C. summer, rows and rows of self-appointed barbecue gurus compete for the title of "Best Barbecue in the Nation's Capital." The event also rounds up concerts, children's activities, and arts and crafts displays—keeping everyone occupied between finger-lickin' bites. • **Last weekend in June/Admission charge**

✳Capital Jazz Fest
Merriweather Post Pavilion, Columbia, Maryland
Not one patch of green can be seen of the lawn at the Merriweather Post Pavilion during the Capital Jazz Fest. Each year, this lively musical event transforms the pavilion into a grassy beach covered with folks and their brightly colored umbrellas, lawn chairs, blankets, and coolers packed with roast beef sandwiches, potato salad, and chilled champagne. The Capital Jazz Fest has become one of the hottest jazz festivals on the East Coast, attracting enthusiasts from as far north as White Plains, New York, and as far south as Charlotte, North Carolina. Two outdoor stages showcase 25 of the jazz world's top talents. Past performers have included Earl Klugh, David Sanborn, Warren Hill, Marcus Johnson, and Nancy Wilson. In 1999, Roy Ayers turned it *out* with his jammin' rendition of "Runaway"! • **First weekend in June/Admission charge**

Black Family Reunion
National Mall, 202/737-0120
Sponsored by the National Coalition of Negro Women, the Black

Family Reunion celebrates the commitments, struggles, and triumphs of the African American family. At the base of the Washington Memorial, folks gather to enjoy the late summer day with their immediate and extended families. Storytelling, music, African dancers, arts and crafts vendors, performances by national urban contemporary groups, and down-home cuisine make this weekend a special event for locals and visitors of all ages. • **Second weekend in September/Free**

✴Taste of D.C.
Pennsylvania Ave. between Ninth and 13th Sts. NW,
202/724-5347
Luscious she-crab soup with a dollop of whipped cream, Carolina gumbo with cornbread, lobster-filled agnolotti, barbecued tofu with couscous, crab cake sandwiches, spicy chicken peanut stew with rice and plantains, and many other dishes tempt the taste buds at Taste of D.C. This lively culinary event features foods from 40 different restaurants, and the portions are full ones, not "tastes" like those at the Taste of Chicago festival. Since the purpose of the D.C. version is to try as many different items as you can stuff your face with, bring a friend and ask for an extra fork so you can share everything—except for the she-crab soup. That you'll want all to yourself! Nonstop live entertainment, a children's pavilion, and a sophisticated selection of original crafts and artifacts add to the weekend's excitement. • **Columbus Day weekend/Free**

Museums and Attractions
Smithsonian Institution Attractions

Washington, D.C., is home to the nation's most famous museum complex: the Smithsonian Institution. Encompassing more than a dozen buildings as well as the National Zoo, the Smithsonian is vast; it is impossible to visit all of the sites in one day. Call 202/357-2700, or visit the Smithsonian Institution Visitor Information Center, located at 1000 Jefferson Dr. SW, for information on specific museums and exhibits.

Muralist G. Byron Peck pays tribute to DC's favorite #1 son, Sir Duke Ellington, as well as beautifies the U Street corridor.

Anacostia Museum of African American History
1901 Fort Pl. SE
Located in the historic Anacostia neighborhood, this museum features revolving exhibits reflecting today's Black culture.

Arts and Industry Building
900 Jefferson Dr. SW
Features exhibits pertaining to African American and Native American cultures.

National Air and Space Museum
Sixth and Independence Aves. SW
The permanent collection includes the "Black Wings: The American Black in Aviation" exhibit.

National Museum of African Art
950 Independence Ave. SW
Dedicated to the preservation of African art.

National Museum of American History
14th and Constitution Aves. NW
Houses an extensive permanent collection chronicling the contributions of African Americans.

Monuments and Memorials

African American Civil War Memorial
10th and W Sts. NW, 202/667-2667
This stunning bronze memorial dedicated to the Black lives lost during the Civil War is inscribed with the names of 208,000 colored U.S. troops and their white officers.

Benjamin Banneker Memorial Circle and Fountain
L'Enfant Promenade and Maine Ave. NW
Not only is Banneker credited with designing Washington's layout, he was also a self-taught scholar and inventor who constructed the nation's first striking wooden clock.

FDR Memorial
1850 W. Basin Dr. SW, 202/619-7222
This beautifully landscaped four-part outdoor gallery memorializes the 12 years of FDR's presidency.

Jefferson Memorial
Tidal Basin south of 15th St. SW, 202/426-6841
A 19-foot-high statue of Jefferson is surrounded by many of his writings, including the Declaration of Independence.

Lincoln Memorial
West Potomac Park at 23rd St. NW
202/426-6841
This memorial provided the backdrop for Dr. Martin Luther King Jr.'s stirring "I Have a Dream" speech. Arguably, it's the most impressive monument in D.C.

Malcolm X and Marcus Garvey Statue
1440 Belmont St. NW
A 12-foot statue honors these two influential African American leaders.

Vietnam Veterans Memorial
Constitution Ave. and Henry Bacon Dr. NW
202/634-1568
More than 52,000 names of those killed or missing in Vietnam are inscribed on the black granite walls of this soul-stirring memorial.

Washington Monument
15th St. and Constitution Ave. NW, 202/426-6841
A free elevator ride to the top offers a panoramic view of the city. Free timed passes are required.

Other Attractions

Corcoran Gallery of Art
500 17th St. NW, 202/639-1700
Inside the Corcoran, a majestic marble stairway leads to the permanent exhibit of the Evan-Tibbs collection, considered one of the most impressive collections of African American paintings in the nation. It includes selections from renowned Black artists such as Aaron Douglas and Sylvia Snowdon. The Corcoran also hosts a delicious gospel brunch every Sunday. • **Admission charge**

Frederick Douglass National Historic Site
1411 W St. SE, 202/426-5961
Abolitionist, activist, and U.S. ambassador Frederick Douglass lived in this stately home in the Anacostia section of Washington from 1877 to 1895. The home affords a spectacular view of the Anacostia River and downtown Washington. The historic site offers tours of the home, a video, and exhibits on Douglass's remarkable life from slavery to freedom. • **Admission charge**

White House
1600 Pennsylvania Ave. NW, 202/456-2200
Free tours; timed tickets are required.

Churches

Ebenezer Methodist Church
Fourth and D Sts. SE, 202/544-9539
This historic landmark is the site of the oldest Black church on Capitol Hill. Ebenezer Methodist opened the first public school for local Blacks in 1863.

First Baptist Church of Georgetown
27th and Dumbarton Sts. NW,
202/965-1899
The first Baptist church in Georgetown was founded in 1862 by a former slave, the Reverend Sandy Alexander. Rev. Alexander grew his congregation from two to 500 during his 37 years as pastor. The church's present mission is to prepare its parishioners to be "viable people facing the twenty-first century."

Metropolitan AME Church
1518 M St. NW, 202/331-1426
Frederick Douglass was once a parishioner at this church, arguably D.C.'s most famous. Erected in 1886, this red-brick Gothic-style building came to house Metropolitan AME when two churches merged. The church, which served as a station on the Underground Railroad, sits on the oldest continuously Black-owned property in downtown Washington. Metropolitan AME is known citywide for its angelic choir.

Mount Zion United Methodist Church
1334 29th St. NW, 202/234-0148
Organized in 1816, Mount Zion United Methodist hosts D.C.'s oldest African American congregation. It too served as a station on the Underground Railroad.

St. Augustine's Catholic Church
1419 V St. NW, 202/265-1470
St. Augustine's is the oldest Black Catholic church in the District of Columbia, founded in 1858 by freed slaves. President Lincoln and his wife helped raise funds to establish the church's chapel and school.

St. Mary's Episcopal Church
728 23rd St. NW, 202/333-3985
Founded in 1827 by 28 Blacks who separated from the segregated
Episcopal Church of the Epiphany, this historic landmark is the first
Black Protestant Episcopal church in the district.

Recreation

East Potomac Golf Course
Ohio Dr. at Hains Point SW, 202/554-7660
Private lessons are available at this 18-hole course, one of the more
popular in the city.

Langston Golf Course & Driving Range
26th St. and Benning Rd., 202/397-8638
Opened in June 1939, Langston Golf Course is known for its symbolic affiliation with the development and desegregation of public
golfing and recreational facilities in the greater Washington, D.C.,
area. One of the earliest golf courses established expressly for African
American golfers, Langston was instrumental in the development of
many players, most notably Lee Alder, one of golf's greatest.

Rock Creek Park
3545 Williamsburg Lane NW, 202/282-1063
This 1,754-acre scenic preserve winds throughout the northwest section of the district all the way into Montgomery County, Maryland.
To take in its most beautiful spots, drive along Rock Creek Park
Parkway, passing under the mammoth-size stone archways that support the streets and bridges above; send shout-outs to the folks picnicking in the park's many recreational areas. Bike paths, riding
stables, tennis courts, nature trails, and an 18-hole golf course are
among the activities afforded nature lovers in Rock Creek Park. The
park's Carter Barron Amphitheater hosts seasonal outdoor concerts,
the Shakespeare in the Park festival, and other events.

About the Author

Carla Labat, like most people, is a lover of great food and fine dining—whether its Oysters Rockefeller served on a plate of rock salt or a flimsy paper plate piled high with a wonderfully sloppy barbecued pork sandwich topped with crisp cole slaw. Her first book, *Satisfy Your Soul: A Guide to African American, African and Caribbean Restaurants*, took her on a four-month eating odyssey across the country, sampling some of the nations best eateries. This latest book not only took Carla back to some of her favorite old haunts, but also introduced her to a couple of new cities, enabling her to expand her list of choice restaurants and her knowledge of each metropolis. Carla is a freelance restaurant critic and travel writer. Her latest reviews on what's hot in the dining industry can be read on her Web page at www.soul-dining.com. Carla lives in McLean, Virginia.

Index

Geographical Index

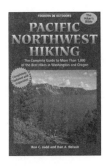

www.ricksteves.com

The Rick Steves web site is bursting with information to boost your travel I.Q. and liven up your European adventure. Including:
• The latest from Rick on what's hot in Europe
• Excerpts from Rick's books
• Rick's comprehensive Guide to European Railpasses

www.foghorn.com

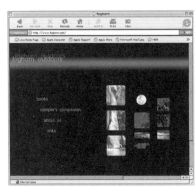

Foghorn Outdoors guides are the premier source for United States outdoor recreation information. Visit the Foghorn Outdoors web site for more information on these activity-based travel guides, including the complete text of the handy *Foghorn Outdoors: Camper's Companion.*

www.moon.com

Moon Handbooks' goal is to give travelers all the background and practical information they'll need for an extraordinary travel experience. Visit the Moon Handbooks web site for interesting information and practical advice, including Q&A with the author of *The Practical Nomad*, Edward Hasbrouck.

FOR TRAVELERS WITH SPECIAL INTERESTS

GUIDES

The 100 Best Small Art Towns in America • Asia in New York City
The Big Book of Adventure Travel • Cities to Go
Cross-Country Ski Vacations • Gene Kilgore's Ranch Vacations
Great American Motorcycle Tours • Healing Centers and Retreats
Indian America • Into the Heart of Jerusalem
The People's Guide to Mexico • The Practical Nomad
Saddle Up! • Staying Healthy in Asia, Africa, and Latin America
Steppin' Out • Travel Unlimited • Understanding Europeans
Watch It Made in the U.S.A. • The Way of the Traveler
Work Worldwide • The World Awaits
The Top Retirement Havens • Yoga Vacations

SERIES

Adventures in Nature
The Dog Lover's Companion
Kidding Around
Live Well

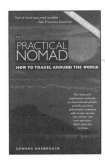
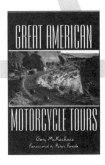

MOON HANDBOOKS provide comprehensive

coverage of a region's arts, history, land, people, and social issues in addition to detailed practical listings for accommodations, food, outdoor recreation, and entertainment. Moon Handbooks allow complete immersion in a region's culture—ideal for travelers who want to combine sightseeing with insight for an extraordinary travel experience.

USA

Alaska-Yukon • Arizona • Big Island of Hawaii • Boston
Coastal California • Colorado • Connecticut • Georgia
Grand Canyon • Hawaii • Honolulu-Waikiki • Idaho
Kauai • Los Angeles • Maine • Massachusetts • Maui
Michigan • Montana • Nevada • New Hampshire
New Mexico • New York City • New York State
North Carolina • Northern California • Ohio • Oregon
Pennsylvania • San Francisco • Santa Fe-Taos • Silicon Valley
South Carolina • Southern California • Tahoe • Tennessee
Texas • Utah • Virginia • Washington • Wisconsin
Wyoming • Yellowstone-Grand Teton

INTERNATIONAL

Alberta and the Northwest Territories • Archaeological Mexico
Atlantic Canada • Australia • Baja • Bangkok • Bali • Belize
British Columbia • Cabo • Canadian Rockies • Cancún
Caribbean Vacations • Colonial Mexico • Costa Rica • Cuba
Dominican Republic • Ecuador • Fiji • Havana • Honduras
Hong Kong • Indonesia • Jamaica • Mexico City • Mexico
Micronesia • The Moon • Nepal • New Zealand
Northern Mexico • Oaxaca • Pacific Mexico • Pakistan
Philippines • Puerto Vallarta • Singapore • South Korea
South Pacific • Southeast Asia • Tahiti
Thailand • Tonga-Samoa • Vancouver
Vietnam, Cambodia and Laos
Virgin Islands • Yucatán Peninsula

www.moon.com

Rick Steves

shows you where to travel and how to travel—all while getting the most value for your dollar. His Back Door travel philosophy is about making friends, having fun, and avoiding tourist rip-offs.

Rick's been traveling to Europe for more than 25 years and is the author of 22 guidebooks, which have sold more than a million copies. He also hosts the award-winning public television series *Travels in Europe with Rick Steves*.

RICK STEVES' COUNTRY & CITY GUIDES

Best of Europe
France, Belgium & the Netherlands
Germany, Austria & Switzerland
Great Britain & Ireland
Italy • London • Paris • Rome • Scandinavia • Spain & Portugal

RICK STEVES' PHRASE BOOKS

French • German • Italian • French, Italian & German
Spanish & Portuguese

MORE EUROPE FROM RICK STEVES

Europe 101
Europe Through the Back Door
Mona Winks
Postcards from Europe

WWW.RICKSTEVES.COM

ROAD TRIP USA

Getting there is half the fun, and Road Trip USA guides are your ticket to driving adventure. Taking you off the interstates and onto less-traveled, two-lane highways, each guide is filled with fascinating trivia, historical information, photographs, facts about regional writers, and details on where to sleep and eat—all contributing to your exploration of the American road.

*"Books so full of the pleasures of the American road,
you can smell the upholstery."*
~ BBC radio

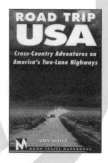

THE ORIGINAL CLASSIC GUIDE
Road Trip USA

ROAD TRIP USA REGIONAL GUIDE
Road Trip USA: California and the Southwest

ROAD TRIP USA GETAWAYS
Road Trip USA Getaways: Chicago
Road Trip USA Getaways: New Orleans
Road Trip USA Getaways: San Francisco
Road Trip USA Getaways: Seattle

www.roadtripusa.com

TRAVEL ★ SMART®

guidebooks are accessible, route-based driving guides. Special interest tours provide the most practical routes for family fun, outdoor activities, or regional history for a trip of anywhere from two to 22 days. Travel Smarts take the guesswork out of planning a trip by recommending only the most interesting places to eat, stay, and visit.

"One of the few travel series that rates sightseeing attractions. That's a handy feature. It helps to have some guidance so that every minute counts."
~ San Diego Union-Tribune

TRAVEL SMART REGIONS

DEEP SOUTH
TRAVEL ★ SMART®

A different kind of guidebook!
Takes the guesswork out of your travels—local authors list only the best places to eat, stay, and visit

Alaska
American
Southwest
Arizona
Carolinas
Colorado
Deep South
Eastern
Canada
Florida Gulf
Coast
Florida
Georgia
Hawaii
Illinois/Indiana
Iowa/Nebraska
Kentucky/Tennessee
Maryland/Delaware
Michigan
Minnesota/Wisconsin
Montana/Wyoming/Idaho
Nevada

New England
New Mexico
New York State
Northern California
Ohio
Oregon
Pacific Northwest
Pennsylvania/New Jersey
South Florida and the Keys
Southern California
Texas
Utah
Virginias
Western Canada

PACIFIC
NORTHWEST
TRAVEL ★ SMART®

A different kind of guidebook!
Takes the guesswork out of your travels—a local author lists only the best places to eat, stay, and visit

Foghorn Outdoors

guides are for campers, hikers, boaters, anglers, bikers, and golfers of all levels of daring and skill. Each guide contains site descriptions and ratings, driving directions, facilities and fees information, and easy-to-read maps that leave only the task of deciding where to go.

"Foghorn Outdoors has established an ecological conservation standard unmatched by any other publisher."
~ Sierra Club

CAMPING Arizona and New Mexico Camping
Baja Camping • California Camping
Camper's Companion • Colorado Camping
Easy Camping in Northern California
Easy Camping in Southern California
Florida Camping • New England Camping
Pacific Northwest Camping
Utah and Nevada Camping

HIKING 101 Great Hikes of the San Francisco Bay Area
California Hiking • Day-Hiking California's National Parks
Easy Hiking in Northern California
Easy Hiking in Southern California
New England Hiking
Pacific Northwest Hiking • Utah Hiking

FISHING Alaska Fishing • California Fishing
Washington Fishing

BOATING California Recreational Lakes and Rivers
Washington Boating and Water Sports

OTHER OUTDOOR RECREATION California Beaches
California Golf • California Waterfalls
California Wildlife • Easy Biking in Northern California
Florida Beaches
The Outdoor Getaway Guide For Southern California
Tom Stienstra's Outdoor Getaway Guide: Northern California

WWW.FOGHORN.COM

CiTY·SMART™

The best way to enjoy a city is to get advice from someone who lives there—and that's exactly what City Smart guidebooks offer. City Smarts are written by local authors with hometown perspectives who have personally selected the best places to eat, shop, sightsee, and simply hang out. The honest, lively, and opinionated advice is perfect for business travelers looking to relax with the locals or for longtime residents looking for something new to do Saturday night.

A portion of sales from each title
benefits a non-profit literacy organization in that city.

CITY SMART CITIES

Albuquerque	Anchorage
Austin	Baltimore
Berkeley/Oakland	Boston
Calgary	Charlotte
Chicago	Cincinnati
Cleveland	Dallas/Ft. Worth
Denver	Indianapolis
Kansas City	Memphis
Milwaukee	Minneapolis/St. Paul
Nashville	Pittsburgh
Portland	Richmond
San Francisco	Sacramento
St. Louis	Salt Lake City
San Antonio	San Diego
Tampa/St. Petersburg	Toronto
Tucson	Vancouver

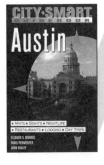

www.travelmatters.com

User-friendly, informative, and fun:

Because travel *matters.*

Visit our newly launched web site and explore the variety of titles and travel information available online, featuring an interactive *Road Trip USA* exhibit.

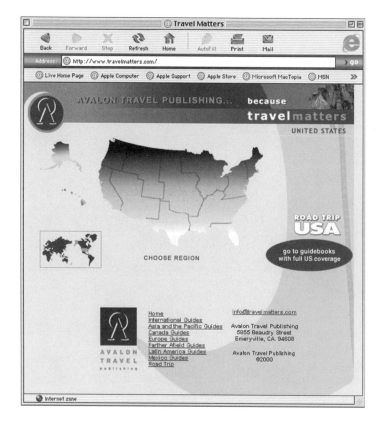